TERENCE CONRAN'S

GARDEN STYLE

BAICOLI
GREEN
SULPHU
HEXYL
Coolglass
Benlate
F M A
LONDO

TERENCE CONRAN'S GARDEN STYLE

CONSULTANT EDITORS
JOHN McGOWAN
AND ROGER DuBERN

PROJECT PHOTOGRAPHY BY
NADIA MACKENZIE

First published in the UK in 1991 as Terence Conran's Garden DIY
by Conran Octopus Limited
37 Shelton Street
London WC2H 9HN

First paperback edition published in 1995 by
Conran Octopus Limited
Reprinted 1997

This edition distributed in Canada by
McClelland & Stewart
481 University Avenue, Suite 900
Toronto, Ontario M5G 2E9

British Library Cataloguing in Publication Data
A catalogue record for this book is available from the British Library

ISBN 1-85029-935-8

Consultant Editors JOHN MCGOWAN and ROGER DUBERN
Project Editor JOANNA BRADSHAW
Editor SIMON WILLIS
Editorial Assistant ROD MACKENZIE
Contributor ELIZABETH WILHIDE

Art Editors HELEN LEWIS, MERYL LLOYD
Illustrator PAUL BRYANT
Visualizer JEAN MORLEY

Photographer NADIA MACKENZIE
Photographic Assistant SIMON ANDERS

Production Manager SONYA SIBBONS
Picture Research NADINE BAZAR

Printed in Hong Kong
Typeset by Servis Filmsetting Limited
Colour separation by Chroma Graphics, Singapore

PUBLISHER'S ACKNOWLEDGMENTS
The publisher would like to thank the following for their invaluable assistance in producing this book:

Jonathan Chidsey, Lady Caroline Conran, Vana Hegarty, Gordon Hurden, Gareth Jones, Sian Jones, Wendy Jones, Harold Lee, Steve Stonebridge and everyone at Benchmark Woodworking Ltd, Alan Rayner and the staff at Servis Filmsetting Ltd, Hickson Timber Products Ltd, Bridget Bodoano and the Conran Shop, the Administrator of Castle Drogo and the National Trust

The projects in this book were specially built by SEAN SUTCLIFFE of Benchmark Woodworking Ltd

Special thanks to SIR TERENCE CONRAN for original project sketches and to PAUL BRYANT for his superb illustrations

SPECIAL NOTE

Before embarking on any of the projects in this book, you must check the law concerning building regulations and planning. It is also important to obtain specialist advice on plumbing and electricity before attempting any alterations to these services yourself.

Whilst every effort has been made to ensure that all the information contained in this book is correct, the publishers cannot be held responsible for any loss, damage or injury caused by reliance upon the accuracy of such information.

DIMENSIONS

Exact dimensions are given in metric followed by an approximate conversion to imperial. Do not mix metric and imperial dimensions when you are making a calculation.

Contents

Introduction

If you have a garden, the chances are that you already 'do it yourself'. Planting, seeding, mowing, turfing, fencing and paving are, for the majority of gardeners, all DIY activities, since few people today have either the space or the means to justify a full-time gardener.

This book is a logical extension of that established outdoor DIY tradition. It contains a range of projects, from the very simple to the more complicated, which shows you how to make a variety of structures, including containers, seats, trelliswork and even a summer house. All of these are important, classic garden accessories, the design of which is too often overlooked.

Achieving success in DIY is to do with confidence. Once you have completed a simple project, this will give you the confidence to move on to a more complicated piece. If you are a DIY beginner, choose the simplest item in terms both of design and tools required and progress gradually as your skills develop.

If the garden is a good place to practise and refine your DIY skills, you can also get away with a lower standard of finish: precision and perfection are not really at home in the garden, where a weathered, rustic appearance can be a positive attribute. Materials need not be expensive and what you make will usually have cost less than the retail product in the garden centre, although this is not invariably the case. You can buy ready-made trellising, for example, for far less than the wood you would need to make it, so to economize by doing-it-yourself you must carefully examine what is commercially available from the garden centre and make the proper comparisons.

The great benefit of DIY in the garden, however, is the degree of satisfaction it affords – the pleasure of making something that has been tailored to suit your own space and needs. What you make will often be better designed than its equivalent in the garden centre; more importantly, it will reflect your own taste and sense of style more successfully.

Terence Conran.

Planning a Garden

In the words of Sir John Soane, good design should contain an element of 'hazard and surprise'. Although Soane was talking about interior design, this important principle applies equally to the disposition and arrangement of outdoor space. Nothing is less memorable than a garden which can be surveyed in a single glance: you want to be able to move through a garden and be surprised by what you discover around each corner.

Fortunately, 'hazard' in gardening is easy to create. Changes of direction, with paths leading around structures which divide and separate different areas within the garden, immediately generate interest. Forms can be created very simply with trelliswork over which climbing plants are trained, providing a sort of growing 'veil' through which to walk.

Even more important are changes in level. In this, as in so much of garden design, there is a great deal to be learned from Japan. Different levels give a sense of movement, transforming even the dullest patch of ground. And because plants like falling over edges or trailing over walls, a change in level provides endless opportunities to blend architectural form with planting, thereby softening the lines of the design.

Trellising, planters adjacent to the house, fast-growing creepers and climbers grown up the walls can all help to blend a house in with its setting, anchoring it to its environment and creating an established garden within a short space of time. One great advantage of garden DIY is that if your house has distinctive architectural details, such as decorative bargeboarding, it is easy to incorporate these features into the design of your garden structures. Something as simple as picking out a colour from a door to use on seating or containers can help to unify the overall design and visually link the house to the garden.

Because the garden is an organic place where things grow, the materials you use for structures and accessories should be natural ones as far as possible. Plastic has no affinity with plants: the two simply do not go together. Artificial materials always stand out in a garden because they do not weather in the way that natural ones do. Wood, stone, terracotta, brick and – for some reason – metal all work well in the garden, harmonizing with one another so that you can vary the textures and surfaces in an interesting way. What is particularly appealing about all of these materials is the way they age and weather, oxodizing, bleaching, staining and acquiring lichens and mosses so that they meld into the garden. Show gardens, because they have not had time to mature, always look too new and clean for my taste. You can encourage ageing if your garden is looking too new by scrubbing salt or domestic bleach into wooden decking to achieve a weathered look or by painting non-pasteurized milk, house-plant food or manure made into a slurry onto concrete or terracotta surfaces to speed up the growth of lichen.

THE OUTDOOR ROOM

Good garden design is a question of creating an outdoor space that reflects your needs, style and preferences, and is at the same time compatible with the materials, structures and details of your house. The garden should be a natural extension to the house, rather than a jarring contrast. Sources of inspiration for garden designs include the ever-popular informal look of the English country cottage, the open-plan architectural terraces of modern town gardens, and the contemplative beauty of Japanese landscape settings.

If the garden needs an element of wilderness and a certain lack of precision to be truly inviting, it is also the place for colour. Far too often, people play safe with garden accessories, sticking to the traditional shades of white or a dark green which fades into the background. Splashes of bright colour are an attractive and appealing feature of Mediterranean gardens and, contrary to popular belief, such vivid accent shades also work in countries where summer light is not as intense. Colour makes a strong positive statement, and is also extremely cheerful in the winter when the garden is least interesting. Yellow, for example, goes equally well with the fresh greens of summer and the greys of winter. Blue (either dark blue or blue-grey) is another good garden colour. If you make your own garden accessories, you can decide for yourself what colour you want to paint them, rather than having to accept the limited and uninspiring shades that are on offer commercially.

Finally, a garden, in the same way as a room, needs a focus of interest: the path must lead somewhere; the view through the pergola must reveal something at the other end; a formal layout of beds demands a centrepiece. Whatever you base your design around should look positive and well-considered, not half-hearted. A large terracotta pot tumbling with colourful plants, an inviting garden seat in a shady place, a patio under a striped awning, a garden pond full of fish or a collection of strange, disparate containers all make good focal points as long as they are properly complemented by their environment. There are many excellent ideas illustrated in this book to stimulate your imagination, but the important point is that these are merely a starting place for your own plans and ideas. Your garden is the place where you can express your own personality and idiosyncracies to create the kind of outdoor room you want to live in, whether it is formal or rustic.

PRACTICALITIES

A new garden should start with a plan which takes into account practical as well as aesthetic considerations. A camera is a useful tool in the planning process: take photographs of the views from the house to the garden (and at the upper levels, too) as well as from the garden to the house. A simple sketch of the plot annotated with rough dimensions will help you to decide on the layout of paths, beds and patio. For a formal design you may wish to work out a strong controlled grid or a symmetrical framework of beds and connecting paths. For a more informal, natural arrangement, it is still important to think about where the paths will go and what shape beds they will create: too often, paths are laid without due regard to the shape of the beds, with awkward and ill-judged results. You should also work out any changes in level required or note existing slopes or steps, as well as features such as mature trees and garden sheds.

Planning a Garden

Although the climate of your garden cannot be altered radically, it can be tempered. Exposure to strong winds can be limited to some extent by the filtering effect of boundary hedging, fencing or trellis. In a dry area, a damp microclimate can be created by the addition of a pond, around the perimeter of which moisture-loving plants can flourish. Shade can be supplied by a variety of means, both manmade and natural, including awnings, arbors, and vines or climbers trained over trellis or wire frameworks. Too little light poses another problem. You cannot, of course, reorientate a garden which faces the wrong way, nor do much about the deep shade cast by high walls. But you can clear out overgrowth, take down fencing and drastically prune overhanging branches to let in as much light as possible. Unfortunately if the sun doesn't shine, there is little you can do about it.

Many other factors will have a bearing on the eventual design:

- The siting of a compost heap, a tool shed and utility area
- Access to water
- The position of eating or sitting areas
- Barbecues
- Areas in which children can play and in which to site play equipment
- Permanent fixtures such as mature trees, existing walls and boundaries
- The presence of any eyesores which may need to be camouflaged
- The need for privacy or security
- Noise from neighbouring gardens
- Special requirements such as the extreme climate of a roof garden
- The amount of time you can spend
- Your budget

All gardens benefit from careful organization. Planting stands a greater chance of success if the basic framework is right.

Design and Detail

Gardens thrive on an element of surprise, hidden corners and changes of level. Decking is a harmonious outdoor surface, and can be planned in advance to provide different seating and eating levels and beds for planting (above). Strategically placed, arbors or trelliswork can act as a focal point in the garden, directing the eye to splashes of colour (above left and opposite).

Colour in the Garden

Colour has long been a neglected element in the garden as far as structures, accessories and garden furniture are concerned (overleaf). Containers, seats, trellis, fences and walls can all be painted to give a positive lift to the overall design of a garden.

PART 1

SEATING AND EATING

In every garden there should be a place where you can sit down, look with pleasure at what you have achieved and think about all the hard work that remains to be done. Any seating area, whether it is a bench in a shady corner or a patio equipped with table, chairs, awning and barbecue, becomes a focal point in the garden's design; its position, accordingly, is part of that initial process of architectural planning. Should it be in sun or shade? In view of the house or in a more secluded location? If you intend to eat outdoors, at least partial shade will be required. Eating outside, preferably in dappled sunlight, is one of the great pleasures of life.

You can sit in the garden to read a book, have a drink, watch the children play, eat a meal or simply take stock of your surroundings, and there are as many styles of garden seat as there are functions for them to fulfil. Which type of seat you choose should reflect the general plan and style of your garden. The quality of light and shade is a very important consideration, not only for personal comfort, but also for good growing conditions and for intrinsic interest.

Seating and Eating

Seats and table tops must be designed so that water does not sit on the surface and rot or rust them away. A fractional tilt to a seat or table top will ensure that water drains off; slats or drainage holes fulfil the same function and there are also new outdoor paints which protect garden furniture to a much greater degree than traditional undercoat and gloss.

Much garden furniture, particularly the cast-iron or painted metal variety, is too ornate for my taste. Tables and seats which are clean-lined, whether they are curved or rectilinear, look much more confident and suit outdoor living much better. Simple garden furniture allows the focus of attention to remain on the planting. This is not to dismiss wrought-ironwork out of hand. Benches with wrought- or cast-iron ends, but plain slatted backs and seats, can be attractive and are more comfortable than all-metal versions which heat up in the sun.

Garden seats can also be amusing. In the nineteenth century, rough-hewn tree branches were nailed together to create whimsical Gothick benches, a kind of visual joke. In a similar vein are sections of tree trunk used as bench supports, a chimney pot filled with sand as a table base or a stone slab inset into a clipped box hedge, with the foliage making a living upholstered back. One of the most irresistible designs is the tree seat, almost a ground-level tree house, which forms a platform around the base of a tree.

In addition to semi-permanent garden furniture, there are many varieties of ready-made garden seat which work equally well indoors. Painted wooden benches, wickerwork, rattan and basket chairs, folding canvas chairs and metal park chairs suit their location and are generally light enough to move easily.

With garden tables, there is the same choice between permanent fixtures and tables which can be set up as required. Stone, marble and ceramic tiles are excellent materials for table tops; folding

Outdoor Living

Stepped timber seating (above) provides interesting and versatile changes of level in a garden. A terrace of herringbone paving and shaded by mature plane trees (right) makes a delightful outdoor eating area.

Overleaf *A range of garden seating ideas.*

Seating and Eating

metal tables, traditionally associated with French parks are more economic.

Seating areas are almost always more pleasurable and useable if there is a degree of shade. If your patio is exposed to the full force of the sun, there are many ways of creating shade that look appropriate as well as stylish. In this area, the yachting world is a fruitful source of visual ideas. Sail-like canvas awnings, varnished wooden frameworks for climbing plants, and canvas in bright clear colours eyeletted and lashed to a simple metal frame all have a faintly nautical flavour. A simple metal armature or framework with a vine trained over is a particularly Mediterranean solution to the problem; narrow gauge trellis overhead breaks up sunlight into a small square grid, taking the power out of it. Shop blinds fitted with a retractable mechanism, canvas clipped on to a wood and wire frame or a large market umbrella are other effective ideas. For a more theatrical effect, a bright, patterned fabric can be knotted and tied to poles like an oversize scarf, or you can borrow ideas from tent design. Plain canvas (perhaps painted on the underside) or broad blue-and-white stripes are crisp, fresh and appealing.

Most people today want their outdoor eating area to be a cooking area as well. A barbecue area is particularly easy to build, a good project for DIY in the garden. Brick or stone are the best materials for construction and you will probably also need to pave around and beneath the barbecue to make cleaning easy. At the simplest level of design, you can buy a mass-produced cast-iron barbecue and simply set it on to a brick or stone slab. If you are building the barbecue as well as its setting, it is best to line it in firebrick as a precaution against the intense heat.

Barbecues should be sited with care. Not only do they generate a great deal of

Garden bench 22
Octagonal tree seat 30
Barbecue 38
Awning 42
Timber table 44
Materials 146

heat, they are also smoky. Avoid positions where smoke and cooking smells will drift into the house – or worse, through your neighbour's windows. Overhanging plants are likely to be singed or even incinerated; adjacent walls will be blackened by smoke, although this is not necessarily unattractive.

You can extend the potential of outdoor eating areas by the addition of good garden lighting. Outdoor lighting calls for a degree of sensitivity, since obvious, glaring fixtures will immediately rob your garden of whatever charm it possesses; on the other hand, subtle, diffused light sources create an instantly magical atmosphere. Garden lighting should be as unobtrusive as possible, with fittings built into walls or shielded in some way.

When you furnish a garden, what you choose should be simple, so as not to compete with the planting; practical, for obvious reasons; and architectural, to contribute to your overall plan or design. You can use this opportunity to go one step further and think about the way you furnish your home indoors as well: a continuation of the same basic attitude will bring the house and garden closer together, to the benefit of both.

OUTDOOR SEATING AREAS

If you intend to use a seating area as a place for outdoor meals you will need to provide a degree of shade or shelter. Sitting in the full glare of the hot midday sun is very unpleasant for any length of time; on the other hand, you do not necessarily want to have to move indoors on account of a few drops of rain. Solutions include integrated terraces and balconies, awnings, and trellis supporting a canopy of vines or climbing plants. Perhaps the most appealing of all in fine weather is a table and chairs placed in the dappled shade under a tree, a natural shelter which filters the light to just the right degree.

GARDEN BENCH

When it comes to garden furniture, people tend to have rather conservative taste. Although they might tolerate modern and even occasionally avant-garde pieces in the home, these are less welcome for outdoor living, where the emphasis has generally been on the traditional. Wrought-iron seating typically has a Victorian flavour, and, in recent years, the designs of Sir Edwin Lutyens have been enormously influential, with their classically inspired curves.

This garden bench with its upright railed back and plain, flat seat and legs owes something to the strict functional beauty of nineteenth-century Shaker furniture. Extremely simple by comparison with much of what is commercially available for the garden, the bench is nevertheless one of the more demanding projects to make. This is partly because garden furniture must be finished to a higher standard than other garden structures, as it will receive closer inspection.

Even if you move your garden furniture indoors for the winter it will have to take some degree of weathering. Allowing water to collect on a surface is the quickest way of causing deterioration and decay. Here the seat slopes slightly so that water drains off and, similarly, where the back joins the seat a narrow gap has been left to allow water to flow down. The straight edges of the legs are bevelled so that accidental knocks by the lawnmower do not cause too much damage.

The height of the back is a critical factor in the design. Equally distinctive is the back's reeded quality. This is, perhaps, not a bench for lounging, although, supplied with a long cushion, it would work very well indoors.

Don't be afraid to let colour make a positive statement in the garden. Yellow and various tones of blue look as good in winter as they do in summer and are more eye-catching than the more sedate shades of dark green or white.

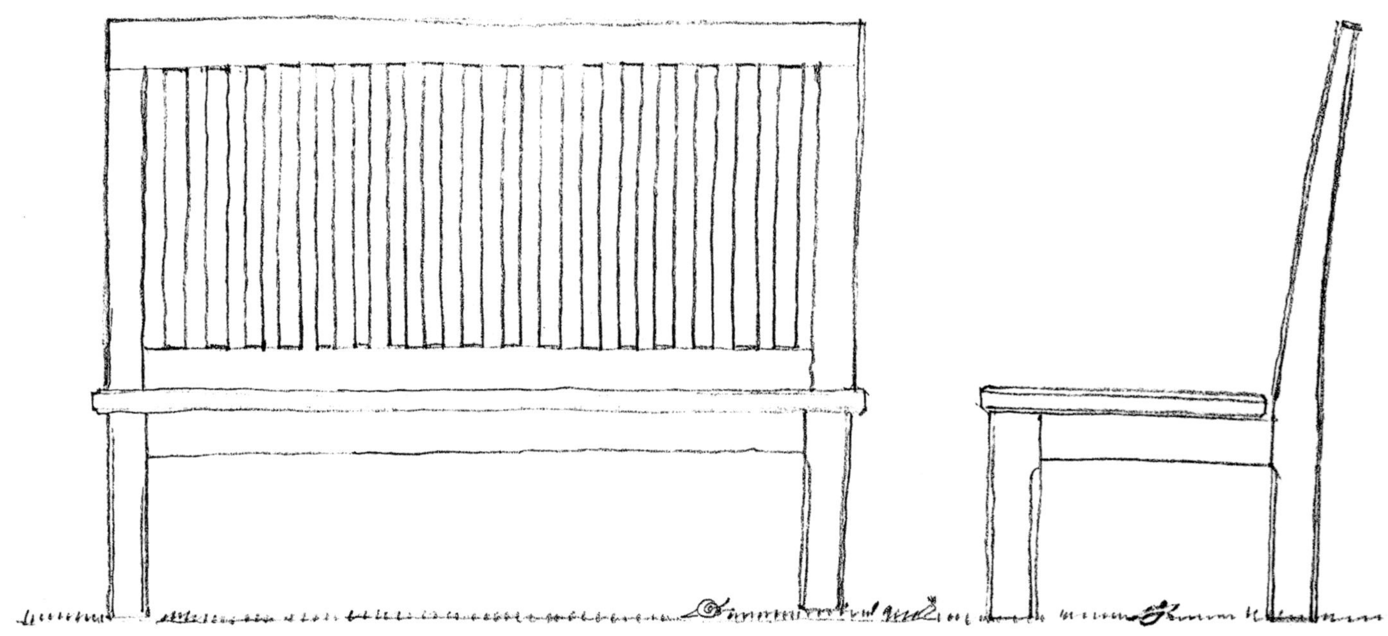

GARDEN BENCH

The garden bench is perhaps the most familiar piece of garden furniture. Building one yourself will almost certainly be cheaper than buying one, and will give you a real sense of satisfaction. If needs be, you can adapt the design shown here to suit the size and proportions of your garden and your individual requirements. Choose the site for your bench with care, positioning it to serve as a focal point that draws the eye in a certain direction; alternatively, you could place it to provide sanctuary in a tranquil, shady corner of the garden where you can retreat to sit in peace, quiet and comfort.

This garden bench could be made from hardwood, but it will be considerably cheaper and more environmentally acceptable if you make it from good-quality softwood. In the latter case, it is important that you treat the timber with good-quality wood preservative at all stages of construction to ensure that it will give you many years of service. A clear wood preservative should be applied to the timber after the component pieces have been cut, but before the joints are assembled; the strength of the joint will not be affected if you allow about 24 hours for the preservative to dry thoroughly before applying the glue. A second coat of preservative should be applied after construction, before the application of the final finish.

Using clear preservative will allow you to keep your options open regarding whether you finish the bench by painting or by applying a water-repellent wood stain of the type used widely on timber window frames. If you finish the bench by painting it, it is a good idea to use an exterior gloss paint or microporous (satin sheen) system. Such paint often contains a penetrating preservative wood primer, and this should be used in preference to a second coat of clear wood preservative.

The ideal way to construct the bench to ensure many years of service is to use traditional mortise and tenon joints for the main frame and dowel joints for the back rest slats and the seat boards. However, if you feel that you do not possess the necessary skills to cut accurate mortise and tenon joints, then the entire bench could be made using dowel joints throughout. If you do only use dowel joints, however, it will be more important than ever to apply a good-quality waterproof woodworking adhesive to each joint before assembly, and to keep each joint firmly cramped until the adhesive is thoroughly set.

MATERIALS

Part	Quantity	Material	Length
BACK LEGS	2	100 x 75mm (4 x 3in) PAR softwood	1035mm (41in)
FRONT LEGS	2	75 x 75mm (3 x 3in) PAR softwood	430mm (17in)*
SIDE FRAME RAILS	4	75 x 50mm (3 x 2in) PAR softwood	480mm (19in)
FRONT RAIL	1	As above	1790mm (70½in)
LOWER BACK RAIL	1	140 x 32mm (5½ x 1¼in) PAR softwood	1790mm (70½in)
UPPER BACK RAIL	1	75 x 50mm (3 x 2in) PAR softwood	1880mm (74in)*
BACK SLATS	32	38 x 25mm (1½ x 1in) PAR softwood	Distance between back rails
SEAT BOARDS	4	140 x 32mm (5½ x 1¼in) PAR softwood	1865mm (73½in)
DOWELS (seat to lower back rail)	5	From 12mm (½in) hardwood dowelling	Approx. 95mm (3¾in)
DOWELS (to join seat boards and fit back slats)	As required	From 8mm (5/16in) hardwood dowelling	Approx. 40mm (1½in)

* Overlength and then cut to size after fixing – see text

TOOLS

- WORKBENCH (fixed or portable)
- MARKING KNIFE
- STEEL MEASURING TAPE
- STEEL RULE
- TRY SQUARE
- PANEL SAW (or circular power saw)
- TENON SAW (or power jigsaw)
- CHISELS
- MARKING GAUGE
- MORTISE GAUGE
- POWER DRILL
- DOWEL or CENTREPOINT DRILL BIT – 8mm (5/16in)
- FLAT BIT – 12mm (½in)
- DOWELLING JIG
- ONE PAIR OF SASH CRAMPS (or webbing cramp)
- SMOOTHING PLANE (hand or power)
- POWER ROUTER and ROUNDING OVER BIT
- MALLET
- ORBITAL SANDER (or hand sanding block)

Adhesives 146
Paint 146
Preservative 146
Softwood 148
Dowel joint 154
Mortise and tenon joint 154

GARDEN BENCH ASSEMBLY

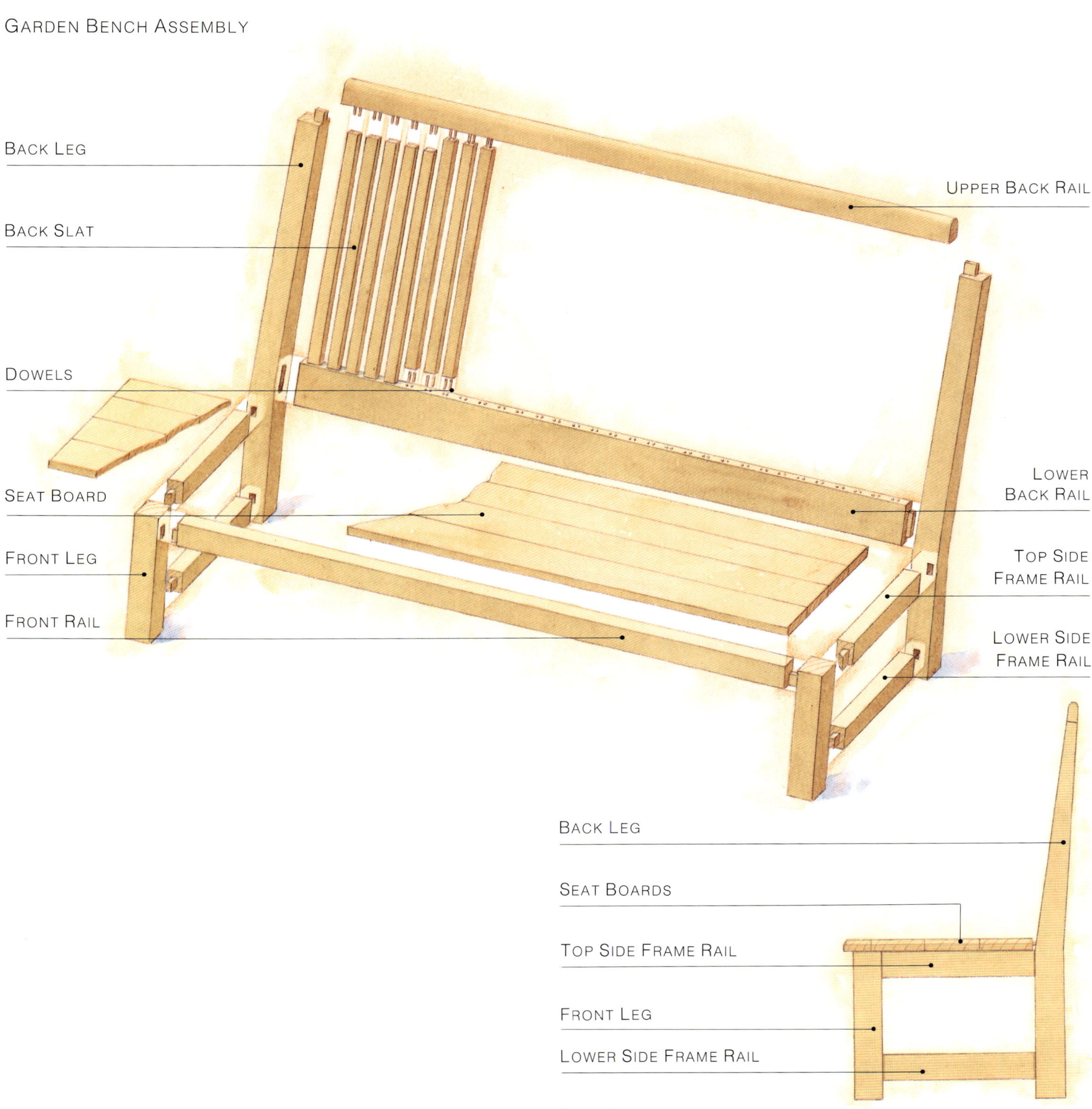

SIDE ELEVATION

GARDEN BENCH

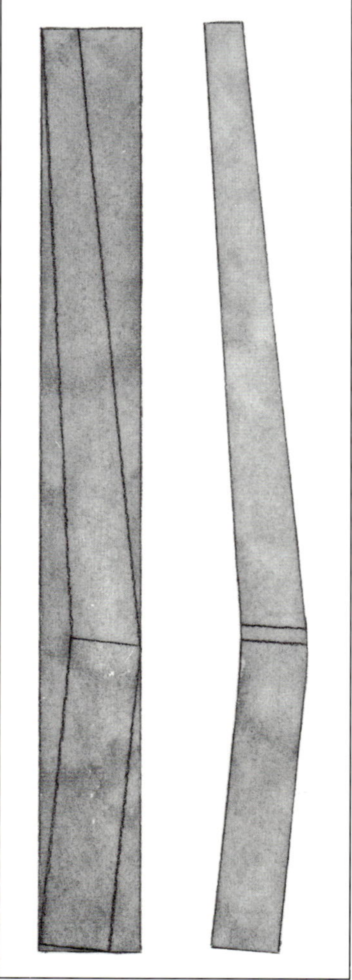

1 Shaping the Back Legs
Lay front leg at an angle on back leg and mark its position. Measure 35mm (1⅜in) in from the back at the top and join marks with top of front leg marks. Cut out around marked lines, curving the shape at the back. Mark off seat thickness parallel with top of front leg position.

SEAT SIDE FRAMES

SHAPING THE FRONT LEGS

Cut the front legs overlength – at least 430mm (17in) long in total – and measure 400mm (15¾in) up from the bottom to mark off the finished length. Square a line around the leg on all faces *(see* **Techniques, page 148***)*. Put the front legs aside for the time being.

SHAPING THE BACK LEGS

The back legs are shaped from 100 x 75mm (4 x 3in) timber. Mark out the legs by laying one of the front legs on the wider face of one of the back legs, sloping at an angle but touching at the bottom and side edges (fig 1). Remember that the front leg is overlength at the top, so align with the finished leg line. Mark round the shape of the front leg onto the back leg.

At the top of the back leg, measure 35mm (1⅜in) from the back face on both sides and join these two points to the top points of the marked front leg position, giving the shape for the back leg (fig 1).

With one back leg marked, cut out around the marked lines, with straight lines at the front face of the leg, but rounding off the angle at the back of the leg to produce a gentle curve. Plane the face edges at the front straight and square to the sides as the joints are measured from this edge.

Use the cut-out back leg to mark the other one and cut it out. When both legs are cut, mark off the seat thickness, parallel with the top of the front leg position, using a seat board and a try square.

MARKING UP THE MORTISES AND TENONS

Take one of the front legs and line one of the side rails (wide face against the leg) to the top marked line (fig 2), taking into account the excess length at the top. Mark off the

Marking square 148
Planing 150
Mortise and tenon joint 154

position of the bottom of the rail onto the leg. Working from this line, mark off the length of the mortise 50mm (2in) up. Square the lines round to the two inside faces *(see* **Techniques, page 148***)*.

For the bottom joint, measure 60mm (2⅜in) up from the bottom of the leg on the back face, then another 50mm (2in) up for the top of the mortise. Transfer all of these lines to the back of the other front leg using a try square. Square the lines of the top mortise round to the inside face of the second front leg.

Using a try square, transfer the length and position of the mortises from the front legs onto the front face of the back legs.

Take a 19mm (¾in) chisel and set a mortise gauge to this width with the stock set so that the mortise is central to the edge of the side rails (*not* central on the legs).

Mark off the top mortises on the front faces of the back legs, and on the two inside faces of the front legs. Measure from the *outside* edge in each case so that the front and upper side rails will be flush.

On the ends of all four side rails, mark off the tenons (fig 3) and also mark off the tenons on the ends of the front rail.

Re-set the stock on the mortise gauge so that it is central on the legs and mark off the lower mortises centrally on the inside faces of all the legs for the lower side rails.

Measure 50mm (2in) in from each end on one of the side rails, and mark the shoulder of the tenon. Square round all faces. Using a try square, transfer the lines onto all the other side rails. Measure 50mm (2in) in from each end of the front rail and square round as before. To ensure a strong construction, it is important that all the lengths between the shoulders on the side rails are accurately marked. Mark the widths of the top tenon 50mm (2in) from the bottom edges of all the *top* rails so that the tenons are bare-faced to the lower edge.

The tenons are central on the two *lower* side rails, so measure 10mm (⅜in) up from the lower edge, then 50mm (2in) for the width of the mortise (fig 3).

CUTTING THE JOINTS

Cut the mortises slightly deeper than 50mm (2in) *(see* **Techniques, Mortise and Tenon Joint, page 154***)* and then the tenons.

Dry assemble the parts to check the fit. The ends of the tenons on the front rail and the ends of the front tenons of the top side rails will all need to be cut at a 45° angle to ensure a tight fit (fig 4).

Cut off the 'horns' (protruding ends) at the tops of the front legs to leave the front legs flush with the upper side rails.

THE BACK

FITTING THE LOWER BACK RAIL

Take a chisel about 12mm (½in) wide and set a mortise gauge to exactly this width. Set the stock so the tenon will be offset to the back on the lower back rail, making a bare-faced tenon joint (fig 1, page 28). Mark the mortise on the inside faces of the back legs, working from the front faces. Mark the bare-faced tenons on the lower back rail.

Align the lower back rail with the mark for the seat at the front so that it is square to the top front face of the back leg (fig 1, page 28). Mark off the position of the rail, and mark a 15mm (⅝in) shoulder at the top and bottom.

On the lower back rail, mark 50mm (2in) in from the ends and 15mm (⅝in) in from the edges for the shoulders. Before cutting the tenons, check that the length between the shoulders is the same as the front rail. Cut the tenons and then chisel the mortises to a depth of 50mm (2in).

FITTING THE UPPER BACK RAIL

Mark 50mm (2in) down from the top of the back leg and square round using a try square. Transfer these lines to the other leg. With the mortise gauge still set to 12mm (½in) set the stock so that it is central at this shoulder line, working from the front face (fig 2, page 28). Now mark off the tenon on both legs.

2 Front Leg Mortises
Mark rail positions on leg. Mortises are central to edge of front and top side rails, central on lower side rail.

3 Front and Side Rail Tenons
Top **Cut bare-faced tenons for front and top side rails.** ***Bottom*** **Tenon is central on lower side rail.**

4 Dry Assembly of Front Legs to Front and Side Rails
Left **Position of cut mortises on front leg.** ***Inset*** **Plan view shows front rail and upper side rail flush with outside edges of front leg.** ***Right*** **Ends of tenons are angled on front and upper side rails.**

Garden Bench

The upper rail should be cut overlength by 50mm (2in), but use the lower rail to mark the exact length between the shoulders and square round the upper rail at each end. From these lines mark 50mm (2in) to the outside (towards the ends).

With the mortise gauge still set for the width of the tenon, mark the mortises on the bottom edge of the rail, working from the front face (fig 2). Mark the width of each tenon to 50mm (2in) from the inside face of the legs so that the tenons are bare-faced.

Cut the mortises to 50mm (2in) deep, and cut the tenons. Dry assemble the back legs to the upper and lower rails to check the fit and cut off the 'horns' (protruding ends) flush with the outer face of the legs.

Shaping the Upper Rail

The upper rail has to be shaped at the back to follow the taper of the back legs (fig 3). Strike a line up each back leg to continue the taper onto the rail and then join up these lines by marking a line along the top edge of the upper rail.

Remove the rail and cut off the waste with a power plane or by using a hand saw. This is a long rip cut and will need care. Finish the taper by planing the surface of the upper rail smooth.

Fitting the Back Slats

The width and spacing of the back slats is a matter of preference. We used 38 x 25mm ($1\frac{1}{2}$ x 1in) slats, spaced about 19mm ($\frac{3}{4}$in) apart.

The easiest way to fit the slats is to use two dowels top and bottom, positioned by means of a dowelling jig. We used 8mm ($\frac{5}{16}$in) dowels, 40mm ($1\frac{1}{2}$in) long. For an even stronger fixing you can use mortise and tenon joints top and bottom, but without a mortising machine it would be a very time-consuming task to make all the necessary joints.

Measure on the back leg the distance from the top of the lower rail to the underside of the upper rail, and cut the slats to this length if you will be fixing them using dowels. Cut the slats about 19mm ($\frac{3}{4}$in) longer at each end if you intend to use mortise and tenon joints.

Detail of the Garden Bench

For decorative effect, the outside edges of the legs, frame rails, seat boards and so on are chamferred before final assembly.

1 Fitting Lower Back Rail to Back Leg

Lower back rail fits square and flush with slope of front face of back leg and will align with back edge of seat boards. Mark mortises on inside faces of back legs and cut bare-faced tenons on lower back rail.

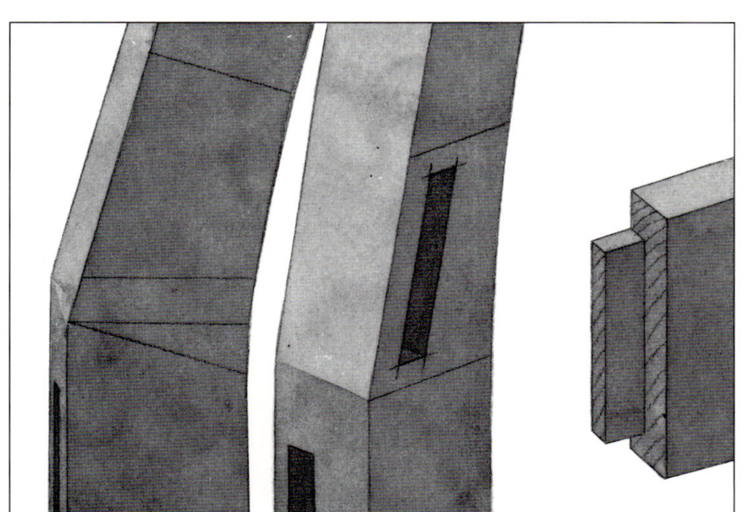

2 Fitting Upper Back Rail to Back Leg

Mark mortise on ends of upper back rail (remember it is overlength) and cut out. Mark rail position on top of back legs and cut bare-faced tenons on legs. Cut excess from ends of rail to fit flush with back legs.

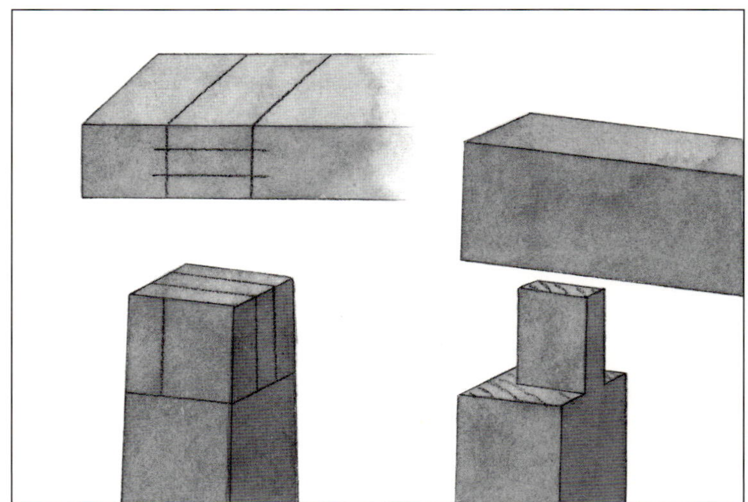

Cramps 145
Folding wedges 148
Drilling 150
Planing 150
Dowel joint 154
Mortise and tenon joint 154

Mark up the ends of the slats for the two dowel holes (fig 4) and, using a dowelling jig, drill the ends of the slats to a depth of 22mm ($\frac{7}{8}$in) using an 8mm ($\frac{5}{16}$in) dowel (centre-point) drill bit.

Mark a centre line along the top edge of the lower rail and the bottom edge of the upper rail for the centre line of the dowel holes.

Work out the positions of the slats along one of these, adjusting as necessary to give an even spacing between the slats. Mark the centres of the dowel hole positions all the way along.

Cramp the two rails together and transfer the dowel centre marks to the other rail. Drill the dowel holes to a depth of 22mm ($\frac{7}{8}$in).

ASSEMBLING THE FRAME

Dry assemble the whole bench. Chamfer the edges of the front and back legs, the lower side rails, the underside of the upper side rails, the edge of the lower back rail and the underside of the front rail using a router with a chamferring bit or a power plane.

Sand all the components to smooth the faces and edges, and to clean off any pencil marks. Glue up the end frames using a gap-filling waterproof glue such as Cascamite, cramping it tightly until the glue has thoroughly dried.

At this point, an adjustment has to be made to the height of the back legs to allow the seat to angle back slightly to assist rainwater drainage. This is done by standing the end frame on a flat surface, such as the workbench, and packing the front edge of the front leg by 15mm ($\frac{5}{8}$in) using a scrap piece of timber (fig 5).

Using an offcut of the same thickness, scribe the back leg and the side and back of the front leg to the correct angle. Cut off the bottoms of the legs to these lines. Repeat for the other end frame. Glue the front rail and the lower back rail into the end frames, then glue all the dowels and slats into the lower back rail. Apply glue to the tops of the slats and to the dowels and seat-back tenons, then tap the upper back rail into place. You will need someone to help you with this.

THE SEAT

CONSTRUCTION

The seat is a solid piece formed by dowelling together a number of narrow lengths of timber. Use a dowelling jig and join to the frame with 8mm ($\frac{5}{16}$in) dowels, 40mm ($1\frac{1}{2}$in) long, spaced about 150–225mm (6–9in) apart.

After dowelling, glue the lengths together using a gap-filling waterproof wood adhesive, such as Cascamite, and hold the assembly together with sash cramps or folding wedges against a fixed batten nailed to a worktop.

When the glue has dried, sand the surface flush and position the seat on the seat bench frame, leaving a 4mm ($\frac{1}{8}$in) wide gap at the back for drainage. Mark round so that there is a 19mm ($\frac{3}{4}$in) overhang at each end and at the front, then trim the seat to this line.

Cut a 12mm ($\frac{1}{2}$in) chamfer on the top edges at the front and sides using a router with a rounding over bit or a power plane.

FIXING

Fix the seat down using zinc-plated shrinkage plates – two at each end and three along the front – and screw into the seat rails and underside of the seat.

To keep the seat rigid so it will not bow in the middle, drill through the back rail into the seat in five places using a 12mm ($\frac{1}{2}$in) flat drill bit. Drill about 50mm (2in) into the seat. Cut five lengths of 12mm ($\frac{1}{2}$in) dowel about 95mm ($3\frac{3}{4}$in) long. Use a tenon saw or the point of a nail to cut two grooves 2–4mm ($\frac{1}{16}$–$\frac{1}{8}$in) deep along the dowel lengths to allow glue and air to escape as the dowels are driven into position.

Apply waterproof adhesive to the holes and hammer the dowels into position using the mallet. After the glue has set, saw off the protruding ends flush with the seat rail.

Chamfer the bottom edges of the legs so the wood will not split if the bench is dragged on the ground. To prevent the legs rotting, fix large, metal hammer-in glides to the bottoms of the legs.

3 Shaping Upper Back Rail
Mark sides and back of back rail to follow taper of back face of back leg. Remove waste and plane smooth.

4 Fitting the Back Slats
Mark slat and dowel positions on rails. Fit slats between back rails using two dowels each end.

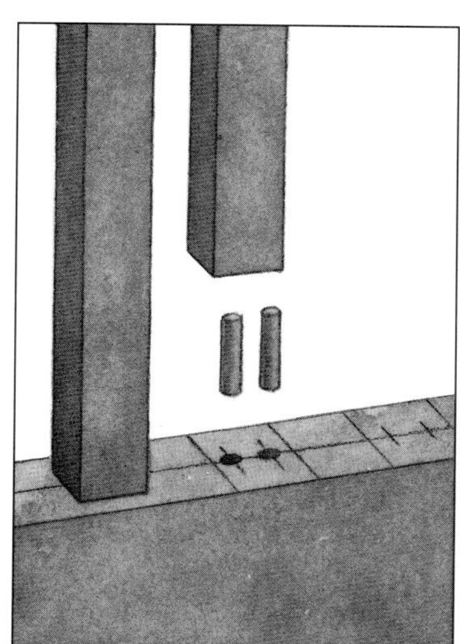

5 Angling the Legs
***Above* Stand bench frame on a flat surface and pack front leg with scrap timber. Scribe legs as necessary.**

6 Cross-section of Seat
***Below* Seat boards are butted up and joined using dowels. Longer dowels fix seat to lower back rail.**

Octagonal Tree Seat

Even in the smallest garden, a tree seat makes an inviting point of interest. Any type of seating really makes a garden look furnished, but a seat which encircles a tree is particularly appealing. Children enjoy playing on, under and around the shady platform and seem to gain endless amusement sitting on opposite sides from each other or their parents.

Although this seat looks complicated, it is actually fairly simple to make. Nevertheless, it is a time-consuming project. Because the back leans inwards, cutting the back slats could have been quite a difficult proposition. To prevent unnecessary complication, a gap has been left between the slats to accommodate any discrepancies that may occur.

Other design simplifications were made. There is a simple bold structure for the frame underneath rather than complicated mortise-and-tenon joints.

Softwood is an easy timber to work with and contributes a great deal to the ease with which a structure like this can be made. But softwood does need to be protected in some way, by treating with preservative, and then by applying a final finish of wood stain or, as in this case, paint. Depending on where in your garden the seat is positioned, you might like to choose a brighter colour: a strong blue would be very effective.

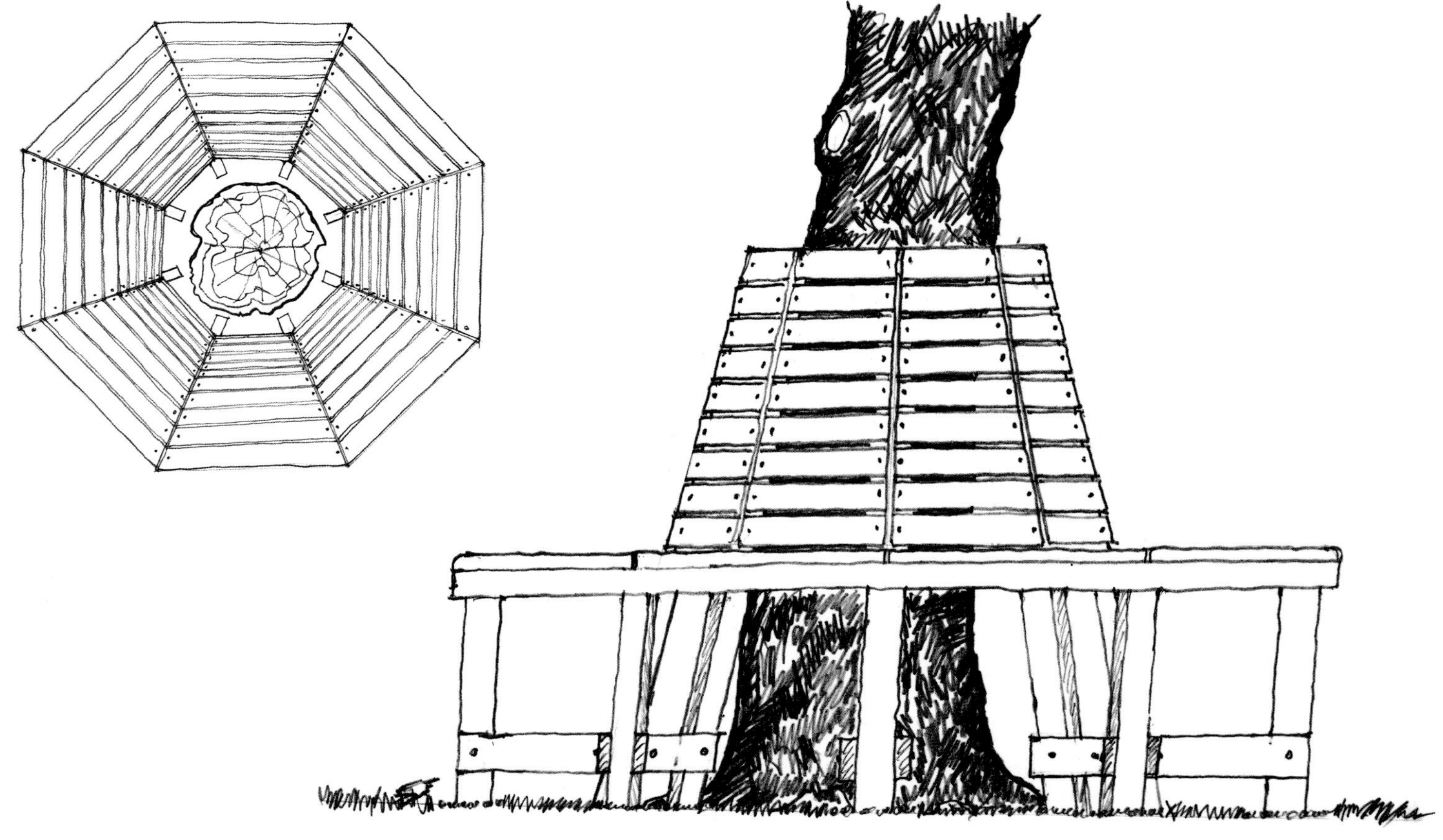

Octagonal Tree Seat

Tools

- WORKBENCH (fixed or portable)
- STEEL MEASURING TAPE
- STEEL RULE
- TRY SQUARE (or combination square)
- SLIDING BEVEL
- PROTRACTOR
- CIRCULAR POWER SAW – preferably bench-mounted (or panel saw)
- TENON SAW
- POWER DRILL
- DRILL BIT – approximately 3mm ($\frac{1}{8}$in) diameter
- COUNTERSINK BIT
- SCREWDRIVER
- CLAW HAMMER
- NAIL PUNCH
- PINCERS
- SMOOTHING PLANE (hand or power)

Materials

Part	Quantity	Material	Length
BACK LEGS	8	75 x 50mm (3 x 2in) PAR softwood	1050mm (42in)
FRONT LEGS	8	As above	500mm (20in)
SEAT FRAME RAILS	32	75 x 25mm (3 x 1in) PAR softwood	530mm (21in)
SEAT SLATS	48	As above	As required
APRON BOARDS	8	As above	As required
BACK SLATS	72	50 x 16mm (2 x $\frac{5}{8}$in) PAR softwood	As required
APRON FIXING BATTENS	8	25 x 25mm (1 x 1in) PAR softwood	150mm (6in) shorter than apron boards

Also required: waterproof woodworking adhesive; 38mm (1$\frac{1}{2}$in) No 8 zinc-plated countersunk wood screws

The size of this eight-sided tree seat is governed by the size of the tree you wish to surround. Remember, you must leave room for the trunk to expand as the tree grows! Some trees grow faster than others: we built our seat around a small walnut tree, which is a slow-growing species, but even so we allowed an internal diameter of 600mm (24in) at the very top of the back support. Quite large tree specimens are available from good garden centres, so it could be worth planting a small 'standard' tree (that is, one with a long trunk) just as the focal point around which to build this seat.

The basic construction consists of eight separate frames on which the seat and backrest slats are fixed. The frames are of a pre-determined size, but the length of the slats is varied according to the internal diameter of the seat.

The seat is made in two sections, dry assembled to each other, so the two halves can be easily unscrewed to fix around the tree.

Seat Frames

Cut the components of the seat frames to length.

Chamfer the front face of each back leg at an angle of 22$\frac{1}{2}$° from the centre line of one of the 75mm (3in) faces (fig 1). It is best to do this using a circular saw canted over at the correct angle – use a sliding bevel aligned on a protractor to set this. Finish off using a hand or power plane for a smooth finish.

1 Chamferring the Back Leg

Draw a line down middle of front face of each back leg. Chamfer legs at an angle of 22$\frac{1}{2}$° from this line.

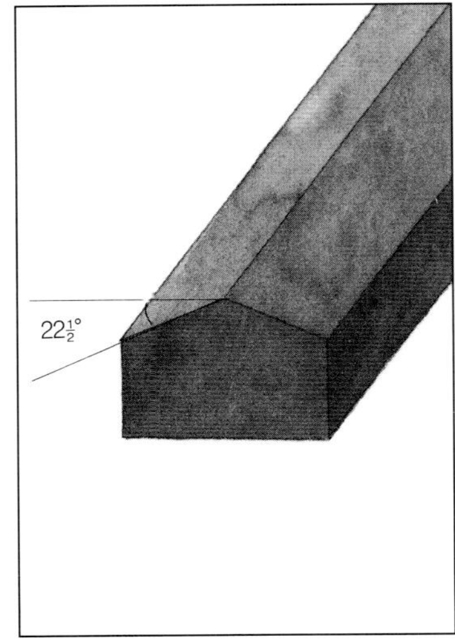

2 Making the Spacing Template

Cut a spacing template from a scrap piece of board to the dimensions shown below. The template is used for accurate positioning of the front and back legs and the seat frame rails to make up the seat frames.

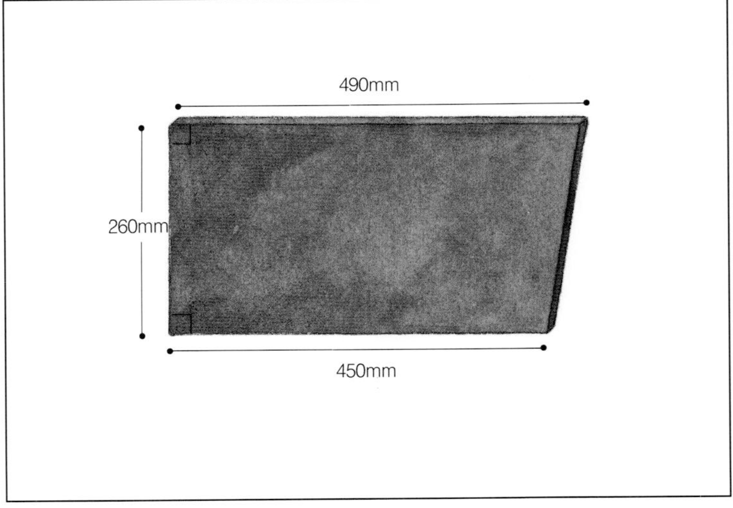

Circular saw **145**
Planes **145**
Softwood **148**

Octagonal Tree Seat Assembly

Octagonal Tree Seat

Detail of Seat Legs

Gravel-filled holes around the front and back legs of the seat frames make levelling easier and keep the legs off water-logged ground, reducing the risk of the wood rotting.

Using a scrap of hardboard or chipboard to the shape and dimensions shown (fig 2, page 32), make up a template for fixing the seat frame rails on to the front and back legs to make up the seat frames.

Temporarily nail a batten to your workbench to give a flat surface to rest the feet of the legs against. Lay the front and back legs of one frame on the bench with two seat frame rails on top and the spacing template between them (fig 1). The back leg must be angled to align with the back of the template and the front leg should be exactly flush with the front edge of the template. The bottom of the legs should be resting against the batten nailed to the workbench.

The bottom seat frame rail is positioned so that it overlaps the front leg by 12mm (½in), while the top frame rail should be flush with the front and top of the front leg.

If a suitable flat workbench is not

1 Making Up the Seat Frames

Lay the front and back legs of one frame on a flat surface so they are flush with template. Top frame rail rests on template and is flush with the top and front of front rail; bottom frame rail overlaps front leg by 12mm (½in).

2 Finished Construction of the Seat Frames

***Above* Glue and screw seat frame rails to legs, then trim overlap at the back so it is parallel with slope of back leg and protrudes 12mm (½in). *Below* Finished frame shows frame rails screwed in position to front and back legs.**

Sliding bevel 144
Drilling 150
Planing 150
Screwing 150

available for this setting out, the pieces can be laid out on a flat floor, with the legs resting against an adjacent wall, so that the wall aligns the base of the legs.

Glue the top of the seat frame rail in place using a waterproof woodworking adhesive (such as Cascamite), then drill pilot holes and screw it to the front and back legs using two screws at each end. Glue and screw the bottom seat frame rail to the legs in the same way.

Turn the frame over and position the other two seat frame rails in the same way, top and bottom. It is very important that these rails are exactly square to the ones on the other side so that the rails will be flush across the top where the seat slats will be fixed (fig 2).

To complete the construction of the frames, the seat frame rails are trimmed off in line with the back leg, but leaving a 12mm ($\frac{1}{2}$in) overlap (fig 2). Strike a line at this position, and then trim off using a panel saw or circular saw.

Repeat the construction for the remaining seven frames.

SEAT SLATS

The seat slats are cut from 75 x 25mm (3 x 1in) PAR (planed all round) softwood. The dimensions of the seat frames are predetermined, so that the number of slats required will not vary, no matter how large the finished seat. What you will have to calculate yourself, however, is the length of each slat. This will depend upon the internal diameter of the seat, itself dependent on size of the tree trunk around which you assemble the project.

To measure up for the seat section, stand the eight frames around the tree roughly in position and spaced at the required distance from the tree, allowing for growth and depending on how large you want the diameter of the tree seat.

MAKING THE SEAT SLATS

When you are satisfied with the spacing of the seat frames, measure the distance between the centres of the back legs at seat height and calculate the average ('x' in fig 3). This will be the length of the inside edge of the innermost seat slats (ours are 380mm [15in] long).

Mark length 'x' on to the back edge of a piece of the slat timber and draw $112\frac{1}{2}°$ angles off at either end using a sliding bevel. You can then use this slat to help draw up a full-size plan of a seat section (fig 4) which will enable you to cut the remaining five seat slats to the correct length.

To make the full-size plan, mark off the back measurement using the innermost slat as a guide for the angles. Extend the angled lines outwards, using the sliding bevel to double check that the angle is $112\frac{1}{2}°$. Returning to the seat frame, measure the distance from the centre of the back leg to the front of the frame ('y' in fig 3). On a full-size plan, mark the length 'y' on the angled lines, and add 20mm ($\frac{3}{4}$in) to allow for the approximate thickness of the apron board at the front of the seat. Join up the two marks 'y plus 20mm ($\frac{3}{4}$in)' at the front of the plan, parallel with the back line, to give the front edge of the seat.

You can now work out the necessary spacing for the slats. Place the innermost slat in position on the full-size plan and roughly cut five more slats, making sure that they are overlength. Bunch the slats together against the innermost slat, measure the remaining distance to the front line of the seat, and divide by five to give the amount of space to be left between each slat. If you want to increase the spacing, at this stage plane the edge of the innermost slat to reduce its width.

Using one of the slats and a spacing batten or spacing blocks cut to the width of the calculated space, draw out all six slats in position on the full-size plan. You will then be able to measure off the plan for the exact lengths of all the slats in each section of the seat.

Cut out all the slats for one seat section, but cut 2mm (about $\frac{1}{16}$in) inside each marked line in order to create a deliberate gap between the ends of the slats. You can use the slats cut for the first seat frame as templates for cutting the seat slats for the other sections.

3 Measuring up for the Seat Slats
Measure distance between centres of back legs at seat height ('x') to calculate length of innermost slat. Measure distance between centre of back leg and front of frame ('y') to calculate spacing between slats.

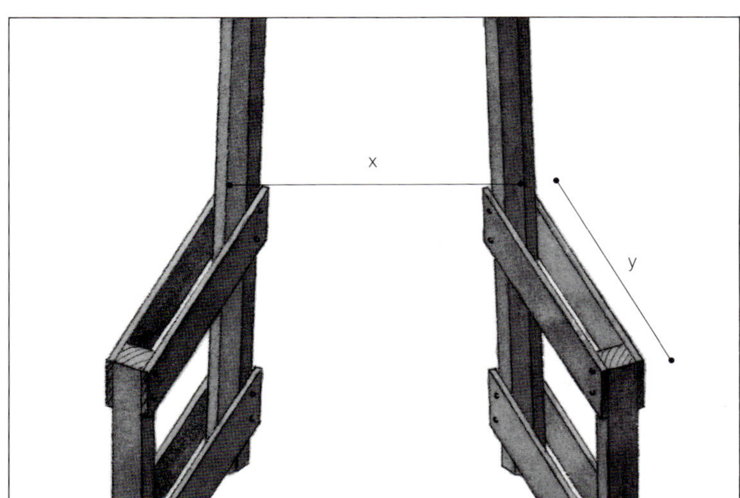

4 Drawing up Full-size Plan of Seat Section
Mark length 'x' and draw lines 'y plus 20mm ($\frac{3}{4}$in)' either end at $112\frac{1}{2}°$ angle. Bunch six slats on plan, measure remaining distance to front and divide by five to calculate spacing. Cut spacers to size, then mark slat positions.

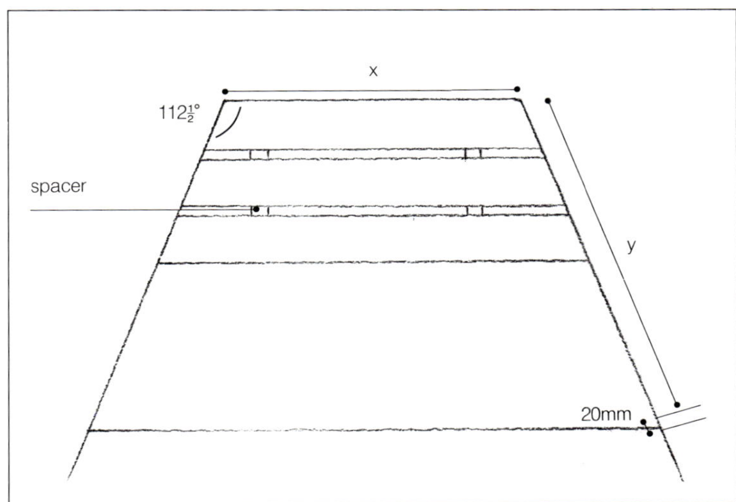

Octagonal Tree Seat

Fixing the Seat Slats

Fix the innermost slats first. Place the first slat across the back of two seat frames, spaced 2mm (about $\frac{1}{16}$in) in from the centre of the back legs, then glue and screw the slat to the top seat frame rails with one screw at each end (fig 1).

Take another seat frame and innermost slat, and space in the same way. Glue and screw in place as before.

Continue in this way for two groups of three sections each. It is very important that you only dry assemble two sections opposite one another, as you will need to remove the slats on two opposite sides of the structure in order to fix the seat frames around the tree.

To fix the subsequent slats, line up the next shortest slat with the innermost slat (fig 2). With the spacing batten (or blocks) between the slats, align one end of the new slat with a batten held against one end of the previously fixed slat. Glue and screw into the top seat frame rail at each end.

Continue with this second size slat all the way round, remembering only to dry assemble where you did before. Carry on in this fashion, one row at a time, assembling without glue those slats in the two sections that are dry assembled.

Before the frontmost slats are fitted, the apron boards must be assembled (fig 3). Cut a piece of 75 x 25mm (3 x 1in) timber to the longest length of the frontmost slat and bevel back the edges at each end so they are in line with the angles of the seat slat. Cut a 25 x 25mm (1 x 1in) fixing batten about 150mm (6in) shorter than the apron board and glue and screw it centrally in place to join the apron board to the frontmost slat. The front edge of the slat must be flush with the front face of the apron board. Repeat the process to make the other apron boards.

Round off the front edges of the frontmost slats to give a smooth finish. Glue and screw into place at the front edges of the frames, remembering not to glue the dry assembled sections.

The Back Slats

The back of each seat section is comprised of nine slats, cut from 50 x 16mm (2 x $\frac{5}{8}$in) PAR (planed all round) softwood. However, because the back legs are angled, the slats are not all the same length; instead, they get shorter as they reach the top.

Decide on the spacing of the back slats, and use scrap pieces of timber of the required thickness as spacing blocks. Lay the spacing blocks at seat level so that you start with a space, then lay the first slat, left overlength for the time being, in position. Mark off the ends in line with the centres of the back legs (fig 4). Set a sliding bevel to this angle, and cut the back slat to the marked length. Use the sliding bevel to mark off the correct angle and cut the first slats for the remaining back sections to length. Glue and screw the first back slats in place to the front of the back legs of all the seat sections, but leave the slats dry assembled in the same sections as you did before on the seat slats.

Use the spacing blocks to position the next length of slat (fig 4), mark off the ends as before, and cut to length. Repeat for the other seven slats in the row around the seat, and fix in place as before.

Continue in this way, row by row, until the seat back is completed (nine rows in our case). If the back legs protrude above the top slats they can be cut flush with the top of the slats for a neat appearance.

Dismantle the dry joints so that the seat is in two 'halves' (actually, two three-eighths).

Assembly

Take the two 'halves' of the seat to the tree and partially re-assemble it without glue so you can mark on the ground where the legs are positioned. Dismantle the seat again.

At the leg positions, dig holes for each of the 16 legs, 150mm (6in) in diameter and 150mm (6in) deep, and fill them with gravel. The gravel provides good drainage, reducing the risk of the legs rotting, and allows you to level the seat easily.

1 Fixing the Innermost Seat Slats
Use plan as guide but cut slats about 2mm ($\frac{1}{16}$in) short both ends. Space slat about 2mm ($\frac{1}{16}$in) in from centre of back legs, then fix between two top frame rails. Work round frames, but *dry assemble* slats on two facing sections.

2 Fixing Subsequent Slats to the Frame
Align next shortest slat with innermost slat: put the spacers or spacing battens in position, align ends of slat with innermost slat, and fix to frame rails. Continue round frame, then repeat for next size slats.

FINISHING

Before painting, it is important to treat the seat with a good-quality wood preservative which can be painted when dry – most clear and green grade preservatives fall into this category. We applied two coats, allowing each to dry thoroughly, and stood the legs in dishes of preservative for a couple of days.

Once the wood preservative is thoroughly dry (allow at least a week), the seat can be painted. We used a microporous paint which needs no primer (apart from preservative) and is intended for outdoor woodwork. The seat can be treated with a water-repellent preservative stain if a 'wood' finish is preferred.

After finishing with paint or wood stain, the seat can be finally assembled around the tree. Make sure the seat is well-bedded in the gravel and stands level on the ground. You can glue all joints at final assembly, or leave two sections of slats 'dry' to allow easy removal of the seat should the need arise.

3 Making the Apron Board

Above **Use fixing batten to attach apron board to frontmost slat.**
Below **Front edge rounded over.**

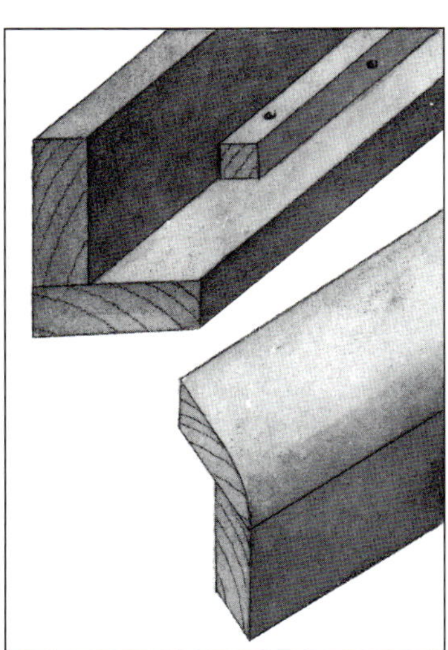

4 Spacing and Fixing the Back Slats

Back slats are initially overlength. Use spacing batten or spacing blocks to position back slat, and mark off ends of slat to line up with centres of back legs. Cut slats to length, then reposition and glue and screw in place.

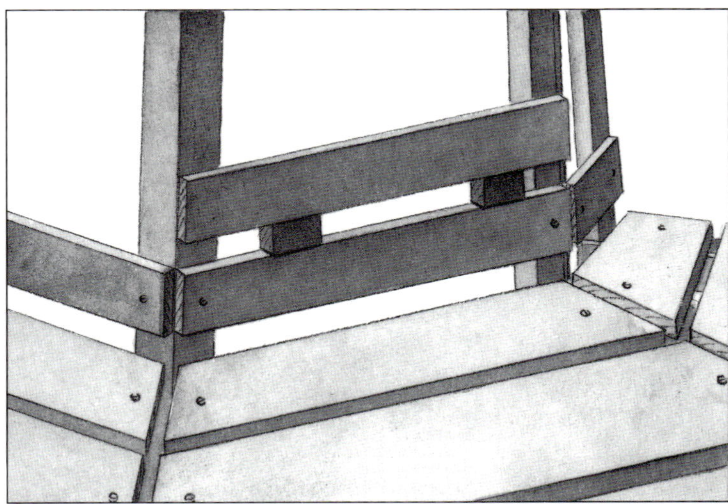

BARBECUE

Most barbecues, whether they are DIY or ready-made versions, have a number of design problems. One common fault is that they are generally too low to work at comfortably, which means the cook spends most of the time crouched awkwardly over the grill. The second problem is that grilling areas are often too small, providing food for only a limited number of people at a time.

This barbecue area corrects both of these typical defects, as well as providing a carefully considered series of spaces and surfaces for serving the food, storing fuel and keeping pans and dishes.

The generous grill area can be temporarily reduced in size if you only want to cook a small amount of food by placing bricks in the middle and confining the space in that way. The grill supports consist of several strips of angle iron cemented into place and these hold the grill tray. The entire structure is built up against a brick wall. With time, the wall will blacken with smoke, but this is not an unattractive effect. If you do not have a similar site for the barbecue, you can build a small brick wall at the back instead or leave the barbecue free-standing.

One particular advantage of this construction is the spaces it provides at either end of the grill area as well as beneath. On top, two quite extensive surfaces can be used as a place for resting pans and dishes of food in preparation. Underneath, timber can be stored. If you use the barbecue often and for long enough, the whole structure will warm up and the timber will be 'kiln-dried'.

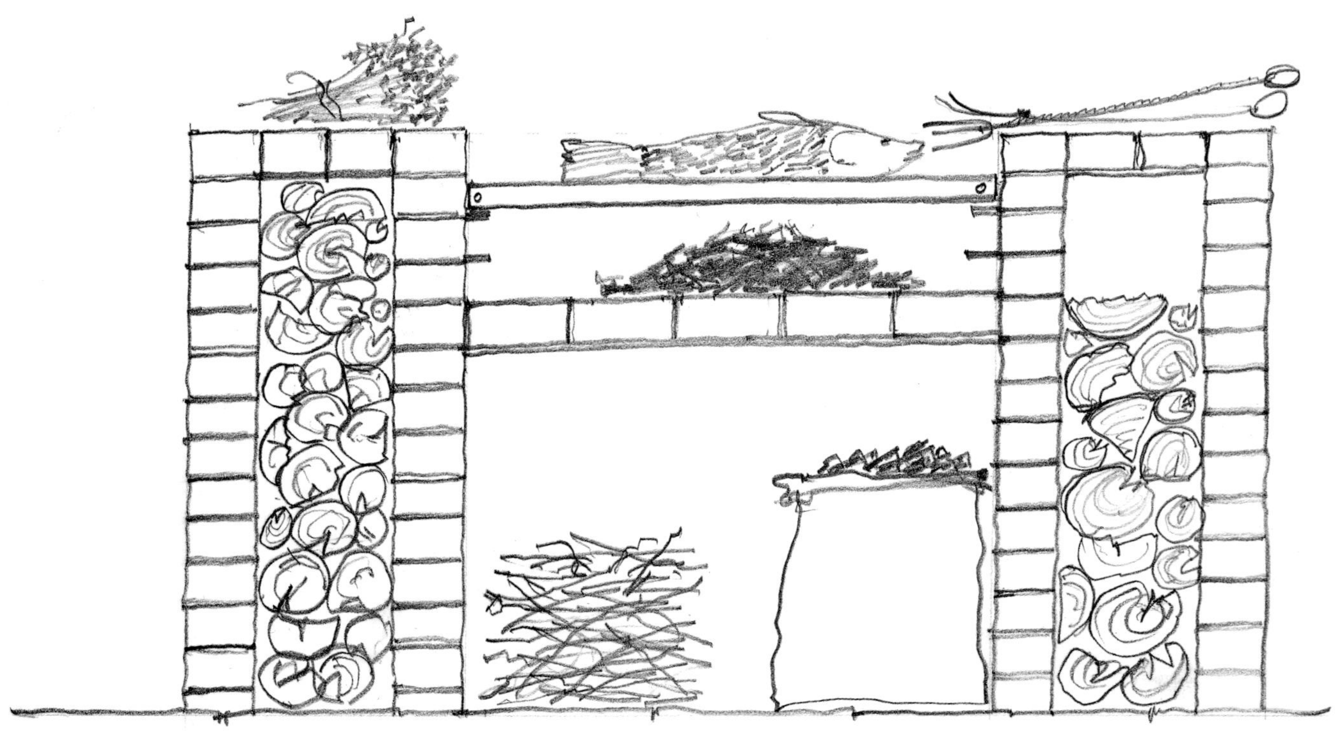

Barbecue

Few pleasures are equal to that of sitting outside on a warm, summer's evening, eating food in the company of family and friends. If you build a barbecue, it will add a second focal point to your sitting-out area, but be careful to site it away from overhanging plants and any other vegetation that might catch fire while you are cooking.

The barbecue here is built from reclaimed bricks which match the wall against which it is built. Second-hand bricks are marginally larger than new bricks, but the dimensions here are calculated in courses rather than specific measurements, and you can use either sort of brick for building this project. The grill area is large enough to cook a substantial amount of food, but you could build the ends closer together if preferred.

The barbecue can be built against an existing wall or it can be free-standing. You can either build it on top of paving slabs, or you can lay paving slabs around the barbecue once it has been built. If you choose the latter option, you will have to cut the paving slabs to fit, and you will also need to dig foundations before laying the first course of bricks. The foundations will need to be 150mm (6in) deep and 200mm (8in) wide around the outline of the barbecue. Lay 100mm (4in) of hardcore in the trench, ram it down, and then cover it with a 50mm (2in) layer of concrete. Check that the surface is level, and then leave the base to dry out and harden for a day or so.

As long as the paving slabs are level and are correctly laid on a firm base, however, it will be easier to build the barbecue on existing slabs. It is a good idea to protect the paving on which the barbecue is to be built with a sheet of thick, heavy-duty polythene. Simply lay the polythene sheet over the paving, build up the barbecue on top of the polythene, and then cut away the protruding sheet afterwards. The polythene will protect the surface of the paving from staining with wet cement while you are building, and will keep the brickwork at the base clean and dry.

Construction

Lay the bricks following the course-by-course plans (figs 1–3; *see also* **Techniques: Bricklaying, pages 156–7**). You will find it helpful to set out this project to ensure that the side walls are built exactly at right angles to the rear wall. A builder's square is quite easy to make from three battens with lengths in the proportion of 3:4:5. These should be nailed together to form a right-angled triangle – a useful size of square to make is a triangle with a base measuring 450mm (18in), a height of 600mm (24in) and a hypotenuse of 750mm (30in). Leave all of the battens slightly overlength, then nail or screw them together to form *exactly* these dimensions. Saw off the surplus afterwards.

Using a tight string line and the builder's square, make sure that the bricks in each course are straight and, using a spirit level, make sure that each course is built vertically.

When the seventh course is reached, bed angle irons across the central section to support bricks forming the firebed. Do *not* lay these bricks for the time being.

Lay the eighth to eleventh courses, and on the eleventh course bed mild steel strips across the side walls to support the 'table' tops.

Spread the mortar on the strips, then lay the twelfth course. Finally, lay bedding mortar on the angle irons in the central section and lay the firebed bricks edge on.

After the mortar has dried out, drill the bricks in the eleventh and twelfth courses to take steel supports (coach screws with the heads cut off are ideal) which will support the food grill tray above the firebed. Measure the size of the central opening and get a blacksmith or steel fabricator to make a grill tray by welding an outer frame of mild steel strips, braced with mild steel strips and fitted with mild steel rods welded about 25mm (1in) apart.

To protect the bricks of the firebed from excessive heat and to keep them clean, at the same time as the grill is made you could get a steel tray made up to cover the firebed.

Tools

- BRICKLAYER'S TROWEL
- POINTING TROWEL
- CLUB HAMMER
- BRICK BOLSTER CHISEL
- SHOVEL
- BUILDER'S BUCKET
- BUILDER'S SQUARE
- SPIRIT LEVEL (long)

Materials

- BRICKS – 231 new or second-hand
- MORTAR – from cement and builder's sand in the proportion 1:6
- STEEL ANGLE IRONS – 4 pieces, 1016mm (40in) long
- MILD STEEL STRIPS – 6 pieces, 100 × 300mm (4 × 12in)
- MILD STEEL – for grill; measure finished barbecue for exact dimensions

1 ***Above*** **Plan View of 1st, 3rd, 5th and 7th Courses**
Lay bricks as shown; bed angle irons to support firebed on 7th course only.
Below **Plan view of 2nd, 4th and 6th Courses**
Cut three-quarter length bricks to enable courses to be staggered.

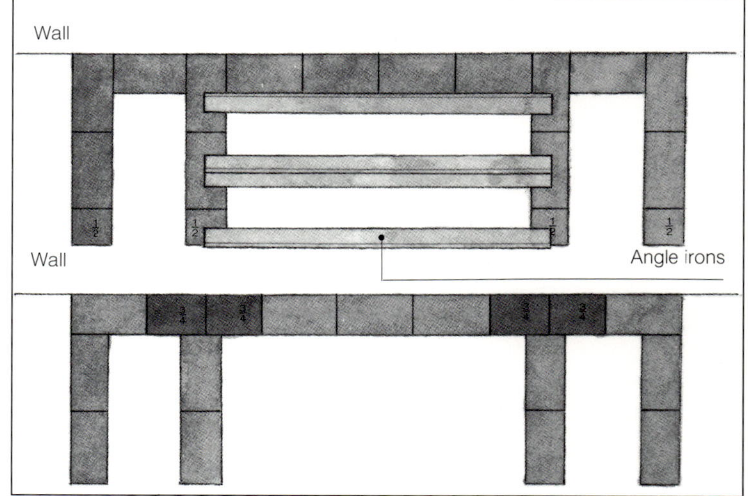

Laying foundations 156
Laying bricks 157

BARBECUE ASSEMBLY

FOOD GRILL TRAY

2½ BRICKS

12 BRICKS

12 BRICKS EDGE ON

FIREBED

STEEL REINFORCEMENT STRIPS

ANGLE IRON

2 ***Above*** **Plan View of 8th Course**

Two rows of 12 bricks are laid edge on above angle irons to form firebed

Below **Plan View of 9th and 11th Courses**

From 9th course, bricks only laid at ends; steel plates above 11th course.

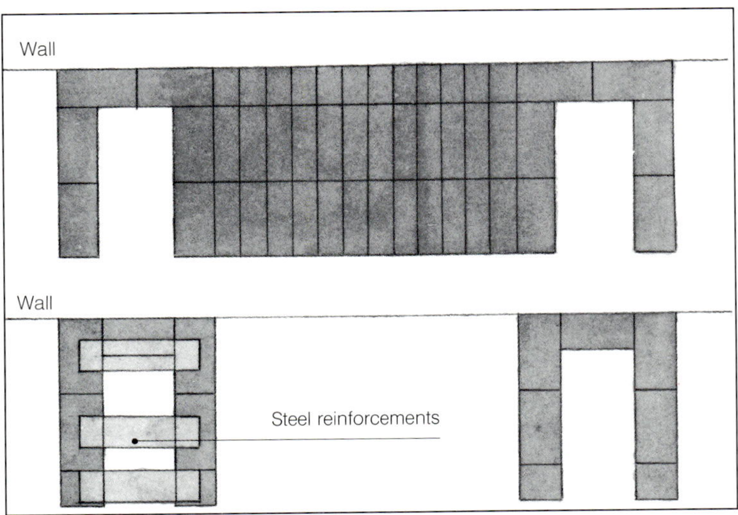

3 ***Above*** **Plan View of 10th Course**

Lay six bricks each end as shown.

Below **Plan View of 12th Course**

Ten bricks each end are laid above steel strips to form top.

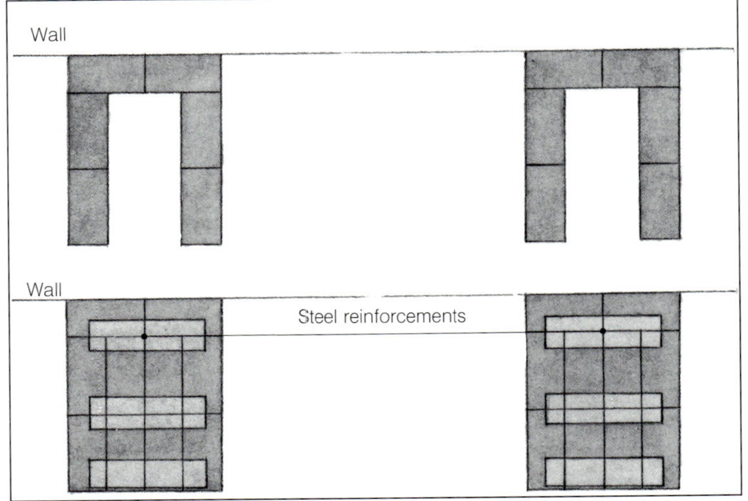

AWNING

An awning over a patio or sitting-out area gives privacy and allows you to use the area in most weather. The awning here is an optional addition to a simple pergola attached to a house wall. It rests on the pergola and can be brought out in sunny or warm showery weather, yet is simple to remove when not required.

You can make the pergola more or less any size to suit your patio or paved area. The structure is made from preservative-treated planed timber; western red cedar is ideal, but ordinary softwood treated with a water-repellent wood stain is a very serviceable alternative.

The supporting posts are made from 100 × 100mm (4 × 4in) timber of sufficient length to give headroom of at least 2.3m (7ft 6in) under the pergola structure. The posts are positioned about 2.4m (8ft) apart and are linked to the house wall by 175 × 50mm (7 × 2in) roof joists. At the front, the posts are steadied and separated at the top by a fascia board measuring 100 × 38mm (4 × 1½in) which runs the entire length of the pergola.

In the example shown, where there is a wall at the end of the terrace, there is no need to position a post and roof joist against the house wall. Instead, a length of 100 × 50mm (4 × 2in) timber is bolted to the wall so that the top of this length of timber is at the same level as the tops of the roof joists. Use expanding wall bolts to ensure a secure fixing.

On the main wall of the house, the roof joists can be supported in galvanized steel joist hangers, which are screwed and wallplugged to the house wall; the roof joists are then screwed into the joist hangers. An alternative method for supporting the roof joists is to rest them on a 100 × 50mm (4 × 2in) timber beam (called a wall plate) which is fixed horizontally to the wall, using expanding wall bolts, so that it supports the roof joists at the correct height. In this case, the roof joists can be fixed to the wall plate by nailing at an angle through the sides of the roof joists and into the top of the wall plate (*see* **Techniques, Skew Nailing, page 151**).

An unusual but practical feature of this pergola is the covered roof section close to the wall of the house. This provides permanent shelter and shade at the back of the seating area, and also strengthens the pergola, prevents sideways movement in high winds, and keeps rain off the house window frames.

The removable awning is made from deck chair canvas and is intended to be fitted during the warmer months of the year. It is draped across the roof joists and is held in place by tapes that loop around the roof joists. The tapes are secured by Velcro fasteners. The awning is stiffened at each end by being folded over and tacked to a 19 × 9.5mm (¾ × ⅜in) strip of hardwood or ramin.

CONSTRUCTION

Start by cutting the support posts to length. You need to take into account that the roof joists are fixed at a slight downward slope, and that you might not have a great deal of flexibility over the height at which you can fix the joist hangers or wall plate onto the wall of your house. You also need to decide how the posts will be fixed at the bottom. The easiest method of fixing the posts is to slot them into socket-type supports which can be screwed to the surface of the patio (fig 2). Alternatively, each post can be fitted over a protruding bolt or bracket cemented into the surface of the paving. Yet another option is to chip a hole through the surface of the patio using a hammer and cold chisel so that the bottom of the post can be concreted in place.

Once the length of post has been decided, the top can be angled and the joint cut to accommodate the roof joist. Saw down to form a slot to suit the width of the roof joist – its actual width will be less than 50mm (2in). Most of the waste can be removed by sawing, and finally the joint (a form of bridle joint) can be cleaned up using a chisel.

If the roof joists are to be fixed to the house wall using joist hangers, these are fixed next. Make sure that they are level by lining them up with

❶ Detail of Top Section

The roof joists are supported by 100 × 100mm (4 × 4in) posts at the front and by the main wall of the house at the back. Shade is provided by the permanent covered section and the removable canvas awning.

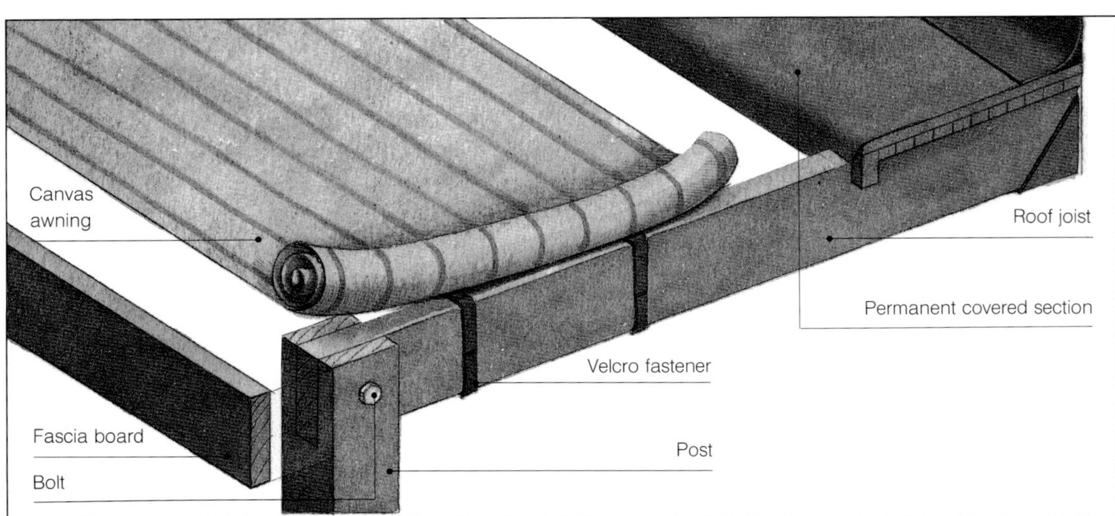

❷ Socket-type Post Supports

Metal support is screwed or bolted to ground. Post slots in support and is fixed by tightening screws at side.

Drilling 150
Expanding wall bolt 151
Skew nailing 151
Fixing posts 152

a line drawn along the wall. Check that the line is horizontal using a spirit level and fix the joist hangers in place using zinc-plated screws into wallplugs. Alternatively, fix the wall plate in place using expanding wall bolts. Slot the roof joists in place between the post and joist hanger or wall plate, and fix with a bolt through the post, and by screwing through the joist hanger. Skew nail the joists if they are resting on a wall plate (fig 3). Nail the fascia board to the top of the support posts.

All that remains is to fix the permanent covered section (fig 4). Nail 38 × 12mm ($1\frac{1}{2} \times \frac{1}{2}$in) cedar or stained softwood slats across the joists finishing with a 38 × 25mm ($1\frac{1}{2} \times 1$in) batten which is notched at intervals to accept the roof joists and is fitted vertically against the lowest slat. The top is covered with a 915mm- (36in-) deep sheet of exterior grade chipboard which is then covered with roofing felt. The roof-to-wall joint is sealed by pressing a strip of self-adhesive flashing strip firmly in place across the entire length of the joint.

3 Fixing the Joists to the Wall

Left **Joist hangers are aligned at correct height and screwed to wall; joists sit in hangers and are screwed in place.** ***Right*** **4 × 2in (100 × 50mm) wall plate fixed horizontally to wall; joists skew nailed in place.**

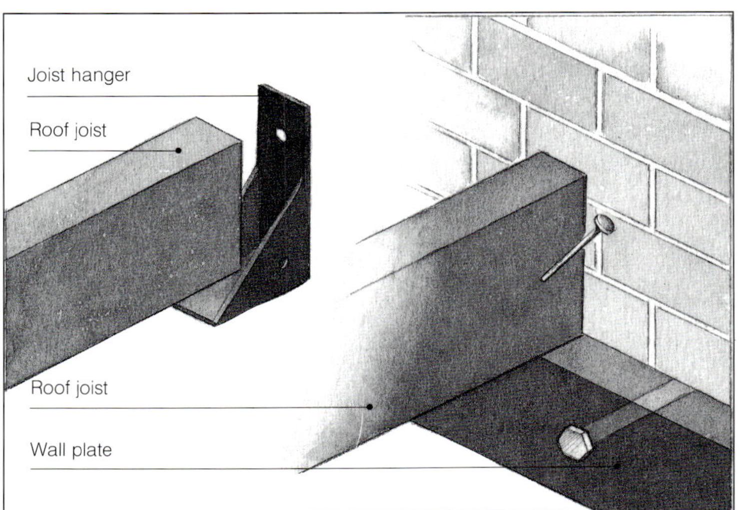

4 Permanent Covered Section

Softwood slats are nailed to roof joists. Batten at front of slats is notched at intervals to accept joists. Section is then covered in exterior-grade chipboard and roofing felt. Seal roof-to-wall joint with flashing strip.

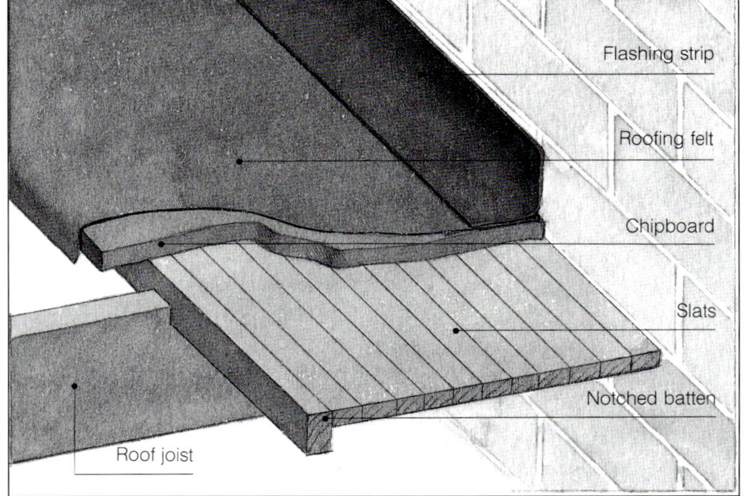

TIMBER TABLE

This sturdy garden table makes an attractive feature in any outdoor setting. The table shown is only 375mm (15in) high, but by increasing the height of the base on which it is built you can make it to any height required. If, for example, you make it about 750mm (30in) high you will be able to sit around it on garden chairs and use it as an outdoor dining table.

Apart from the brick base, the table is made entirely from solid timber. Preservative-treated quality softwood is ideal; hardwood could be used, but because of the large quantity of timber required, its cost would be prohibitively high.

The table top is made from 75 x 50mm (3 x 2in) timber, in the form of 12 square frames which become progressively larger from a central block. There is a gap of about 5mm (¼in) between each square, which is created automatically by using 50mm (2in) wide PAR (planed all round) timber for the table top. PAR timber is sawn to its nominal width – in this case 50mm (2in) – and then each face is planed about 5mm (¼in) so that the actual width is about 45mm (1¾in).

CONSTRUCTION

Start by building a base from brick, stone or reconstituted stone-and-concrete blocks *(see* **Techniques, page 156/7** *)*; the base should measure 560 x 560mm (22 x 22in) and it should be about 225mm (9in) high if you want to make the table as shown in the photograph. The height could be increased to as much as 600mm (24in) if an outdoor dining table is required.

The table top is fixed on two diagonal supports which are fitted to the base plinth to form an 'X'. Cut cross halving joints *(see* **Techniques, page 152** *)* at the point where the supports intersect (fig 2). For neatness, the ends of the supports are sloped as shown in the side view (fig 2). The last 300mm (12in) is sloped from the full depth of 75mm (3in) to 25mm (1in) at the end. Assemble the supports by gluing the cross halving joint with waterproof woodworking adhesive and then cramp the supports until the glue sets, checking first that the supports are exactly at right angles.

If you are unable to buy preservative pressure-treated timber, then at this stage it is wise to treat the supports with a good quality water-repellent preservative; apply a second coat of preservative 24 hours later.

The supports are fixed down to the base plinth using expanding wall bolts into holes drilled in the base plinth and recessed into the supports. Before tightening these bolts, check that the supports are absolutely level using a spirit level and put packing pieces underneath them to adjust as necessary.

FORMING THE TABLE TOP

The table top consists of concentric 'frames' which fit one inside the other down to the solid block

MATERIALS

Part	Quantity	Material	Length
PLINTH	As required	Bricks or concrete blocks	As required
TABLE-TOP SUPPORTS	2	75 x 50mm (3 x 2in) PAR timber	1700mm (67in)
TABLE-TOP FRAMES	4	75 x 50mm (3 x 2in) PAR timber	1200mm (48in)
	4	As above	1100mm (44in)
	4	As above	1000mm (40in)
	4	As above	900mm (36in)
	4	As above	800mm (32in)
	4	As above	700mm (28in)
	4	As above	600mm (24in)
	4	As above	500mm (20in)
	4	As above	400mm (16in)
	4	As above	300mm (12in)
	4	As above	200mm (8in)
	4	As above	100mm (4in)

ALSO: about 15m (48ft) of 9.5mm (⅜in) diameter hardwood dowel to be cut into 100mm (4in) lengths for joining corners; 4 expanding wall bolts for fixing down table-top supports; waterproof woodworking adhesive.

1 Brick Plinth Base

Table rests on brick or stone plinth built to required height. Fill middle with rubble topped with concrete.

2 Making the Table-top Supports

Cut cross halving joints in the supports so that they meet to form an 'X', with the supports exactly at right angles. The ends of the supports are sloped on the underside through the last 300mm (12in).

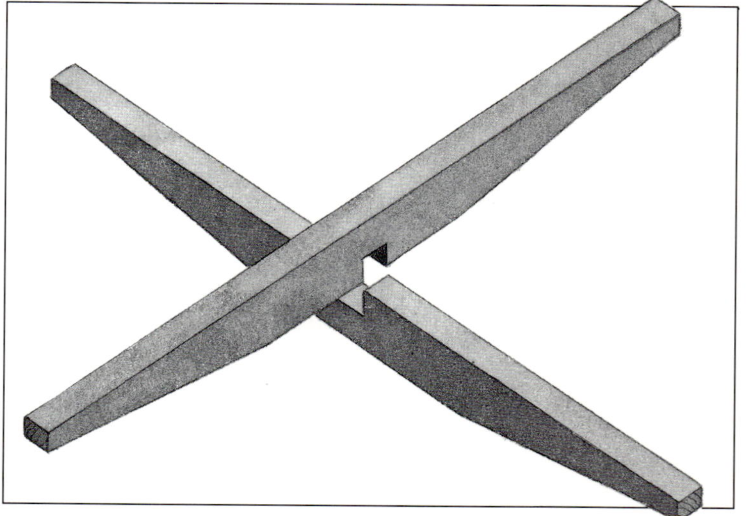

Preservative 146	**Halving joint 152**
Softwood 146	**Dowel joint 154**
Sawing 148	**Mitre joint 154**
Expanding wall bolt 151	**Laying bricks 157**

formed of four pieces in the centre. Although the timber is 75 × 50mm (3 × 2in), the 'frames' are formed just like giant picture frames, with the corners mitred at 45°. The easiest way to cut these mitres is to use a power saw with the blade tilted to a 45° angle. You can use an ordinary portable circular power saw with the timber held securely in a vice, but it will be even easier if you hire or buy a mitre cut-off saw, a radial arm saw, or a circular saw table for the purpose.

Cut the largest frame so that it gives external dimensions of 1200 × 1200mm (48 × 48in). Apply waterproof woodworking adhesive to the mating parts of each joint, then draw them together with frame cramps before drilling into the joint with a 9.5mm ($\frac{3}{8}$in) drill bit, keeping the bit at a 90° angle to the joint. Drill two holes in each joint and then drive 9.5mm ($\frac{3}{8}$in) long wooden dowels into the holes, after coating the dowels with waterproof woodworking adhesive. Before applying the adhesive, make a shallow saw cut along the length of each dowel, which will help to ensure that not all of the glue will be driven out when the dowel is inserted. At this stage, make sure that the dowel is long enough to protrude from the hole at each end; when the adhesive has set, the ends of the dowels can be sawn off close to the sides of the frame and the surface then neatly planed smooth to give an unobtrusive fixing. Make up the remaining frames in the same way to the dimensions specified in the Materials chart (opposite).

The central block is formed by cutting four pieces of 75 × 50mm (3 × 2in) timber sections which are joined by dowels to form a square block. The frames are treated with two coats of water-repellent wood preservative to ensure longevity before being assembled on to the timber supports.

The table-top frames are fixed to the table-top supports using waterproof woodworking adhesive and dowels inserted into holes drilled vertically down into the supports and vertically up into the undersides of the table-top frames.

3 Fixing Table-top Supports to Plinth

Use expanding wall bolts to fix the supports at each corner of the plinth. Drill the plinth to accept the wall bolts and drill 50mm (2in) deep holes to recess the bolts in the supports. Check supports are level before final fixing.

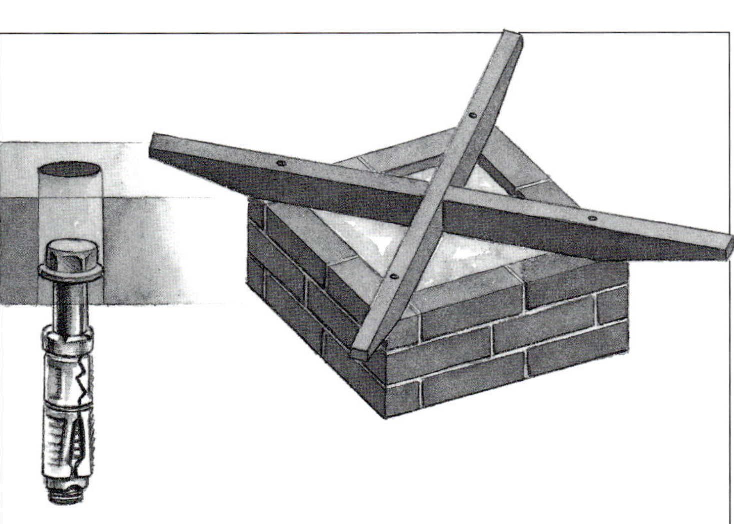

4 Forming Table-top Frames

Cut 45° mitres at corners and fix using waterproof adhesive and dowels through the sides.

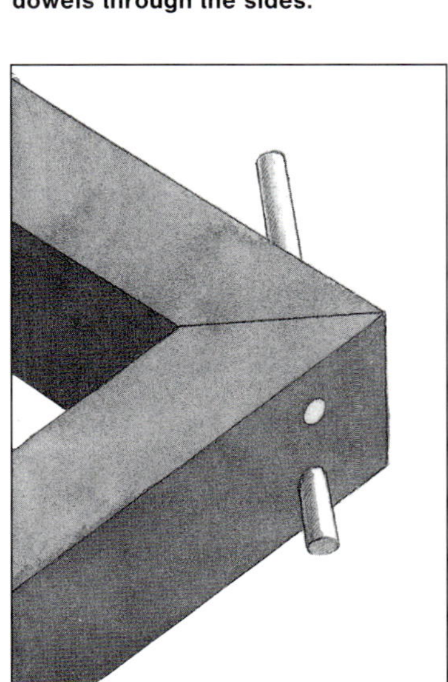

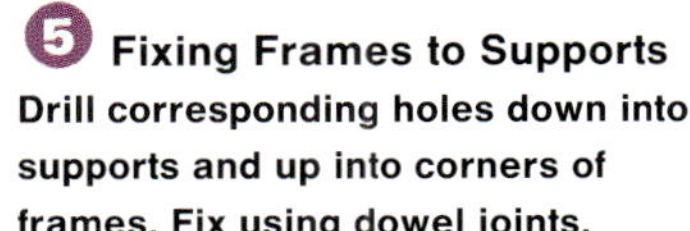

5 Fixing Frames to Supports

Drill corresponding holes down into supports and up into corners of frames. Fix using dowel joints.

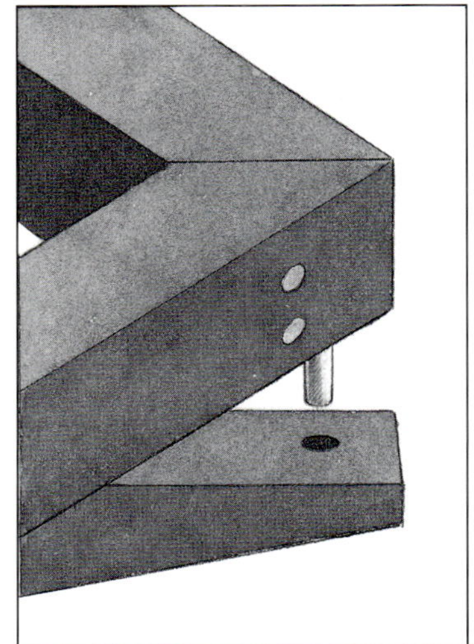

PART 2

GARDEN HOUSES

The garden house is a subject in itself. At one extreme, garden houses can be supremely romantic, providing a true retreat from the world; at the other, they can be as mundane as a shed. In between come summer houses, gazebos, pavilions, follies, greenhouses, workshops, Wendy houses, studios, offices and garden rooms. One could even include dovecotes, pigeon lofts, rabbit hutches, dog kennels and chicken coops, since animal houses so often accompany human ones. But whatever their ultimate function, there is something uniquely appealing about buildings on such a small scale. For the garden designer, they are places where wit and imagination, as much as practicality, can come into play.

Children have inspired some of the most charming versions of the garden house, while animal houses, when they are decorated rather than strictly functional, also tend to be designed to amuse and appeal to children. More than any other type of garden structure, the many varieties of garden house offer the opportunity to use bright paints, providing a much-needed splash of year-round colour in the garden.

Garden Houses

The summer house or garden retreat has a long tradition in Europe and an even longer tradition in the Far East. As a pavilion or gazebo it was essentially built to provide a platform from which to view a garden, or, in Eastern terms, to contemplate nature. However, from the eighteenth century onwards, the nature of the garden house evolved from being a viewing place to a kind of architectural attraction in the garden. Chinese pavilions, Japanese tea houses, miniature thatched cottages, classical temples and Gothick grottoes were some of the styles that were enthusiastically embraced.

As a rule, follies of this kind really need acres of parkland to act as a foil for their charms; today, however, garden houses are usually simpler in design, reflecting their essentially practical nature. Nevertheless there are many attractive 'ordinary' buildings to act as inspiration, including bathing huts, lodges and gypsy caravans. Painted wood, clapboarding, shingle and exterior-grade plywood are all good basic construction materials. Roofs can be tiled, felted or made of corrugated iron; for a truly rustic look, you could seek out a thatcher, or have the roof covered in turf. Building a garden house can be an exercise in creative salvage and recycling for those with that kind of imagination and skill.

The degree of finish depends on the ultimate use of the house: a building which must function as an annexe for overnight guests obviously needs to be completed to a higher standard of comfort than one which merely serves as a place to read a book or escape from the rain. If you are going to use the house as a studio or office, for example, you will need to lay on electricity; in other cases, having a supply of water might be a distinct advantage. Similarly, building permission may have to be sought from your local authority or government department, depending on the intended size and function of your shed or house.

Site is an important issue. A summer house or pavilion plays an obvious role in the layout of the entire garden. If you are going to sit there and admire nature, the view must be worthwhile. Paving and

Home from Home

The garden house – shed, pavilion, workshop or summer house – is innately appealing (left and far left). Part of the charm of these small-scale buildings is their forthright style and use of simple materials.

Ample garden storage is an invaluable asset (above). Wall-mounted racks are generally a good idea; hanging tools saves floor space and prevents tines and blades becoming damaged. Ceiling hooks can be used to suspend baskets and trugs.

planting should be planned taking into account the site of the building as far as possible. You could arrange for a pavilion to be set at the end of a walkway to give impact to a formal design, placed on a higher level to offer a commanding view, or secreted in a sheltered corner to add a sense of mystery and surprise.

Although there is nothing mysterious or romantic about a garden shed, with a little thought it need not be the unlovely and somewhat blatant feature common to so many gardens. A garden shed which functions as a true garden room for maintenance of tools, potting up and storing seeds and bulbs is an invaluable resource in any household.

Storage is one of the main requirements. You will fill a shed very quickly with outdoor and garden equipment, so it is important to build or buy one which is big enough for your needs. The first consideration is likely to be providing an efficient system for storing garden tools, seeds, bulbs, fertilizer and so on.

In addition to tool storage, you will need floor space for big items, which may include a lawnmower, bicycles, garden furniture, awnings and umbrellas packed away during the winter, portable barbecues and large toys. You will also need somewhere to put bags of compost and charcoal, as well as a dry, high shelf for storing fertilizers and pesticides out of the reach of children and animals. Ceiling hooks can be used to accommodate baskets and trugs; shelves will take pots and seed trays. It is also useful to have somewhere cool and dark for storing bulbs or root vegetables during the summer or after the harvest.

One advantage of a well-planned storage system is that you can see at a glance if anything has not been put back. But the benefits are not merely practical. As well as providing an efficient area to work, a carefully organized garden room or shed, with its array of traditional garden tools and equipment, can be as pleasant a place in which to spend time as a kitchen.

As far as site is concerned, there is no reason why a shed needs to be in full view. You may not have all that much choice when it comes to position, but it is a good idea to place the shed out of the way, near a compost heap or bonfire site. Alternatively, you can create a utility area by positioning the shed near an existing garage, dustbin store or greenhouse and screen the view by adding trellis panels and climbing plants.

Off-the-peg sheds, which come in ready-to-assemble packs, are rarely as attractive as those you design and build yourself. But there are ways of improving the appearance of the standard shed which are especially useful if you have little choice about where the shed is positioned. Many examples look better if they are simply painted. Good quality brick paviours laid around the base, plant tubs filled with flowers and trellis with plants trained over will all help to connect the shed to its surroundings, making it look less brash and out of place.

Summer house 52
Nesting box 78

GARDEN RETREATS

A garden house can provide a secluded spot for sitting and watching the world go by (far left, centre and far right). If you want to disguise a structure or hide an ugly shed from view, fast-growing climbers such as Russian vine (Fallopia aubertii) *or mile-a-minute* (Polygonum baldschuanicum) *are the answer.*

ANIMAL HOUSES

Coops, dovecotes, bird-houses and the like can be the excuse for wit and decorative flair to come into play. These structures provide a good opportunity to practise DIY skills.

SUMMER HOUSE

Most people could well do with the extra space that a summer house provides. And although this is the perfect place for storing tools, bulbs and seeds, or potting up and a variety of other garden chores, you need not necessarily put it to horticultural use. A DIY workshop, an artist's studio, a guest annexe, the ultimate play house – it is easy to think of a host of functions for this kind of structure to fulfil, although the use it is put to can mean that you will have to seek planning permission before you start building. It could prove invaluable as a home office or study, offering an important psychological separation of home and work for those who work at home. And it is substantial enough to serve as a pavilion on a village cricket green.

The house may appear a daunting prospect for all but the most ardent DIY enthusiast; but the skills you require are well within the average range of ability and there is no need for the kind of refinement demanded by furniture-making. There is no sophisticated jointing and there are few techniques which should not already be familiar. The cost of materials, all readily available, are roughly the same as a family holiday, which makes it fairly reasonable, unless you put a high price on your own time and labour. The major commitment is time. Working alone during the evenings and weekends, it should take about three months. Full-time, with one or two willing assistants, it might only take a couple of weeks.

As far as the design is concerned, there were a number of influences. The idea to use corrugated iron (actually profiled steel) for the roof came from the houses of the Australian outback. The shape of the roof was suggested by the roofline of the traditional cricket pavilion. In different colour combinations, the house acquires quite different aspects: green and white for a cricket pavilion; pale pastels for a seaside look; vibrant blues, greens and pinks to suggest the Caribbean.

The project is a major undertaking. We would recommend that you attempt most of the other projects in the book before tackling this one. But if the demands are high, so are the rewards. What could be more satisfying – or useful – than building your own garden house?

Summer House

A summer house, somewhere in a secluded part of the garden, is a delightful retreat to be savoured when you want to relax away from the bustle of the house. This design captures all the magic, charm and intrigue required from a garden hideaway and just invites you to explore inside. The size of the room is approximately 3.6 × 2.4m (12 × 8ft) which is a comfortable size to furnish with wicker chairs yet remain cosy and intimate. The extended roof covering over the veranda gives the impression of greater size while providing a 1000mm (39in) deep protected area on showery days when you want to sit outside. The size of the base is partly dictated by the area that can be built upon without the need of planning permission. However, check with your local authority, since the use to which you put the building will also affect the need for permission.

The red-and-blue colour scheme chosen here not only accentuates the design and materials but is fun, too. By changing the colour combinations you can substantially alter the finished look of the building; a few suggestions for alternative colours are illustrated on page 67.

The basic structure rests on a level base of concrete slabs which in turn support timber joists. The veranda is treated slatted wood, while the interior floor is exterior-grade plywood finished, in this case, with floor paint, although you could equally use carpets, tiles or boards. It would be perfectly possible to extend the walls to take in the veranda area if you require more indoor floor space. The interior walls are also clad with plywood to give the structure rigidity – between this and the outdoor boarding is a layer of insulation. The level ceiling is covered in tongued-and-grooved boards and is also insulated. You could leave the roof structure exposed if you wanted, although you would lose a lot of heat in cold weather as a result. If you require heating, a paraffin heater or a fan heater are the best options.

The chains leading down from the guttering at the four corners of the building act in the same way as the drainpipes, conducting water down to the ground, where four soakaways are dug: a feature of traditional Japanese houses.

The illustrations below and opposite give an overall impression of the construction of the front, back and side walls and of the roof. However, in addition to the project text and illustrations, you may also need to refer to the sections on Materials and Techniques (pages 146–7 and 148–57) when further guidance is needed on individual stages of the construction.

Tools

- PORTABLE WORKBENCH
- STEEL MEASURING TAPE
- STEEL RULE
- TRY SQUARE or COMBINATION SQUARE
- ADJUSTABLE SLIDING BEVEL
- PANEL SAW (or circular saw)
- POWER DRILL
- DRILL BIT – 12mm ($\frac{1}{2}$in) and 3.2mm ($\frac{1}{8}$in)
- SPANNER
- HAMMER
- NAIL PUNCH
- PINCERS
- CHISEL
- MALLET
- TIN SNIPS

WEATHERBOARDING
ROOF CAPPING
LEAD FLASHING
WEATHERBOARDING
POST
PAVING SLABS

CEILING JOIST
MAIN ROOF TRUSS
INTERMEDIATE
PURLIN
RIDGE PURLIN
RAISED ROOF PURLIN
JACK RAFTER HEAD PLATE
END JACK RAFTER
GUTTER
SHORT CEILING RAFTER
NOGGIN
INSULATION
POST
PLYWOOD FLOOR
JOIST

Summer House: Foundation and Base

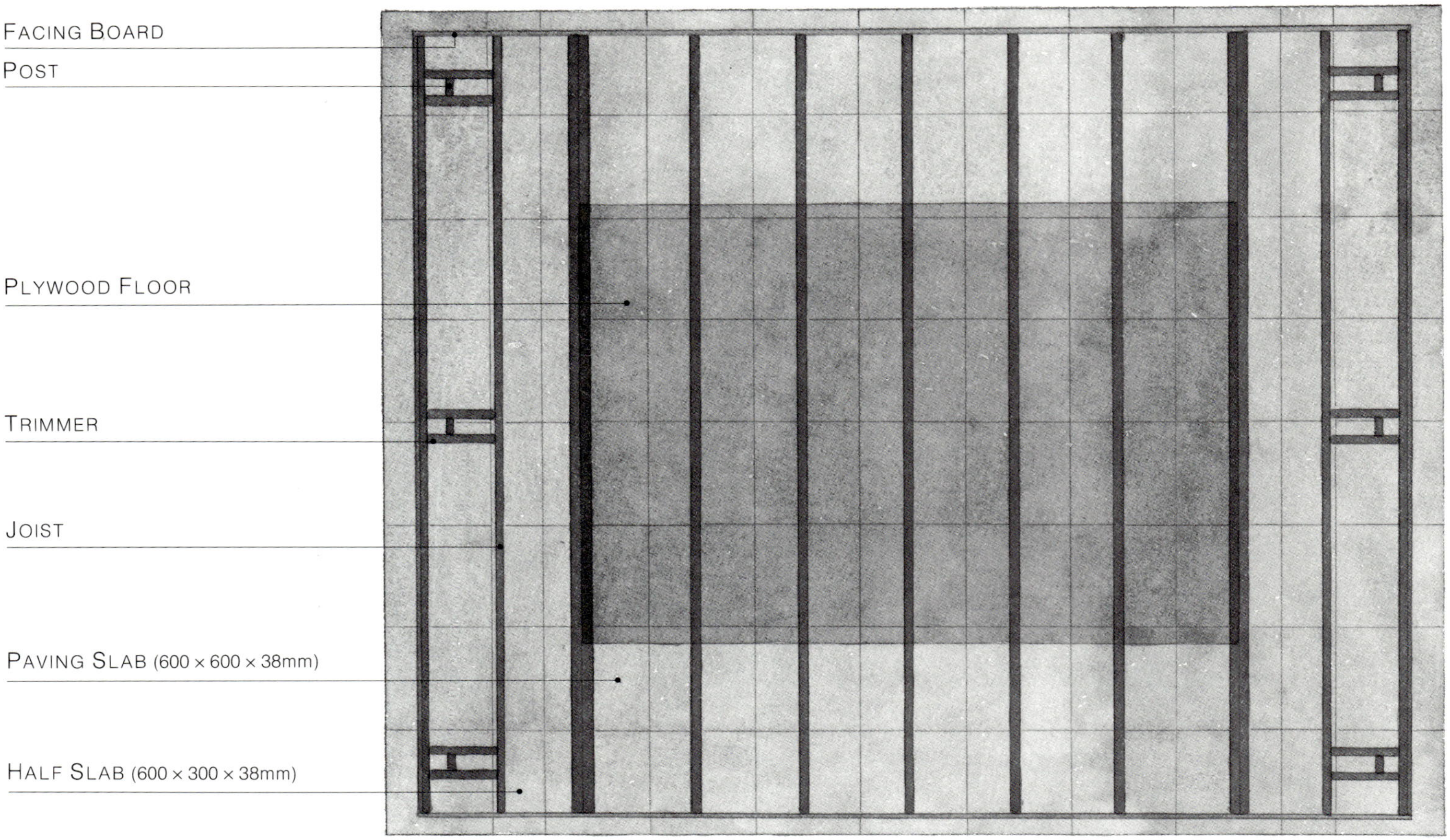

Facing Board
Post
Plywood Floor
Trimmer
Joist
Paving Slab (600 × 600 × 38mm)
Half Slab (600 × 300 × 38mm)

Base Assembly

1 Setting Out Position of Base

Use pegs and stringline to set out base outline. Two sizes of slabs are used – 600 × 600mm (24 × 24in) and 600 × 300mm (24 × 12in) – to ensure joists are supported centrally while leaving a narrow border around house perimeter.

Stringline
Paving slab
½ Slab
Peg

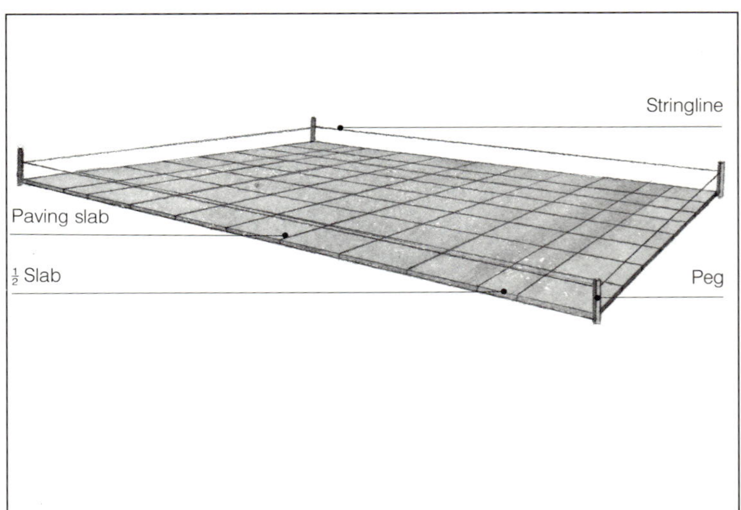

Concrete 147

Concrete paving slabs 147

FOUNDATION AND BASE

Set out the site to be covered by the complete base using four corner pegs and a string line (fig 1). Choose a sheltered part of the garden: this will minimize the risk of structural damage in storms and high winds. The summer house is not anchored to the ground, so you must site it with care.

Avoid sloping terrain as this would need a lot of excavation work for a level base to be laid.

The base can be laid using either paving slabs or concrete. If you choose slabs, then you will need 72 slabs measuring 600 × 600 × 38mm (24 × 24 × 1½in). You will also need 16 half-size slabs (600 × 300mm [24 × 12in]). These are required so that a narrow border remains around the walls while the joists rest centrally on the slabs (Base and Floor Assembly illustration).

The slabs should be laid on a 1:5 mix of cement to sharp sand. You need to build in a slope of 1 in 60 from front to back to ensure that rainwater drains away and does not lie alongside the joists and cause them to rot away.

Alternatively, if you use concrete you will have to dig out about 125mm (5in) of soil and lay a foundation of well-compacted hardcore covered with a 50mm (2in) layer of concrete mixed from one part cement to five parts ballast.

You will have to set up a formwork (wooden frame) of timbers to retain the concrete, again having first pegged out the site. The formwork timbers should be held in place using stakes driven into the ground. Old floorboards, or similar, are ideal as formwork. Do not forget to build in a slight fall in the formwork from front to back.

When the base is completed you can lay out the joists. Use 100 × 50mm (4 × 2in) sawn timber for the floor joists, making sure that it has been thoroughly treated with preservative. Ideally, pressure-impregnated timber should be used. There are 13 joists in all, with a double row being used to support the end walls. The outer joists support the veranda floor at each end.

Each joist should be laid on a strip of bituminous felt to serve as a damp-proof membrane and to prevent moisture seeping up through the base. Since the base has a slight fall built into it from front to back, you will need to lay small packing pieces about every 600mm (24in) under each joist to bring it level. This is important since you want to have a level floor.

Next lay the summer house floor (fig 3). This is 19mm (¾in) WBP plywood and the area is nominally 3.6 × 2.4m (12 × 8ft). The sheets should be fixed to the joists using 38mm (1½in) No 8 screws at 400mm (16in) centres around the edge. Fix the middle sheet first and then a sheet either side, cut to fit as needed. Next lay 50 × 19mm (2 × ¾in) packing strips of plywood on which the front and back walls will sit.

The end joists, which will support the veranda floor, can be removed temporarily since they will be a hazard while the summer house is being constructed.

2 Setting Out and Levelling Floor Joists

Timber joists are laid down at 600mm (24in) centres. A double row is needed to support the end walls. Since the slabs are laid to a slight fall, packing pieces are needed below the joists to level them.

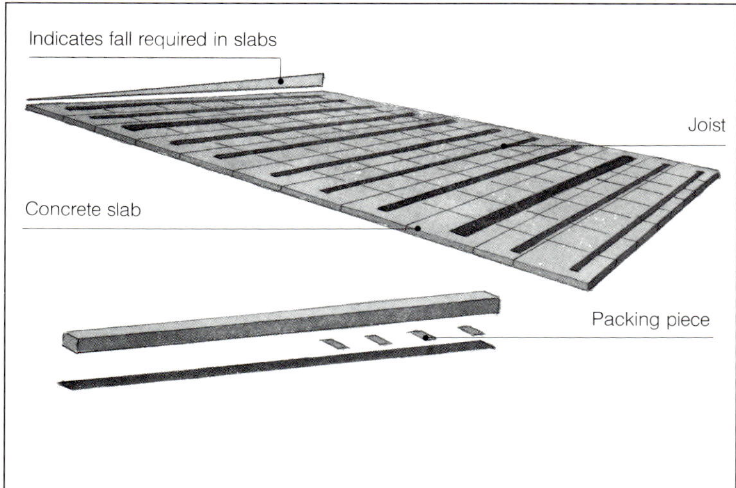

3 Laying the Plywood Floor

The floor is formed from 19mm (¾in) thick WBP plywood screwed to the floor joists using 38mm No 8 screws. Lay the middle panel first and then one other panel on each side.

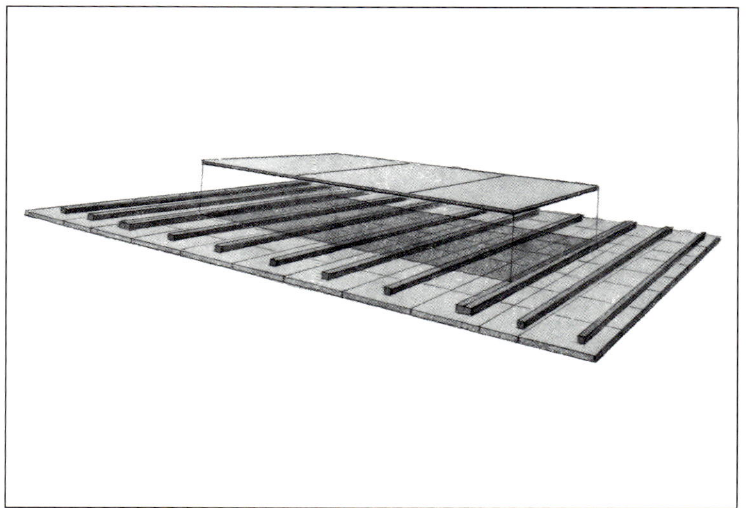

SUMMER HOUSE: WALL ASSEMBLY

WALLS

The inner faces of the walls are made from 12mm (½in) WBP plywood. Cut out the pieces needed for each of the four walls. The window openings, front and back, are about 700 × 600mm (27½ × 23½in) and the doorway is about 2000 × 810mm (78 × 32in). If you intend to buy the door ready-made then tailor the door opening to the required size – remember to allow for the dimensions of the door frame reveal.

Taking each wall by turn, lay out the 50 × 50mm (2 × 2in) studding at the centres shown (fig 1). Note also that the short horizontal noggins are intentionally slightly misaligned in order to stagger the screw fixings in the panels.

Lay the plywood panels on the studding with the inside surface uppermost – these will form the internal walls of the house (fig 2). Use 38mm (1½in) No 8 screws to fix the panels to the studs at 400mm (16in) intervals. Countersink and fill all of the screw heads.

The door and window openings are all framed with 50 × 25mm (2 × 1in) trimmers skew nailed to the studs using 50mm (2in) nails *(see* **Techniques, page 151***)*.

The walls are joined together using 125mm (5in) long 12mm (½in) diameter bolts. If you position all four walls (fig 3) using a helper and temporary supporting struts, you can drill bolt holes at the corners through adjoining vertical studs. Cramp each corner before drilling the holes and fixing the bolts, leaving a little 'play' at this stage for final adjustment of the four walls. Four bolts are needed at each corner at the approximate positions indicated (fig 1, back wall). The order of assembly is to offer up the front wall to one end wall and bolt together; then bolt the back wall to the other end wall; finally, bolt the two remaining corners together.

When all the walls have been joined and are square, the sole plates of each wall (fig 2, front wall) can be nailed to the joists using 100mm (4in) nails at approximately 400m (16in) centres.

1 Assembling Framework for each Wall

The illustrations show the arrangement of the 50 × 50mm (2 × 2in) studding for each of the four walls. *Top* Front frame with allowance for the door and windows. *Middle* Rear frame with a window opening. *Below* Solid end walls.

Drilling 150
Screwing 150
Skew nailing 151
Butt joint 152

WALL FRAME ASSEMBLY

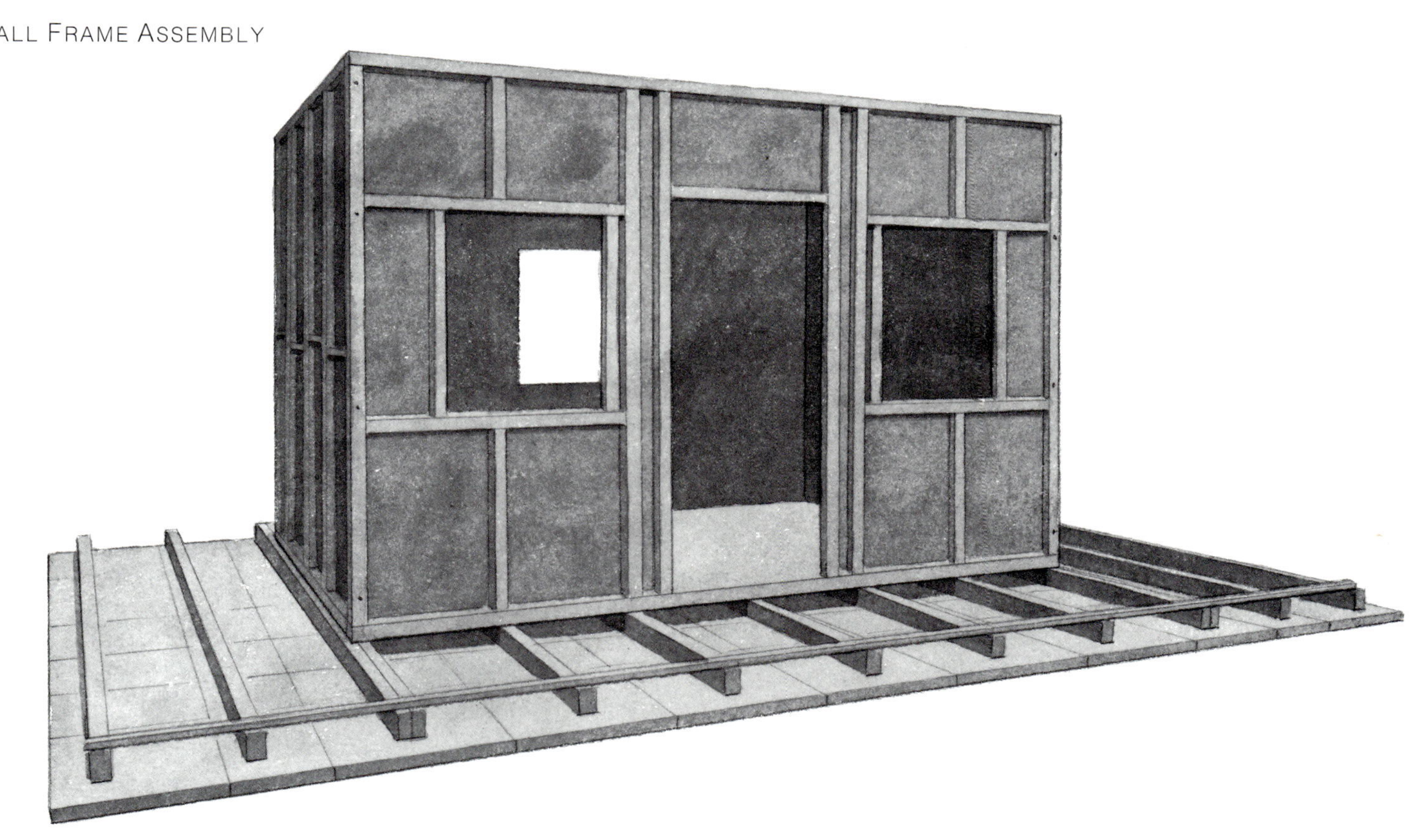

2 Adding Inner Walls to Frames

The inner walls are formed from 12mm ($\frac{1}{2}$in) thick plywood. The front wall is made from five pieces with cut-outs for the windows in the side sections. The sheets are fixed to the frame using 38mm No 8 screws.

3 Joining the Four Frames Together

Each studding framework is joined together using 125mm (5in) long bolts. Using a helper, supporting struts and cramps, keep the frames aligned at the corners. Drill holes for four bolts at each corner and bolt together.

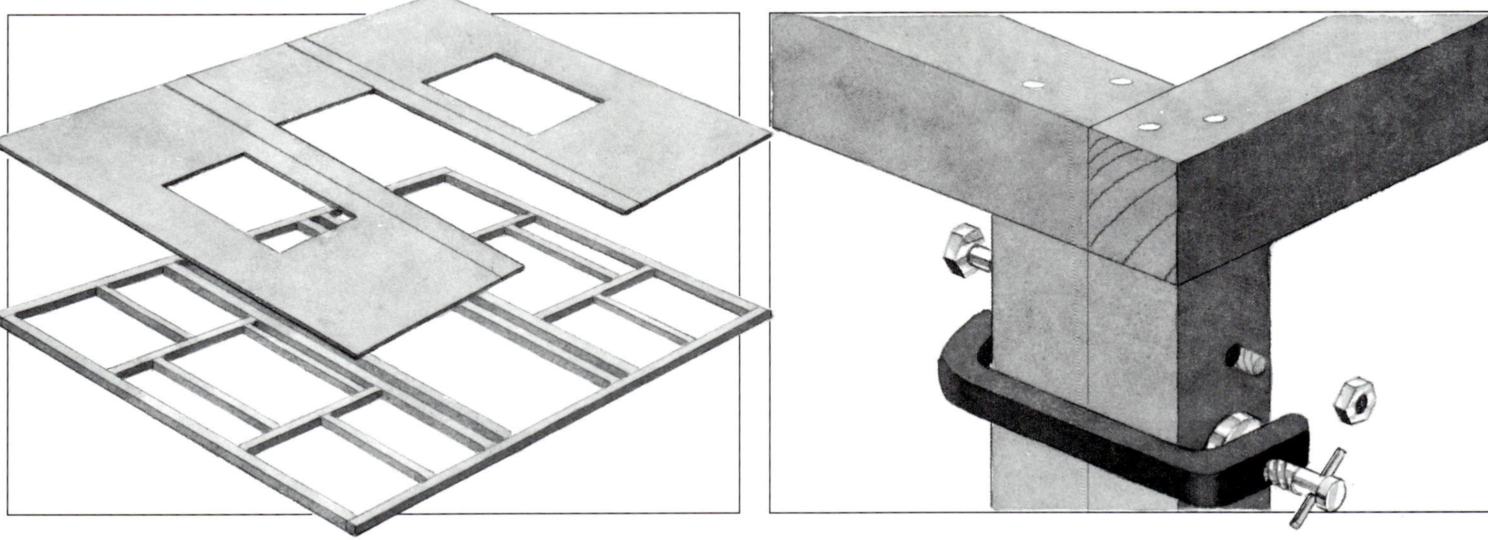

Summer House: Roof Assembly

Layout of Roof Timbers

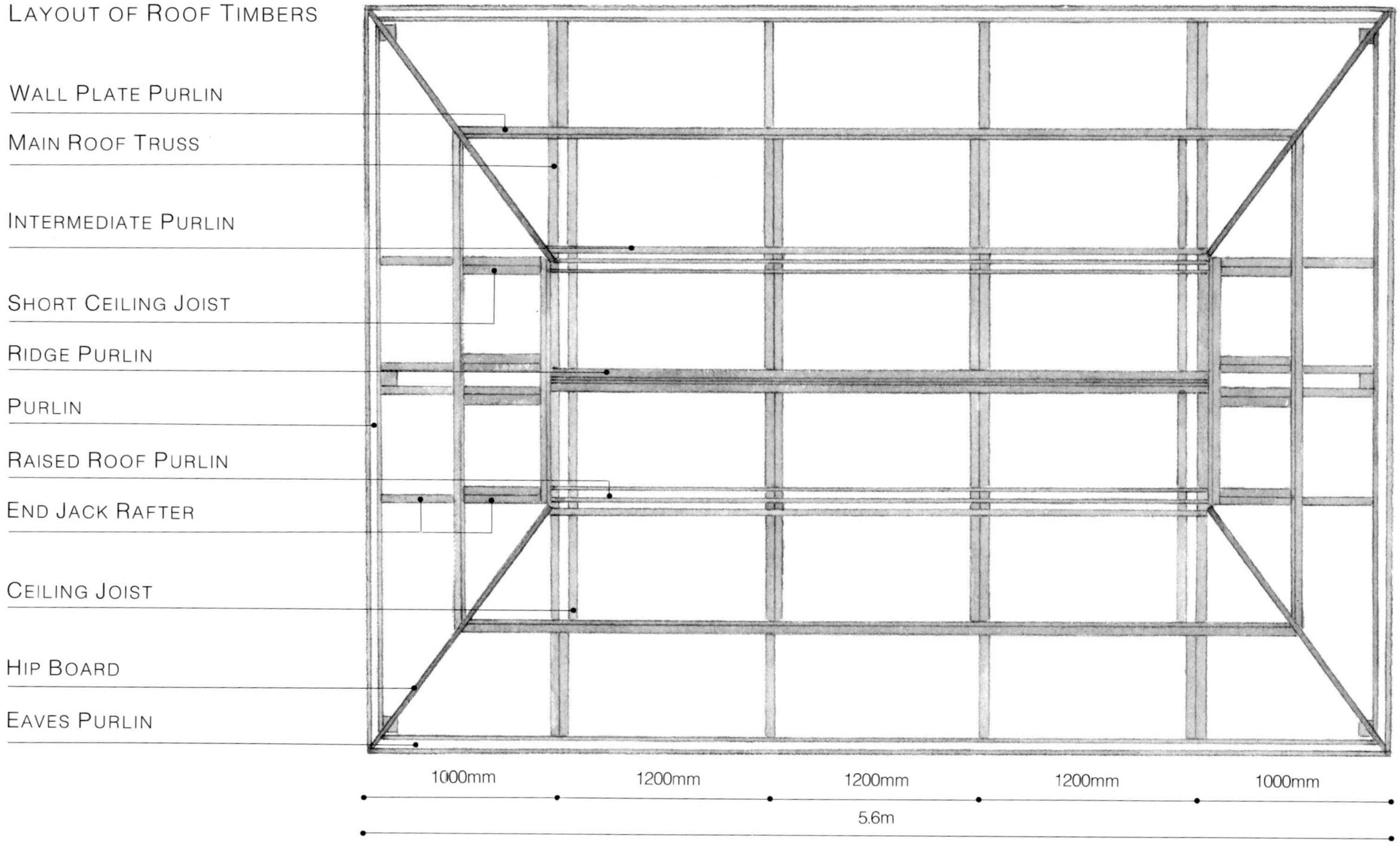

Wall Plate Purlin
Main Roof Truss
Intermediate Purlin
Short Ceiling Joist
Ridge Purlin
Purlin
Raised Roof Purlin
End Jack Rafter
Ceiling Joist
Hip Board
Eaves Purlin
1000mm
1200mm
1200mm
1200mm
1000mm
5.6m

Section across Length of Roof

Main Roof Truss
Jack Rafter Head Plate
Short Ceiling Rafter
Post

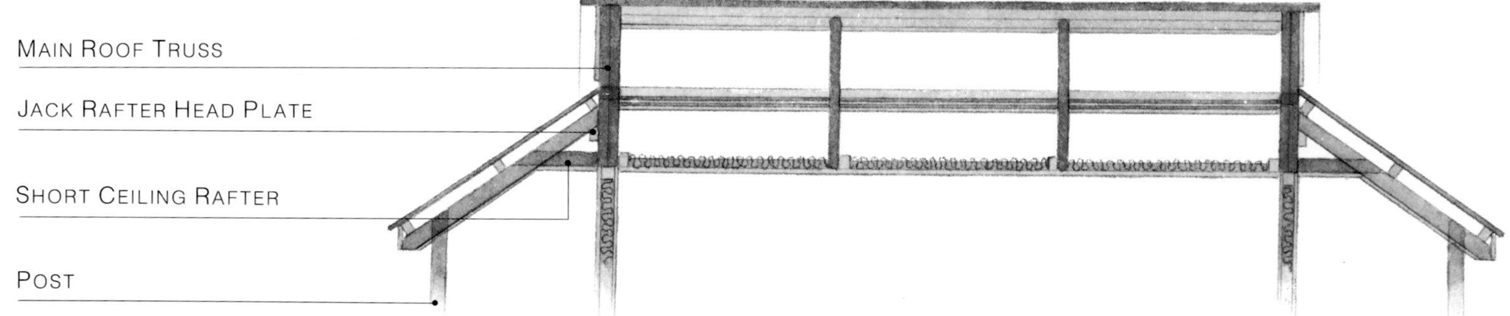

Fixings 147
Sawing 148
Skew nailing 151
Mitre joint 154

ROOF

The striking, veranda-covering roof of this summer house is a fundamental part of its design. It consists of a pitched roof clad with sheets of corrugated steel and with a 'hip' at either end projecting out to cover the sides of the veranda. It is quite complicated, so it is strongly recommended that you spend a little while studying the plans, and then tackle the construction one step at a time as described here. The positions of the rafters and purlins will become much clearer as you start to fix the pieces together.

MAIN TRUSSES

Start by making the four main roof trusses. Each truss, a triangular-shaped frame mitred at the top, is made from two 75 × 50mm (3 × 2in) angled rafters each about 2.6m (8ft 8in) long (allowing for them being overlength), reinforced with a triangular plywood gusset at the top, and braced with a ceiling joist at the appropriate level.

The rafters are cut at an angle at the top, butted together and held at the correct angle by being nailed to a 12mm (½in) thick triangular plywood gusset. Each triangular plywood gusset is pitched at 26°, and this controls the angle of all the rafters. The rafters are prevented from spreading by the ceiling joists which are bolted to them towards the bases of the rafters.

All the main trusses are the same, except that the two end trusses have double rafters, formed by bolting pairs of rafters together using 12mm (½in) coach bolts with steel timber connectors on the bolts sandwiched between the two timbers. Similar sized bolts and steel timber connectors are used to bolt the ceiling joists to the rafters.

Ensure that the four main trusses are cut and nailed at the same angle: nail up the first truss on a flat surface, and use this truss as a template for nailing subsequent trusses.

Make all the rafters about 200mm (8in) overlength; they can then be cut to the correct length after fixing. Nail the top firrings in place.

FIXING MAIN TRUSSES

Lift the main trusses on to the walls, spacing them approximately 1200mm (48in) apart. Do not forget to position the double rafter trusses at each end. Make sure that all the trusses are square and vertical, and then nail them down to the head plates of the front and back walls, using 150mm (6in) round head nails which should be skew nailed into the head plates (*see* **Techniques, page 151**).

Temporarily hold the trusses in place so that they are vertical: nail long battens diagonally across the rafters to act as bracing (fig 1, below). Position the battens carefully so that there is enough room to fix the purlins at the ridge, wall plate and eaves levels.

FIXING PURLINS

Cut and fix the ridge purlins (horizontal timbers) in place. These are the same overall length as the front and back wall structure and are fixed to the firrings on either side of the apexes of the main trusses.

Cut the eaves purlins (positioned at the front and back to support the outermost edges of the pitched roof covering) 2.5m (8ft 2in) overlength to give an overhang of 1250mm (49in) at each end (fig 2). Fix in place by nailing into rafters.

Next cut the front and back wall plate purlins (the ones above the eaves purlins), approximately 650mm (25½in) overlength at each end to allow for trimming later. Nail in place on the rafters (fig 2). Remove the diagonal bracing and cut and fix the two intermediate purlins (one each side) midway between the ridge and wall plate purlins. These butt up against the ends of the firring pieces, which should now be cut to length. The intermediate purlins are about 300mm (12in) overlength each end for cutting back at an angle later.

MAKING THE RAISED ROOF SECTION

The firrings act as packing over the rafters. Fit a second purlin close to the lower end of the firring pieces to form the raised roof section.

1 Construction of Main Roof Trusses

Each truss is formed by nailing it to a pre-cut 12mm (½in) thick plywood gusset pitched at 26°, and then braced by a ceiling joist for stability. End trusses have double raters. After positioning, rafters are braced by purlins.

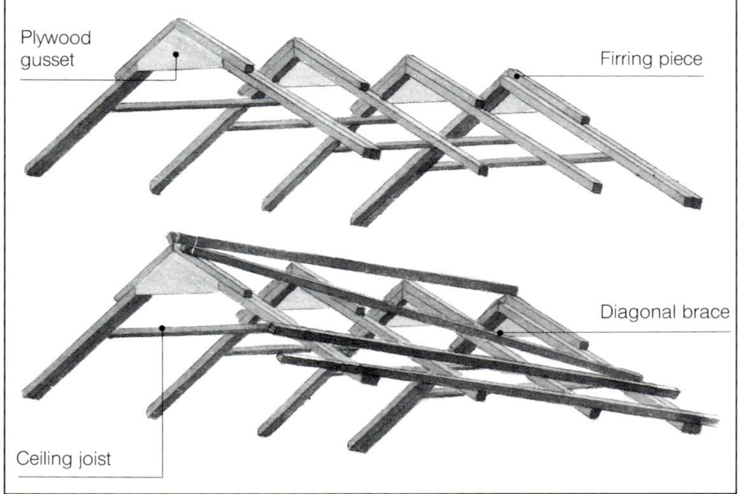

2 Fixing the Purlins to the Roof Trusses

With trusses spaced along the head plates on the walls, and held upright by temporary diagonal braces, cut and nail the ridge purlins in place. Note that eaves, wall plate and intermediate purlins are left temporarily overlength.

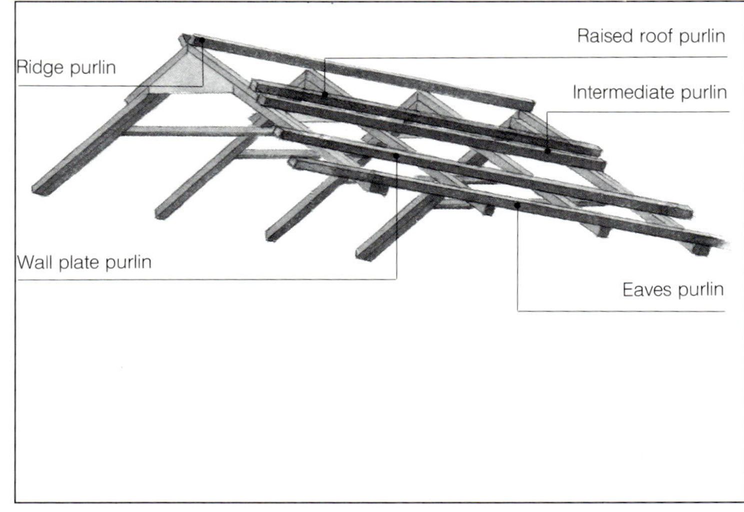

Summer House: Hip Roof Assembly

Setting Out Hip Roof At Each End

Measure 1000mm (39in) along the top outer edge of the eaves purlin, measuring from the outer face of the outside truss. Tack a line from this point (string will do) to where the end lean-to roof meets the end truss. This should form a roof pitch at the ends of about 36°. Make up a triangle of plywood or scrap battening to this angle and use it to check the roof pitch during all stages of construction (fig 2).

Tie another string line from the top of the first eaves purlin (1000mm [39in] from the face of the end truss) to the top of the corresponding eaves purlin on the opposite side (1000mm [39in] out from the end truss). From this point, take another string line up to where the end lean-to roof meets the end truss. With these string lines in place, 1000mm (39in) out from the end truss, the general arrangement of the roof hips and pitch down to eaves level on the lean-to roofs at each end of the building will become apparent.

Cut the end jack rafters (four at each end) overlength, and also the short ceiling joists for the ends (again, four at each corner). Both are cut from 75 x 50mm (3 x 2in) sawn timber (fig 6).

Cut the jack rafter head plates (which support the jack rafters against the end trusses). Nail or bolt these to the end trusses as shown (fig 3), and after fixing trim the ends of the head plates to the slope of the main roof rafters.

Use an adjustable sliding bevel to set the angle required for the ends of the jack rafters where they butt against the end trusses, and trim the ends of the jack rafters to this angle. On the underside of each rafter cut a birdsmouth (notch) so that the rafter will sit neatly on the head plate. The eaves ends are left overlength for the time being.

Nail the four jack rafters and the four short ceiling joists in place at each end. Check that the top of the rafters are aligned and slope in line with the previously fixed string guidelines. Make sure that the undersides of the short ceiling joists are horizontal and are in line with the undersides of the ceiling joists at the front and back of the building.

Note that in the centre of the ends there are two rafters fixed 75mm (3in) apart (fig 4). Later these will be bolted to the central veranda support post.

Cut the 150 x 25mm (6 x 1in) hip boards (rafters) overlength and hold them as close to their final position as possible so that the correct angles can be marked on the ends of the front and rear purlins which rest against the hip boards and which are now cut to length. Again, an adjustable sliding bevel is used to mark these angled cuts, which are angled in two directions to ensure that the ends of the purlins fit tightly against the hip boards when these are fixed in place.

At the top, the hip board is notched to fit over the jack rafter head plate (fig 3), and the end of the hip board is angled so that the hip board fits tightly against the main end truss. This angle needs careful marking with an adjustable sliding bevel to ensure an accurate fit, particularly of the support notch at the top end. The top surface of each hip board should be lined up with the top of the purlins.

The hip boards can now be fitted and held in place by nailing to the ends of the front and rear purlins.

Next, cut and fasten by nailing the three 75 x 50mm (3 x 2in) purlins on the lean-to roofs at the ends of the building. They must be cut to length and angled so that they butt tightly against the hip boards at the ends, and align at the corner hips with the front and back purlins.

Cut and fit the 75 x 75mm (3 x 3in) veranda support posts in the middle of the end sections to fit between the concrete base and the twin central jack rafters. The base of each post should sit on a small piece of lead, which seals the end grain very effectively. Using timber connector plates and 12mm (½in) diameter coach bolts, drill and bolt to the floor joists at the base and between the twin jack rafters at the top. Leave overlength for the time being, and later trim flush, angled with the tops of the purlins.

1 Cross-section of the Width Showing the Raised Roof Section

Note how the firring pieces lift the ridge and raised roof purlins to create the raised roof section. Also look at the eaves area and note how the truss ends are trimmed vertically, level with the front top edge of the eaves purlin, to give a plumb fixing for the fascia board to which the gutters are fixed.

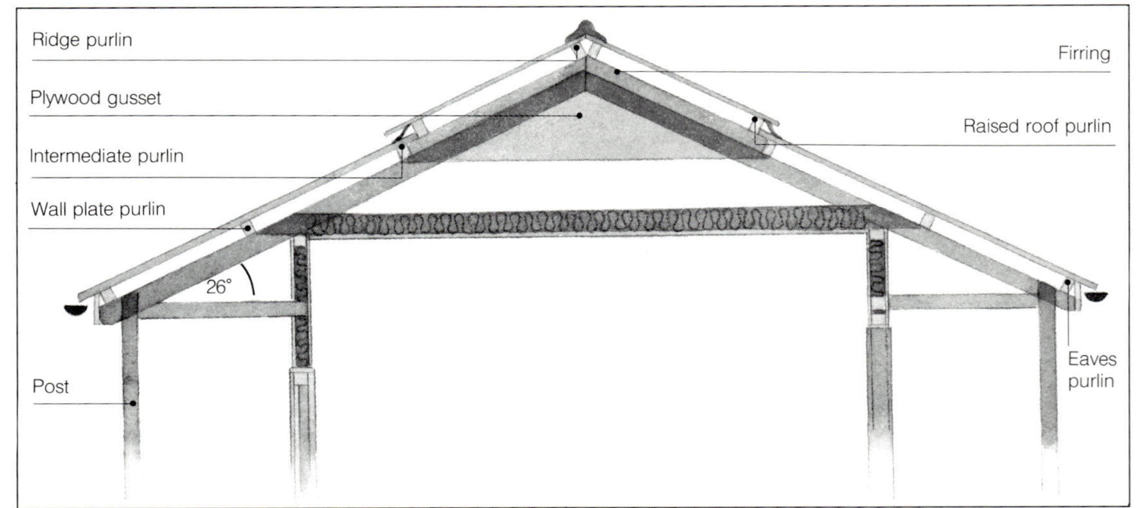

2 Trimming the Rafter Ends

Sliding bevel marks rafter ends (shown without eaves purlin). Use a template to check roof pitch.

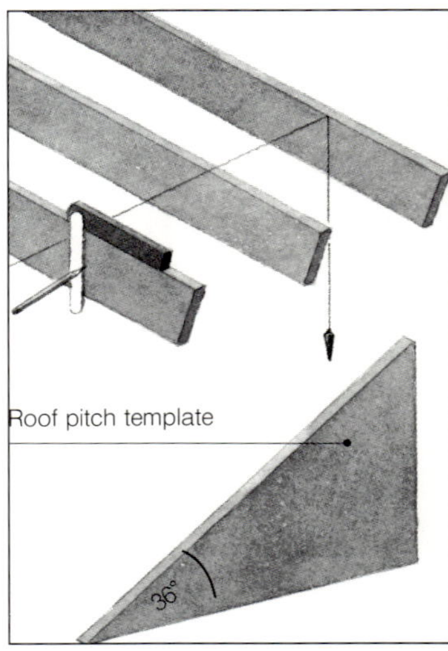

Sliding bevel 144
Sawing 148
Nailing 150
Fixings 151

HIP ROOF ASSEMBLY

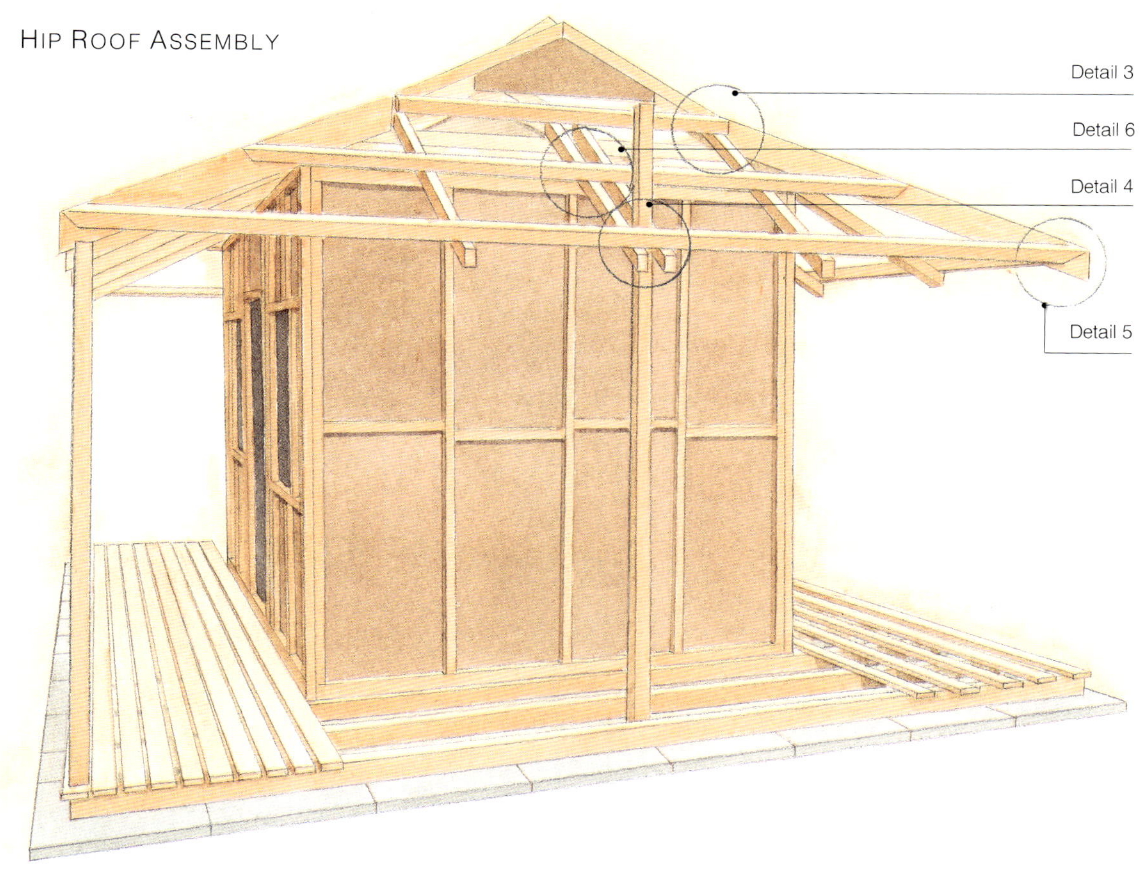

The 75 × 75mm (3 × 3in) corner veranda support posts fit between the concrete base and the top sides of the hip boards. Allow 25–30mm (1–1¼in) clearance from the eaves purlins. The undersides of the hip boards are notched to take posts, and the top ends of the posts are cut out with matching notches which allow them to be bolted to the hip boards (fig 5). Cut the post tops to the same angles as the roof pitches and to the level of the purlins.

FITTING FASCIA BOARDS

Use a sliding bevel to mark the rafter ends with a vertical line where they will be trimmed. When the fascia boards are fixed on to the rafter ends they will be upright, allowing gutters to be fitted. Trim the rafters in line with the top of the eaves purlin. The bottoms of the rafter ends are trimmed level with the bottom of the fascia boards, either before or after the fascias are fixed. Also trim the ends of the hip boards to take the fascia boards.

Cut the fascia boards from 150 × 25mm (6 × 1in) sawn timber.

3 Hip Board/Head Plate Join

Notch hip board to fit over jack rafter head plate. Angle board end to fit against truss. Purlins fit against hip.

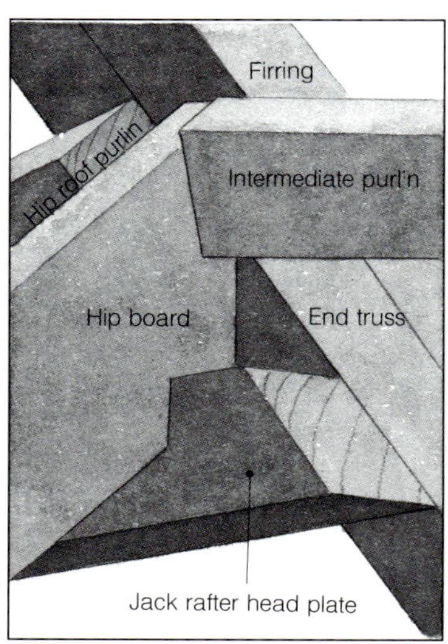

4 Intermediate Veranda Support Post

Posts bolt between central jack rafters. Saw tops level with purlins.

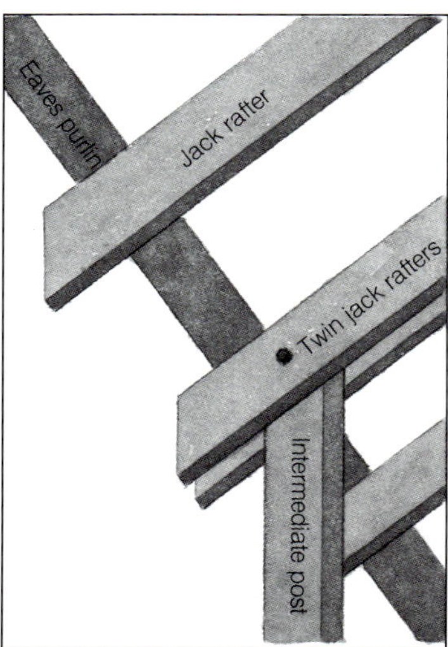

5 Corner Post/Hip Board Join

Notch hip boards for corner posts, which are slotted to fit over hips. Bolt and trim tops to roof slope.

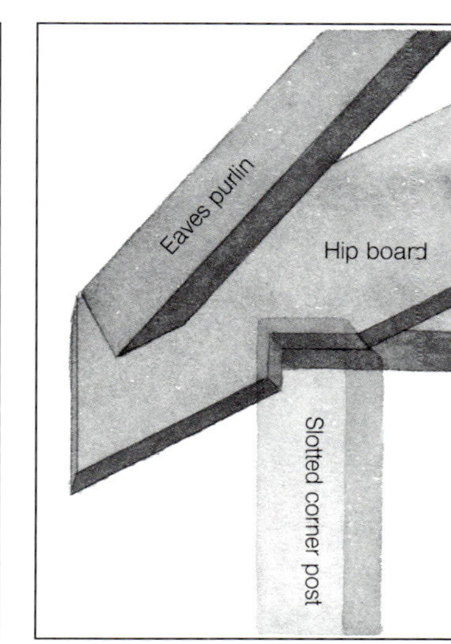

6 Jack Rafters/Ceiling Joists

Underside view of the jack rafters nailed to short ceiling joists. Tops of rafters must align.

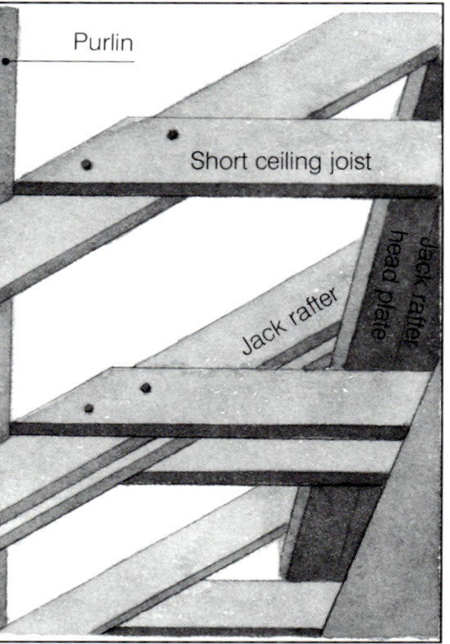

Summer House: Roof and Detailing

Fitting Corrugated Metal Roof

You can buy corrugated metal sheets cut to any size. Fix the lower sections first by nailing through the peaks of the corrugations into the purlins and screwing through the valleys using special self-sealing screws. Make sure that adjacent sheets overlap by at least two corrugations on each side of the panels.

Fix a lead flashing along the lower purlin of the raised roof sections and press the lead down on to the lower roof sheets using a roller. Apply a similar strip of flashing from the main end trusses on to the end lean-to roof sheets (fig 1). Nail 12mm (½in) feather-edge boards to the end trusses to form gable ends *(see* **Techniques, page 151**).

Finally, fix the raised-roof corrugated sheets, screwing and nailing (as above) into the firring pieces. Adjacent sheets must overlap at least two corrugations on both sides of each panel. Fit and fasten metal capping pieces to the ridge and hips of the hip roof sections.

1 Lower Roof Flashing

Lay lead flashing along the lower raised roof purlin; roll the flashing on to the lower roof sheets.

Detailing

With the main walls constructed and the roof in place, the final detailing jobs can be completed.

Between the wall studs on all four walls, fit 50mm (2in) thick Rockwool wall batts for insulation (fig 4). The material is semi-rigid and, if necessary, can be held in place by tapping panel pins into the studs in much the same way that glass is held in a window frame.

The window and door frame reveals are then cut to length from 125 x 25mm (5 x 1in) PAR (planed all round) softwood and temporarily screwed in place (figs 2 and 3). Make up the window frames from 50 x 50mm (2 x 2in) timber screwed together, and then nail through the outsides of the frames to fix the glazing bars (these are stocked by timber merchants). Screw the frames into the reveals.

The weatherboarding can now be nailed in place on each wall, starting at the base and working upwards (fig 4). Cut the boarding to fit neatly around the window and door frames *(see* **Techniques, page 151**).

Cut and nail in place the 150 x 25mm (6 x 1in) fascia boards to the eaves and the 50 x 50mm (2 x 2in) rafter ties.

Closing battens are needed at the four corners of the summer house to close off the end grain of the weatherboards. The battens should be cut to length and fixed temporarily in place.

Having checked everything over you can now start to decorate. Remove the closing battens while

Paint 146
Nailing 150
Screwing 150
Fixing cladding 151

the weatherboards are treated with exterior grade preservative, stain or paint, then paint the battens in a contrasting colour before nailing them back in place.

The door and window frames can now be painted, along with the roof and fascia board.

Now fix the guttering, giving it a slight fall towards each corner, where a small hole should be cut. Fix a chain through each outlet and run it down to the ground to channel rain water into a soakaway. Alternatively, you could fit a combined stopend and downpipe outlet at each corner of the guttering; however, this will mean that you will not be able to run the chains down to the ground at the exact corners of the summer house – to the detriment of the overall design.

If the external joists were temporarily removed while the project was being built then relay them now on a strip of bituminous felt and fix them to the veranda support posts as described earlier (page 62).

The 'duckboard' floor of the veranda is now formed by screwing 75 × 25mm (3 × 1in) slats to the joists leaving 19mm (¾in) spaces between them. Use 50mm (2in) long No 8 screws.

The window can now be glazed using 3mm (⅛in) glass held in place with glazing bars pinned to the frame. It is important that the glazing bars are fixed square to each other so that the glass will slot comfortably in place. Check each 'window' for square by measuring the diagonals, which should be equal. When ordering the glass, buy it 2–3mm (about ⅛in) smaller than the window opening, both in width and height, to allow for normal expansion.

If you prefer, you can buy a ready-made ledged and braced door; alternatively, you can make one using tongued-and-grooved boarding with 100 × 25mm (4 × 1in) timber for the ledges (cross rails) and braces (diagonals). The door can be full-length or a stable door as here. If you choose the latter, you simply make the two smaller doors with a lower ledge for each one. In a full-length door, only one central ledge is needed.

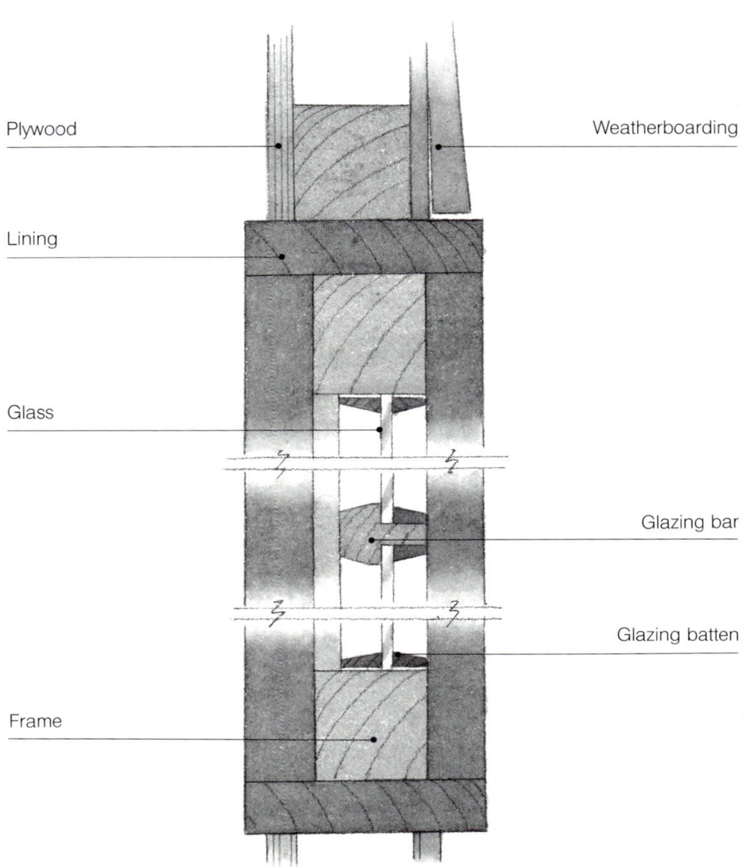

2 Fixing the Door Head
Screw door lining to the studwork, with 25 × 12mm (1 × ½in) doorstops nailed to sides and top of frame.

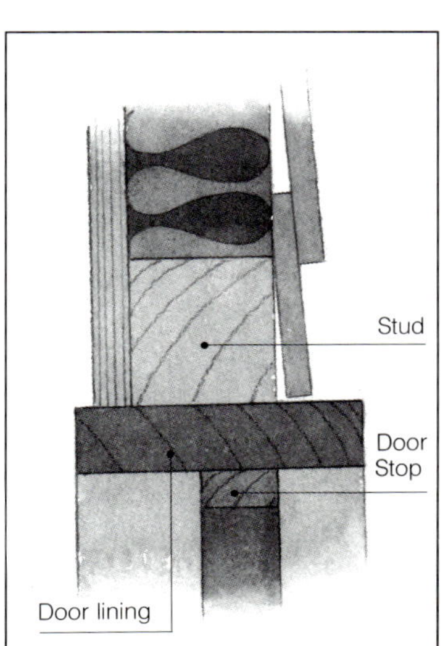

3 Window Frame Assembly
Above **The top and bottom sections of the frame are fixed to the 125 × 25mm (5 × 1in) linings.**

4 Fixing Weatherboarding
Below **Exterior walls are formed from overlapping boards nailed to the studwork; work from bottom up.**

Summer House: Detailing

A ledged and braced door is made by simply nailing the boards to the ledges and braces. It is constructed by laying the top and bottom ledges on a flat surface and then screwing the tongued-and-grooved boards to them (*see* **Techniques, page 151**). The boards should overlap the ledges by about 25mm (1in) at either end.

The diagonal brace is then fitted by notching it into the ledges and, again, screwing through the door and into the brace. The purpose of the brace is to transmit the weight to the hinges and so prevent the door from sagging. It is important that the braces are fixed the right way round as shown (fig 1).

Use two butt hinges to hang each door. These are fixed to the end grain of the ledges. If you make a framed door then also use butt hinges: two 75mm (3in) sizes for each half of a stable door, or three for a full-length door.

Next, fit the 25 × 12mm (1 × ½in) door stops – two vertical pieces and a horizontal top piece – to the door reveal (fig 2, page 65). These stops must be positioned accurately: hold the door in place and mark the positions of the stops immediately inside its closed position. This ensures that the stops are fitted accurately. Here, they are positioned about 25mm (1in) back from the front of the door reveal.

Complete the interior by cladding the ceiling using tongued-and-grooved boards, not forgetting to insert Rockwool insulating bats between the joists (fig 2), held in place by panel pins as with the walls. The walls can be decorated according to your requirements using exterior paint, varnish stain, or microporous paint.

Finally, at each corner, dig a 300 × 300 × 300mm (12 × 12 × 12in) soakaway hole and fill with shingle or pebbles (fig 3). Bed the ends of the chains into them so that they are held tautly in place.

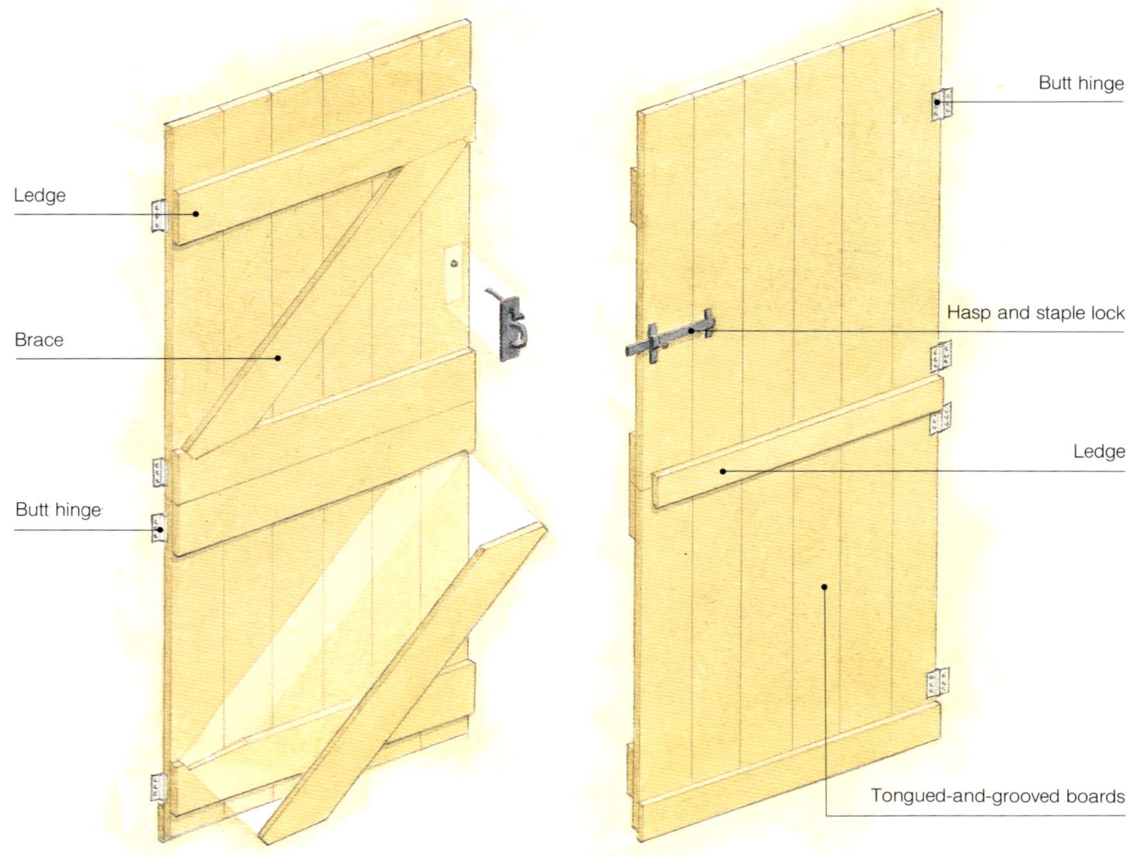

1 Door Assembly
Above **The ledged and braced door can either be a stable door (as shown) or a single unit.**

2 Insulating the Ceiling
Clad the ceiling with tongued-and-grooved boards, and place insulating batts between the joists.

3 Making the Soakaways
A chain conducts rainwater from the gutters to a soakaway – a hole filled with shingle or pebbles.

Paint 146
Screwing 150
Nailing 150
Fixing cladding 151

DEN . . . GAZEBO . . . HIDEAWAY . . . CHALET . . . SHANTY . . . BOTHY . . . HUNTING BOX . . . CROFT . . . PAD . . . OUTHOUSE . . .

SHACK . . . PLAY HOUSE . . . SNUG . . . CABIN . . . SHED . . . BOLT HOLE . . . STUDIO . . . PAVILION . . . LODGE . . . RETREAT . . .

POTTING SHED . . . HUT . . . SANCTUARY . . . HIDEY-HOLE . . . CUBBYHOLE . . . HAVEN . . . GARDEN ROOM . . . .

Summer House

A Change of Scenery

In a secluded part of the garden, the summer house can be used as a simple retreat. The interior is large enough to function as a tool room and potting shed (right) or as a cosy study or home office (opposite).

JOHN PEED
& SON.
SEED and BULB
MERCHANTS,
SPECIALITIES.
CALADIUMS.
GLOXINIAS.
BEGONIAS.

Play House

A Home of Their Own

Whether as a private den away from their parents or as a 'real home' on a miniature scale, a play house in the garden will give children hours of fun and laughter.

A play house in the garden will attract children like bees to a honey-pot. Play houses are excellent for developing children's learning skills, encouraging them to exercise their imaginations. As they play with other children, they will develop inter-personal skills at the same time as enjoying hours of fun. Depending on the age of your children, you can decorate the interior for them, or encourage them to equip it and paint it themselves. In the latter case, make sure that they only use non-toxic paints, which should also be washable, so that the walls can be painted time and again.

By keeping internal fixtures to a minimum, the children can use the play house to represent a variety of structures: from a hospital to a shop, an adult living room to an office, or as a den away from the grown-ups.

When children finally outgrow the play house, it can be adapted without too much expenditure or alteration for use as storage space for garden equipment.

The model shown in the photograph is situated in the grounds of Castle Drogo, a Lutyens house near Exeter now administered by the National Trust. The play house was built *circa* 1909 as a birthday present and was transferred to its present home from a house in Sussex *circa* 1928.

Our plans show how a play house of a similar style could be constructed. For all the framework timber use 38 × 38mm ($1\frac{1}{2} \times 1\frac{1}{2}$in) PAR (planed all round) softwood, as accuracy is important. All the relevant dimensions are shown on the illustrations. Glued and nailed butt joints are used throughout.

PLAY HOUSE ASSEMBLY

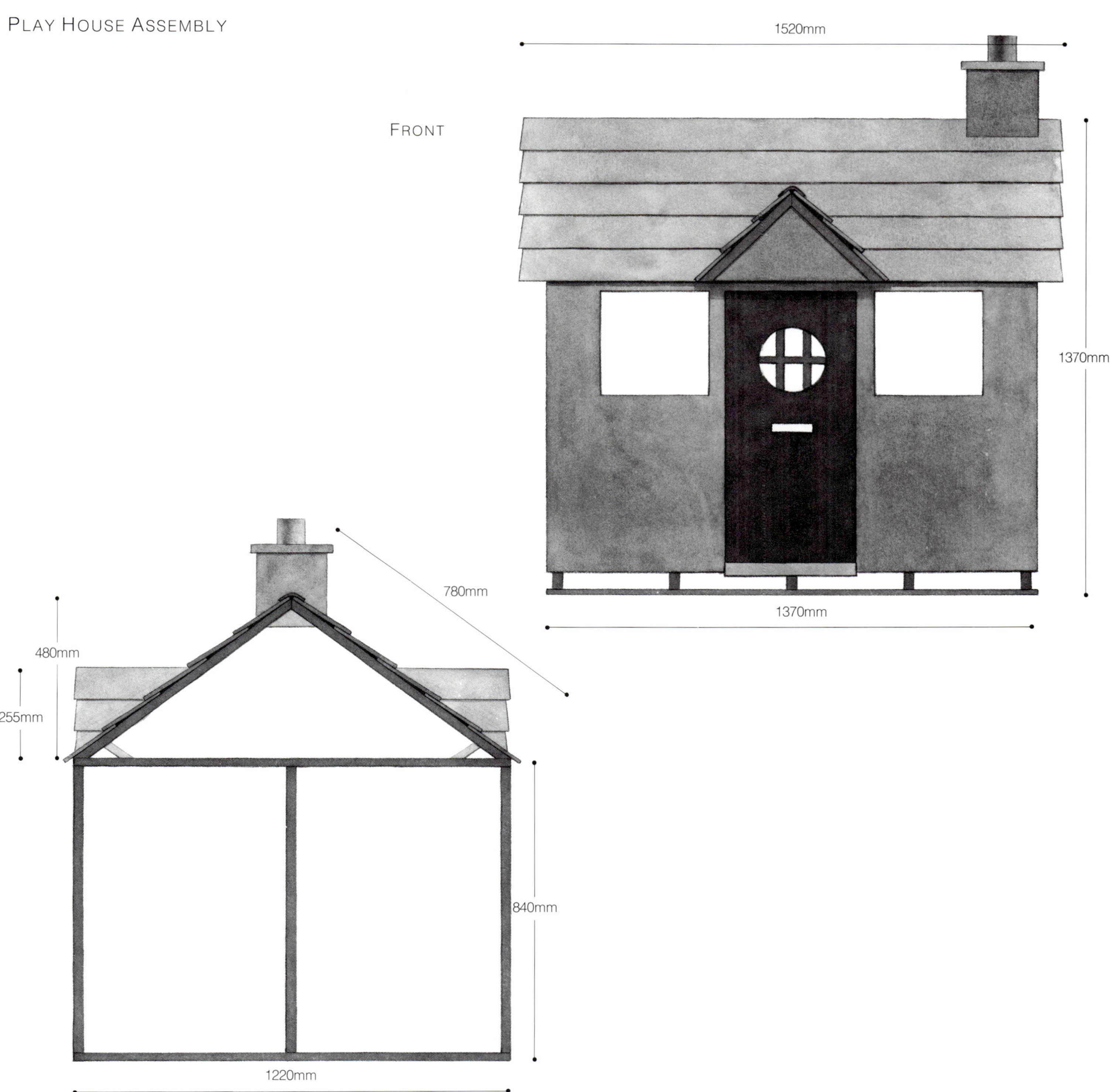

Play House

Base

A solid, level base is essential, otherwise it will not be possible to build the house. The simplest method is to lay paving slabs on sand. To prevent damp in the soil creeping up and attacking the floor, lay a polythene membrane below the sand.

The base should be made slightly smaller than the house so that the wall cladding extends just beyond it all round. This means that rainwater running down the walls will not trickle inside the house, but will instead drip onto the ground.

The overall area of the house is 1370 × 1220mm (54 × 48in) and the base is 5mm ($\frac{1}{4}$in) less all round at 1360 × 1210mm ($53\frac{1}{2} \times 47\frac{1}{2}$in). The floor itself is constructed as a normal house floor with floorboards nailed at right angles to joists. For the joists, use 50 × 25mm (2 × 1in) rough sawn timber. Five joists running from front to back will be sufficient. The two end joists should be just inside the ends of the floorboards, and the other three should be spaced equally between.

The floorboards can be square edged or tongued-and-grooved. The former simply butt up to each other, while tongued-and-grooved boards interlock. You can use either 125mm (5in) or 150mm (6in) wide boards for the floor; thicknesses range from 12–32mm ($\frac{1}{2}$–$1\frac{1}{4}$in), but buy the thinnest available.

Lay the five joists on the ground, then nail one end board at right angles to each joist. Repeat for the other side. Use 50mm (2in) lost head nails and punch the heads below surface.

At this point, the floor will be held solidly in position so that you can add more boards, making sure that square edge boards butt up closely and that tongued-and-grooved boards are tightly interlocked. You will probably have to remove the last board, fixed earlier, to trim it to size before refixing it.

Walls

Fix 19mm ($\frac{3}{4}$in) thick marine plywood over the softwood framework. The front of the house is split into two separate frameworks with the door in the middle. The two frameworks are identical with allowance made for a window on either side. The windows can be any size provided that they look right proportionately – here, 300mm square (12in square) is about right.

The top horizontal member holds the two frames together, but until the side and back frames are added it will be flimsy. So, as a temporary support, add a strut across the doorway as shown (fig 1). This can be nailed in place and removed when the frameworks have been joined and the wall panels added.

Light through the front windows is unlikely to be sufficient: a window up to 500 × 380mm (20 × 15in) can be built into the rear wall.

The side walls are plain. Use a top and bottom horizontal member for rigidity and to strengthen each plywood wall panel.

Assembling the Walls

The front and back wall frames are screwed to the base using 75mm (3in) No 8 screws. This is especially vital in exposed positions where high wind could turn the house over. The horizontal members on each side are now fixed, together with the central supports.

The plywood wall panels can now be cut to size and nailed to the frames using 38mm ($1\frac{1}{2}$in) nails, again punching the heads below the surface. When these are in place, the house will be very solid. Remember to cut the panels to extend just below the base.

Roof

First fix the dormer roof in position. This is made from two A-shaped frames joined with a glued mitre joint and reinforced with two 38mm ($1\frac{1}{2}$in) corrugated fasteners. Plywood offcuts nailed in place strengthen the roof-to-wall joints and reinforce the mitre joint at the apex of the A-frame, while a batten the length of the side wall frames runs between them at the apex. These frames are then clad with featheredge facing boards, nailed in place with 50mm (2in) lost head nails.

Start at the bottom and work up to the ridge. The boards are nailed

1 Constructing the Front Framework

Build all of the frames from 38 × 38mm ($1\frac{1}{2} \times 1\frac{1}{2}$in) PAR softwood. Brace the opening for the door at the front and allow for a window on either side. Dormer roof frame rests centrally on top.

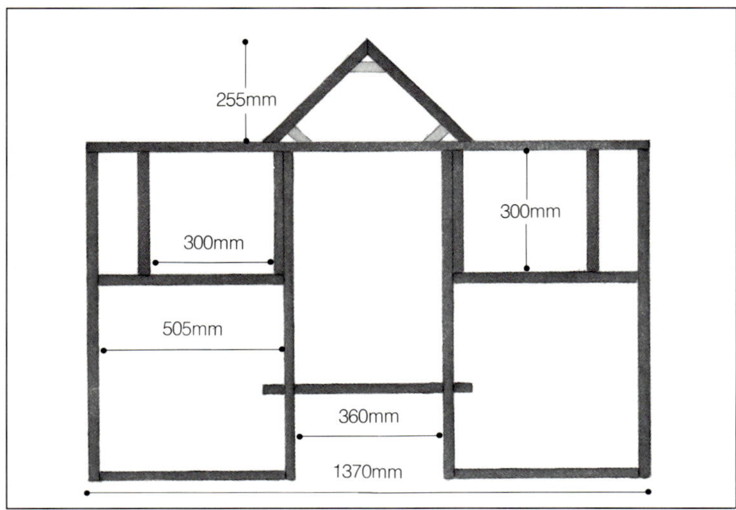

2 Constructing the Back Framework

The back frame is a very simple construction of glued and nailed butt joints. A central window can be fitted at the back to improve the amount of light inside the play house.

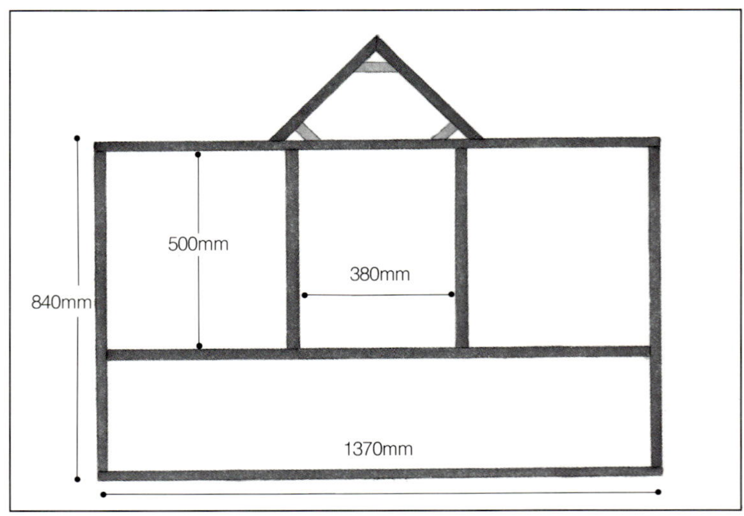

Sanding block 145
Paint 146
Concrete paving slabs 147
Nailing 150
Screwing 150
Fixing cladding 151
Butt joint 152
Mitre joint 154

with the thinner edge uppermost so that the thicker edge of the board above overlaps it by 12mm ($\frac{1}{2}$in) *(see* **Techniques, page 151** *).*

At the top, you will probably have to trim the last board to fit. The ridge is sealed by fixing self-adhesive aluminium flashing tape in position. Cut the strip to the required length from the roll, peel back a little of the backing paper and position the tape on the roof. Press the tape into place with a cloth, peel back more of the backing paper and continue in this manner until the ridge is covered. Do not peel away all of the backing paper at once – the adhesive is powerful and will start to stick itself to the roof in the wrong place. Add two triangular plywood panels to enclose each end of the dormer. These are inset into the A-frames and glued in place.

When the dormer is complete it can be lifted into place and screwed and glued in place to the top of the wall frames.

The main roof is constructed similarly except that the A-frames are fixed in place and then the feather-edge boarding, cutting it to fit around the dormer as necessary.

Use plywood offcuts to strengthen the joints as before, and use triangular plywood panels inset into the A-frames and glued in place at either end.

WINDOWS

You have a choice for the windows: you can either use plain acrylic sheet, or else you can decorate it with self-adhesive lead strips as imitation leaded lights. A similar effect can be achieved with self-adhesive black tape. An alternative is to use thin battens to form small 'windows' within the main frame. For safety reasons, do not use glass.

DOOR

Construct the door from floorboards and fix two 100 × 25mm (4 × 1in) battens horizontally to serve as bracing and to prevent the door warping. Alternatively, you can use shiplap cladding smooth side out, which will give slightly better weather resistance *(see* **Materials, page 146** *).*

CHIMNEY

The chimney is an optional extra. Make it from plywood offcuts joined with 25mm square (1in square) plywood strips in each corner, or use plastic joint blocks. A piece of plastic pipe forms the pot.

PAINTING

Before painting, all the timber which the children will be able to touch should be very carefully smoothed by sanding it down with a power sander to remove any splinters.

Use masonry paint for the main walls and treat the door with primer, undercoat and exterior gloss. Coat the floor with an appropriate wood dye and exterior-grade varnish or a varnish stain; alternatively, it can be painted with masonry paint.

GUTTERS AND PIPES

The gutters and drainpipes are purely decorative. Use offcuts of plastic guttering – the smallest section made for sheds will do. Make the drainpipes from waste pipe held in place with pipe clips.

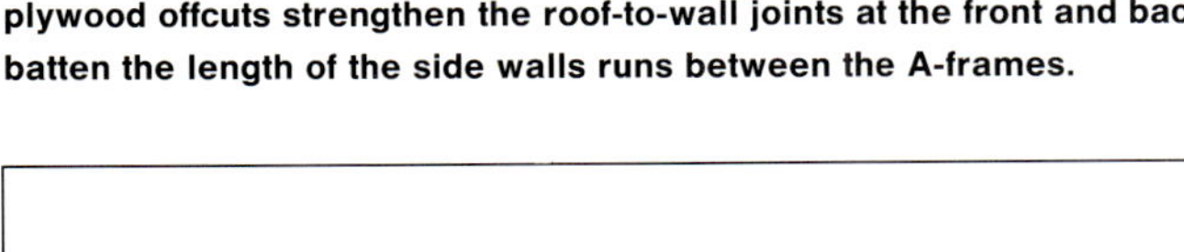
3 Constructing the Dormer Roof Frame
Re-inforce the A-shaped frames with plywood offcuts at the apex. Additional plywood offcuts strengthen the roof-to-wall joints at the front and back. A batten the length of the side walls runs between the A-frames.

4 Making the Door
Make door from floorboards braced top and bottom. Weather bar at bottom throws rain clear of the base.

5 Making the Chimney
This is purely decorative. Angle the plywood to sit on the apex of the roof. Add plastic pipe to form pot.

Rabbit Run

Run Rabbit, Run

Pet rabbits can exercise in safety if you build a rabbit run. The dimensions can be adjusted according to the size and number of rabbits. The enclosed end section provides shelter in bad weather.

An enclosed run such as this will provide your rabbits with an area for safe daytime exercise. One section of the run is fully enclosed for occasions when the weather turns nasty. Be sure to anchor the run firmly to the ground to ensure that the rabbits cannot escape.

Treat all the timber with a good quality wood preservative that will not harm your rabbits and allow it to dry thoroughly. For the side cladding panels use 6mm (¼in) thick marine or WBP grade exterior plywood; use the same material for the doors, but use 9mm (⅜in) thickness for the floor.

Make up four A-shaped frames using 50 × 25mm (2 × 1in) softwood and strengthen them with 25 × 25mm (1 × 1in) cross pieces. The apex of each frame needs to be mitred and this joint can be secured with a 25mm (1in) wide corrugated fastener. The other joints in the frame are secured using 38mm (1½in) No 8 rustless screws. Use waterproof adhesive on all joints.

Position the frames at 600mm (24in) spacings, then link them at either side with 1800mm (72in) lengths of 38 × 6mm (1½ × ¼in) plywood battens, top and bottom, fixed in place using 25mm (1in) No 8 screws driven into the A-frames.

Add the floor to the section that will be beneath the side cladding panels, pinning it to the two cross rails at the bottom of the A-frames with 25mm (1in) panel pins.

Use 12mm (½in) plastic-coated wire netting, which should be cut to finish 50mm (2in) inside the position of the plywood side panels. Use 19mm (¾in) netting staples to secure it to the frame of the run and secure it very strongly with staples at 75mm (3in) intervals. Cut out a triangle of netting for the back frame of the run and secure it in the same way as for the sides. Pin the side panels in place on the frame, enclosing the edges of the netting. The frame battens will create a small gap between the A-frame and the side panels – add a filler piece if you want the panels flush.

The outer door should be cut out to sit snugly inside the end frame. Add small spacer blocks to bring it flush with the frame, then add a turnbutton for each corner to hold it in place. Make a turnbutton from an offcut of the 6mm (¼in) plywood and a 25mm (1in) No 8 screw. Drill 12mm (½in) ventilation holes in the door and nail an offcut of wood to act as a handle.

The internal door is pinned in place inside the rabbit run to give access between the covered and uncovered sections. Drill 12mm (½in) ventilation holes and cut the entrance with a jigsaw or coping saw.

Add a capping of roofing felt to seal the apex of the roof. Use bitumen-based adhesive to attach it.

Drilling 150
Nailing 150
Screwing 150
Mitre joint 154

RABBIT RUN ASSEMBLY

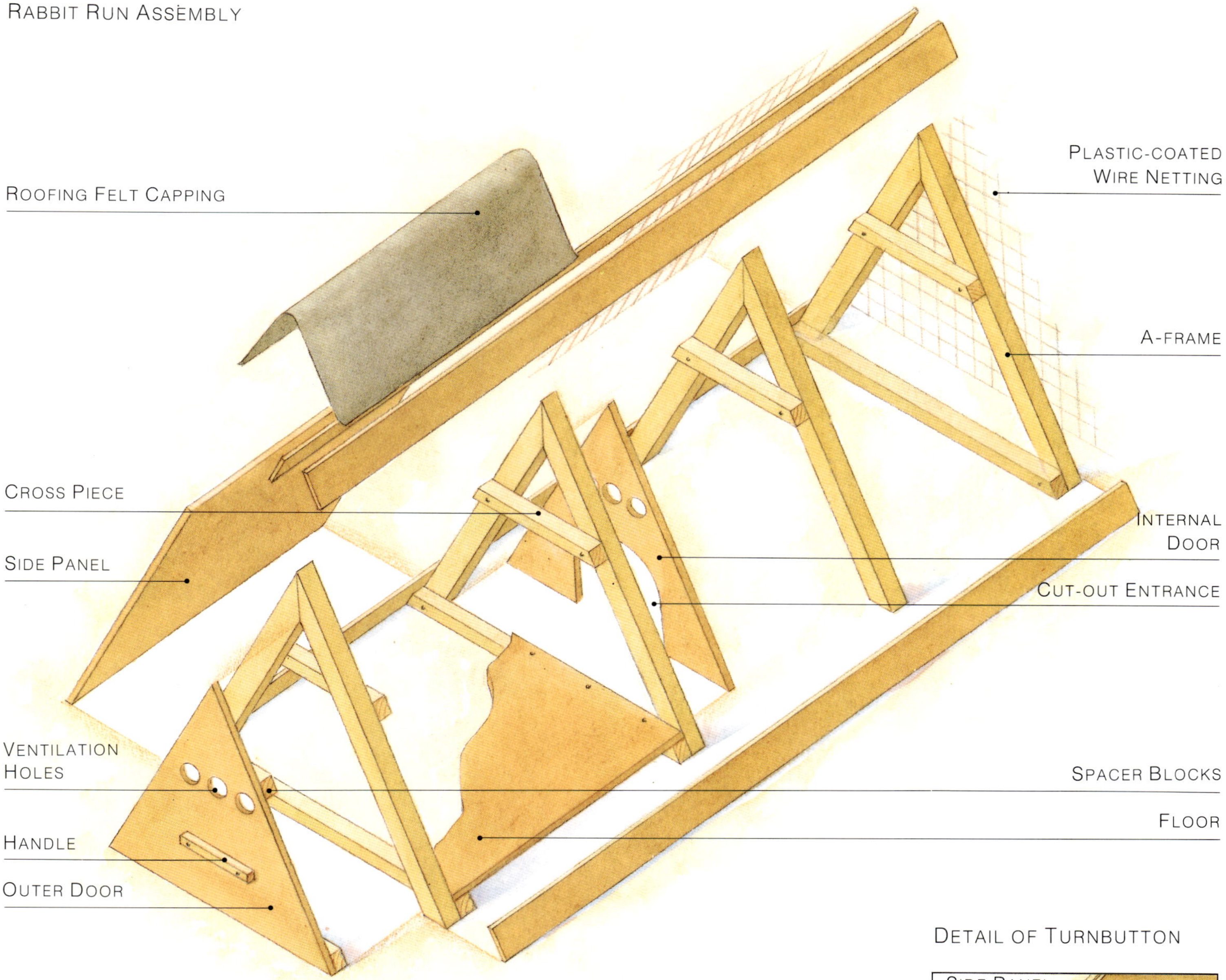

ROOFING FELT CAPPING

PLASTIC-COATED WIRE NETTING

A-FRAME

CROSS PIECE

SIDE PANEL

INTERNAL DOOR

CUT-OUT ENTRANCE

VENTILATION HOLES

SPACER BLOCKS

FLOOR

HANDLE

OUTER DOOR

DETAIL OF TURNBUTTON

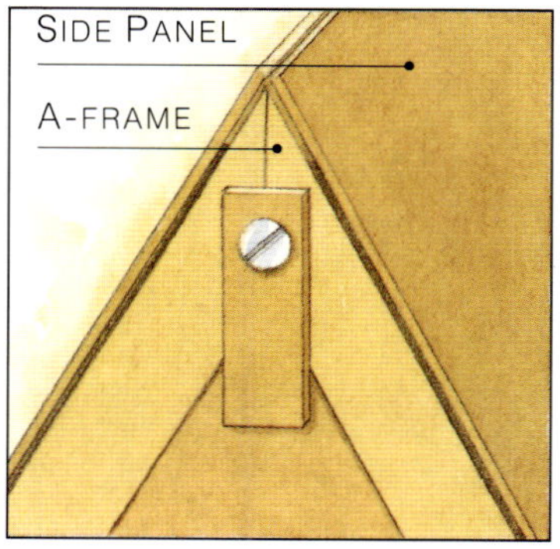

SIDE PANEL

A-FRAME

NESTING BOX

The introduction of a nesting box to your garden will help to conserve bird life and provide entertainment for the family. Given time, the birds will gain in confidence and come closer to your home.

The sizes given for this particular box (similar to the one in the photograph) are not critical so they can be altered by 25–50mm (1–2in) if preferred. The only thing that must be specific is the diameter of the entrance hole since this will govern the species of bird that will be encouraged to nest. The height that the box is sited above the ground is also important, but is generally not as critical as that of the entrance hole. A table of entrance hole diameters and above-ground heights is given opposite.

Rough-sawn timber is ideal for boxes, and a thickness of 16mm ($\frac{5}{8}$in) makes jointing easy. All joints are butted, and secured with waterproof wood adhesive and galvanized or alloy nails. Wood is a good insulator against heat and cold, it resists condensation and blends well with any environment.

First, cut out the two side pieces, each measuring 200 × 120mm (8 × $4\frac{3}{4}$in). Next, cut a groove along the inside front edge of both pieces to serve as a channel for the door to slide in. The channels must be perfectly aligned; marking out, therefore, must be very accurate.

If you have a router then the channels can be cut out quickly and precisely using a straight-sided router bit. If you do not have a router then use a marking knife to scribe the edge of the groove. Next, use a tenon saw to cut the groove to the required depth along each edge before paring out the waste with a chisel. Work slowly and carefully until the sides and base of the channels are flat.

The back panel is a complete piece, shaped to support the roof panels. In position, it is slightly inset between the side panels.

The front is constructed from two separate pieces. The top triangular section is fixed to the roof and has a hole of the required diameter drilled through it. The hole can be drilled using either an auger bit or, if you have one, an expansive bit fitted in a wheel brace.

Should you not have a bit suitable for cutting large diameter holes then use a padsaw or jigsaw. First, drill a hole inside the outline of the hole to leave a starting position for the saw blade. Drill the hole with a normal twist drill. Cut out the shape carefully and finish by sanding the edges (*see* **Techniques, page 149**).

The door is cut to dimensions of 200 × 160mm (8 × $6\frac{1}{2}$in). A rebate is taken from each side so that the door sits neatly in the side panels.

The rebate is cut easily with a router and straight-sided bit or with a tenon saw and chisel (*see* **Techniques, page 150**).

The roof is comprised of two panels; each panel measures 215 × 155mm ($8\frac{1}{2}$ × 6in). The roof is joined at the top using a mitre joint. The joint, as throughout, is glued but this time it is secured with a 25mm (1in) corrugated fastener, which is tapped home flush with the surface.

When all the pieces have been cut to size, treat the exterior faces and edges only with a water-based wood preservative. It is best to leave internal faces untreated to avoid any toxic risk to the birds.

To assemble the box, first join the two side panels to the floor and then add the back panel.

Make up the roof, including the triangular front section, and attach this to the lower part.

Finally, with the sliding door in the closed position, drill a hole through either side of the nesting box and into the door to a depth of 25mm (1in). Insert a 50mm (2in) galvanized steel nail into each hole to hold the door in place. The holes should be of a diameter to give the nails a tight but sliding fit.

BACK GARDEN BIRD-LIFE
A nesting box provides a safe haven for small birds and their young. By encouraging birds to nest in your garden, you will derive personal satisfaction and the enjoyment of observing wildlife close at hand.

Siting is not crucial, although a location within view of your house is obviously desirable for the family's enjoyment. Try to avoid anywhere where water is likely to cascade down, and, if your garden is exposed, position the box on the most sheltered side to avoid strong winds. Most birds prefer a direct flight line to the entrance.

If you are lucky, the box may lodge conveniently in the fork of a tree, but in most cases some form of fixing will be required. The simplest way is to secure plastic-coated garden wire to the back of the box using fencing staples, and then to wire the box to a tree trunk. With an immature tree, attach the wire fairly loosely to allow for growth of the trunk. It is best not to nail or screw directly into the trunk or branch of a tree as this may damage it.

Alternatively, you can place the nesting box on top of a post. Sink a post support into the ground at the chosen site and insert a 75 × 75mm (3 × 3in) post cut to the appropriate height (*see* **Techniques, page 152**). Remove the sliding door from the nesting box, drill a pilot hole through the base and into the post, and screw in place.

Remember to clear out the nesting box annually, after the fledglings and their parents have flown.

Cutting a circle 149
Cutting rebates 150
Drilling 150
Nailing 150
Screwing 150
Butt joint 152
Fixing posts 152
Mitre joint 154

SPECIES	HOLE DIAMETER	HEIGHT ABOVE GROUND
BLUE TIT	25mm (1in)	2–5m (6–15ft)
GREAT TIT	28mm (1⅛in)	2–5m (6–15ft)
COAL TIT	25mm (1in)	1m (39in)
MARSH TIT	25mm (1in)	1m (39in)
WILLOW TIT	25mm (1in)	1m (39in)
NUTHATCH	32mm (1¼in)	4–5m (12–15ft)
TREE SPARROW	32mm (1¼in)	4–5m (12–15ft)

NESTING BOX ASSEMBLY

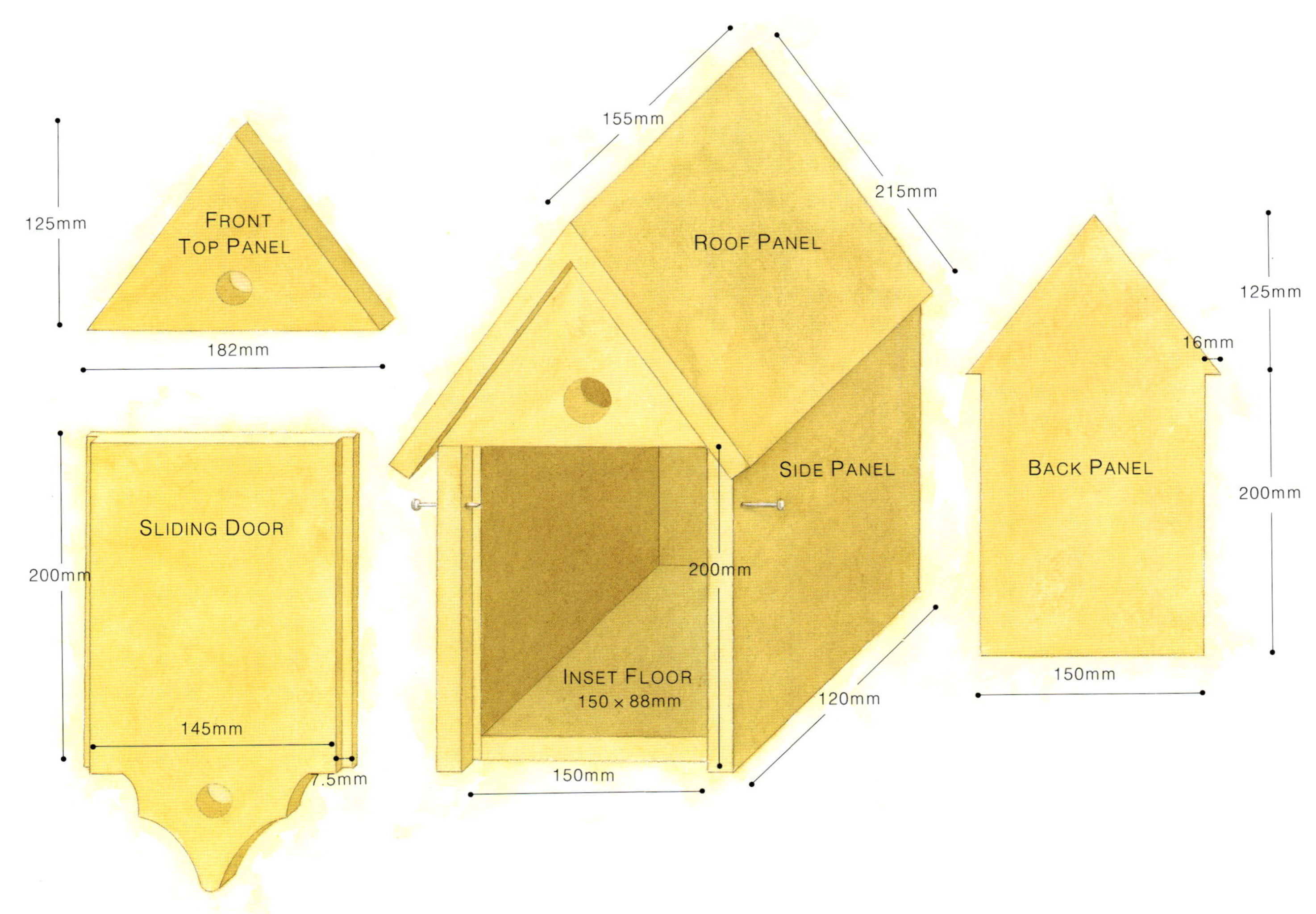

PART 3

PATIOS, PATHS AND PONDS

The contrast between various garden surfaces – hard and soft, paved, turfed, planted or water-filled – gives a garden its fundamental shape and design. Considerations such as where to build a patio or a flight of steps, which area to link with paths or how to edge a flowerbed are not details to be decided piecemeal but basic issues which should be resolved at the outset.

All gardens, even informal ones, need some hard surfaces. Modern gardens are generally small and demands on the space available are high. One of our most important requirements today is that the garden should function as an extension of the house, as an outdoor room, which usually means that there must be some sort of paved seating area for relaxation. And there will always be the need for paths to connect one part of the garden to another, as a practical surface for walking and tending beds, and visually to divide flowerbeds from the lawn. Wherever possible, construct hard surfaces from natural materials that weather and age, and allow plants or grass to grow in the crevices of paving and paths, softening the edges so that these areas blend harmoniously with the rest of the garden.

Patios, Paths and Ponds

Because hard surfaces are relatively expensive, fairly permanent and take time and effort to install, it is critically important to work out your ideas on paper first. This is also the stage at which to plan changes of level or to work out how to accommodate an existing slope in the form of steps or terraces. Look at the shapes – the overall pattern – that the paved areas will create. Make sure that paths do not leave useless margins of lawn or awkward-shaped flowerbeds. Plan the connections so that the paths really go somewhere, rather than meander aimlessly. Establish the basic proportion of patio to lawn so that the paving reinforces the overall design of the garden. A formal layout, for example, usually relies on a strong, symmetrical grid which can be expressed in a higher proportion of paths and paved areas. In a town garden, you may decide to dispense with a lawn altogether and work out a series of connecting paved areas and raised beds.

The range of materials suitable for hard surfacing is so great that there really is no need to rely solely on concrete. All the natural materials are much more sympathetic in the garden and they not only work well with plants but also with each other, so that you can mix materials to create interesting contrasts of texture and pattern. Bricks can be laid to create herring-bone or basketweave patterns as well as simple coursing; be sure to choose frost-proof varieties for outdoor use and avoid ugly stock bricks which never weather. Stone – including York stone, slate and granite sets – is traditional and expensive but can sometimes be reclaimed much more cheaply from building sites or builders' yards. Gravel can be rather dull; pebble paths are much more positive. Sea pebbles, in particular, set into concrete look wonderful laid in a mosaic. Treated wood is an excellent garden material. Railway sleepers, which have a uniform thickness and are already treated against rot, can be put to a number of uses, from making steps to forming the sides of raised beds. Slices can be cut from the trunks of fallen trees, treated, and used end grain-on for paths, steps and patios. Decking, as a terrace or around the perimeter of a pond, is contemporary-looking and absorbs the heat of the sun to make a warm, comfortable surface.

Whatever material you choose will probably depend to a large extent on the amount of money you can spend, but try to form some kind of connection with the overall style of the house and the materials from which it is built. This is an important consideration, particularly for terraces or patios that immediately adjoin the house and create a relatively large surface area which has an impact on how the house is viewed.

If you cannot avoid the use of concrete, there are many ways of improving its rather dull and uniform appearance. Paviours are much better than a poured concrete slab and can be enormously improved if, instead of setting them in cement, they are laid with gaps in between. You can then fill the gaps with pebbles or plants such as creeping thyme or camomile to soften the edges. Choose paviours of a neutral shade and let colour come from lichens and mosses: you can encourage lichen to grow by treating concrete with non-pasteurized milk or houseplant food. Even if most of the paving is concrete, an edging of brick or another more harmonious material will lift it out of the ordinary.

A path makes a good edge for a flowerbed or herbaceous border, separating planted areas from lawn and making mowing easier. In the absence of a path, beds need some form of containment. Conventional edging includes brick,

Outdoor Flooring

The surfaces you choose for outdoor flooring can reinforce the overall style and design of the garden. A regular gridded pattern of smooth stone slabs suits the modern formal style of a town garden (above). Deck boarding is particularly sympathetic surrounding the perimeter of a pool, where it makes a comfortable surface for bare feet (above right). Slate tiles create a sleek paved area in a town garden (above far right). For a more informal, country setting, a sweep of large cobblestone makes an attractive paved area (below right).

Ponds 94
Timber 146
Laying bricks 157

looped wire which also serves to prop up plants, and concrete bricks. Traditional terracotta edging, particularly the Victorian rope design, is also available. Less conventionally, you can make effective edging with whatever comes to hand: slivers of stone, old roofing slates or thin horizontal slats of treated hardwood nailed to posts.

Water is one of the most delightful of all the elements in garden design, providing another contrast of surface, and retaining its interest even in winter when the garden is bare. A sheet of water, reflecting the sky, has always been a feature of formal designs; surrounded by moisture-loving plants and filled with fish and lily pads, a pond can come close to fulfilling everyone's dream of having a river running through the garden. Moving water – a jet, a fountain, a cascade or a water sculpture – adds another dimension, that of sound. The tinkling noise of running water in the garden is extremely pleasant and restful.

There are also good practical reasons for incorporating water in a garden design. A pond or pool provides a supply of water at air temperature, which presents far less of a shock to young seedlings than water from a hosepipe. Even in a dry

COOL WATER

Formal pools of water can be incorporated into even the smallest town garden (right and above right), although pools designed to look like natural lakes need more space around them to be successful.

SURFACE INTEREST

A contrast of different surfaces – terracotta, stone, brick or concrete – enlivens a garden design (opposite and above opposite.).

area, a pond will create its own microclimate where you can grow species such as arum lilies, irises and other plants which flourish in damp conditions. And you do not have to stock your pond with fish for it to be attractive to insects, butterflies and other wildlife.

In whatever form, water is a natural focal point in the garden. If the garden slopes, it is a simple proposition to create channels where water flows down the incline and collects in a pool, to be pumped back by an inexpensive recirculating pump. In hot countries, water in channels or running down steeped terraces has long been a means both of irrigating vegetable crops and, in courtyard gardens, of cooling the air. A still pool of water in a geometric shape is often the centrepiece of a formal garden, and formal cascades, for example, were an important feature of Italian Renaissance gardens. Sunken or raised pools in rectangular, circular, square or L-shapes are relatively easy to build from concrete block with waterproof facing, the edges softened by clumps of rushes and irises. And in a small town garden, the suggestion of water can be created very simply by the addition of a water sculpture. Water falling over large urns, slabs of stone or boulders is much more effective and attractive than a waterfall or fountain which involves a contrived, rather crudely cast garden ornament.

Informal ponds and pools, where the intention is to create as natural an effect as possible, demand a larger garden to be successful. Groups of boulders, timber decking, dense perimeter planting and perhaps a flat, low bridge can give an informal pond a Japanese quality. Water on this kind of scale demands more attention and general maintenance than a simple formal pool if it is to be convincing and appealing.

Water Sculpture

The delightful sound of running water in the garden is especially restful and pleasing. A water sculpture can be made very simply and economically, requiring only a minimal outlay for a small pump and the careful installation of a power supply.

This fountain consists simply of a large ribbed terracotta pot set into a pool which is in turn sunk into the ground and overhung with a brick surround. The dimensions have been calculated using standard bricks as a module.

A black polythene pond liner is fitted inside the pool, and bricks and a tile used to make a central platform on which the pot rests. A waterproof power cable runs from the pump through a special conduit to connect with the main power supply. A word of caution: special care must be taken to ensure that there is no leaking where the cable exits from the pool. It is also vital to lay the correct conduit for the cable so that it cannot be accidentally cut when digging above it.

An earthenware pot makes the best choice for the sculpture since terracotta is easier to drill than stoneware. A copper pipe is inserted through a hole drilled in the base of the pot. When the pool is filled with water, the pump sends a jet of water up through the pipe to fill the pot and overflow down the sides.

During the winter months, the power supply should be switched off and the pot emptied to prevent the risk of it being cracked by a hard frost.

WATER SCULPTURE

The sight and sound of moving water is one of the most pleasurable experiences to be had in a garden on a hot summer's day. You need not go to the trouble and expense of installing an elaborate pond complete with waterfall, fish and plants to enjoy this in your own garden – you can build this simple yet very effective water sculpture. The size of the pool is entirely optional, as is the centrepiece. We chose a pot with ridged sides since it gives an interesting surface for the water to splash on to and run down.

A submersible pump pushes the water up and out of the pot. As the pump is electrically operated from the house supply, it makes sense to keep the water sculpture as close to the house as possible since this saves having to run the buried cable a long way. The submersible pump can be hidden beneath the pot or in a corner of the pond to be covered by pond weed or water lilies.

With any water feature in the garden, safety must be paramount: a child can drown even in shallow water. If you have children and choose to install a pool then do make sure that it is made child-proof.

TOOLS
HAND SAW
SPADE
SPIRIT LEVEL
SANDING BLOCK and ABRASIVE PAPER
STEEL RULE
TROWEL (if paving laid on mortar)
CLUB HAMMER
POWER DRILL
ADJUSTABLE SPANNER
HACKSAW
SCREWDRIVER

MATERIALS

Part	Quantity	Material	Length
POT	1	Terracotta	As required
TUBE	1	12mm (½in) copper tubing	Height of pot
TILE	1	Terracotta	300 x 300mm (12 x 12in)
PAVING SLAB	1	Concrete	600 x 600mm (24 x 24in)
SIDES OF POOL	4	19mm (¾in) shuttering plywood	As required

Also required: 1 submersible pump and outdoor cable; 12mm (½in) compression tank outlet; jubilee clip and rubber washers; PVC or butyl pond liner; sand for lining pond; bricks for supporting terracotta tile and for pool surround; sand or soil for bedding brick surround

BUILDING THE POOL

Choose a level site and mark out the ground using a string line and pegs or a hosepipe. This will give you a good idea of whether the position and size is satisfactory. Our pool is 1000mm (39in) square.

Dig out the hole to a depth of about 300mm (12in). The four sides should be tapered outwards slightly and the base should be flat – check this using a spirit level.

Cut out four pieces of plywood to form the sides of the pool. The top edge of the plywood should align with the level of the surrounding soil once you have cut around the edge of the pool to bed the brick or stone surround which will lie flush and overlap the edge of the pool slightly. In our case, the plywood was 220mm (8¾in) deep. Place the plywood pieces in position and sand them carefully to remove splinters.

Bed down a paving slab in the middle. If you lay it on sand it will be simple to level. Lay a sand screed across the excavation, covering the slab by about 12mm (½in).

The brick or paved surround will be far more appealing if weathered, second-hand material is used. Dig out the area around the pool to the width and depth required for the bricks or slabs being used. In our case, the area was 425mm (17in) wide all round to allow for a double row of 225mm (9in) bricks overlapping the pond edge by 25mm (1in). The depth was approximately 80mm (3⅛in) to allow for the 65mm (2½in) brick depth plus a 15mm (⅝in) layer of fine soil or sand underneath. If you excavate to a depth so that the brick surround will be level with the lawn, mowing will be easier.

FITTING THE LINER

The length of liner should be twice the pool depth plus the overall length of the pool (including the brick surround); the width of liner should be twice the depth of the pool plus the overall width.

Lay the pond liner in place following the manufacturer's instructions. Allow the excess edges of the liner to lap up over the sides of the pond, then weight it down temporarily while the pond is being filled. The weight of the water will gradually force the liner to stretch to the shape of the plywood walls. Check with the instructions as to how long you should allow the liner to stretch until it will be smooth.

Remove the temporary bricks and trim the liner to leave about 150mm (6in) to lie below the brick surround.

Next, lay the bricks. Lay the course surrounding the edge of the pool first so that the bricks will overlap the water by 25mm (1in). It is a good idea to lay the corner bricks first and then to rest a straight-edge and spirit level across them; bring them level by adjusting the bed of sand or fine soil below and tapping each brick with the shaft of a club hammer. It is then easy to fill in the remaining bricks, levelling each one with neighbouring bricks, and filling in the gaps with sand or soil so that plants and moss can grow up in the cracks. Although reasonable alignment of the bricks is important, second-hand bricks can tend to be slightly off centre, but that gives the surround a rustic charm. However, it is important that the surface is level so that no-one will trip. Note the brick arrangement used to turn the corners (fig 1)

PREPARING THE POT

The base of the pot sits on a 300mm square (12in square) terracotta tile, itself supported by two levelled bricks, laid edge on and spaced at the required distance (fig 2). The water level should be slightly above the tile so that the bottom of the pot is just submerged. The pump is placed below the tile.

Drill a 19mm (¾in) diameter hole through the centre of the base of the pot to take a 12mm (½in) tank outlet fitting. Use a tungsten carbide drill bit at slow speed. A larger hole is needed in the tile to take the pipe from the pump; to make this, drill a series of small holes closely together in a circle. As the small holes are joined up, a larger hole will automatically be formed.

FITTING THE PUMP

Fit the compression tank outlet through the holes in the pot and tile ensuring that rubber washers are used on both sides and that the nuts are not overtightened, otherwise the

Ponds 94
Sawing 148
Drilling 150
Laying bricks 157

pot could crack. Using a hacksaw, cut a length of copper tube to extend from inside the compression joint to the rim of the pot (fig 3).

Attach the rubber tube from the pump to the compression outlet, if necessary using a jubilee clip to secure it. If the base of the pot is too thick then there might not be sufficient thread left to attach the tube. If so, screw on an extension piece.

The pump is powered from the house electrical supply. It can be operated directly from the mains but it is safer to feed it back through a transformer situated in the house which makes the supply low voltage for safety but adequate to power a pump. The cable should be armoured for outdoor use and laid in a plastic conduit underground and fed into the pool from below the brick surround. There may be local regulations about this, so check first.

You can then switch on the power supply to the pump and enjoy the results. It is a good idea to remove the pot and store it inside during the winter as it may crack in freezing weather.

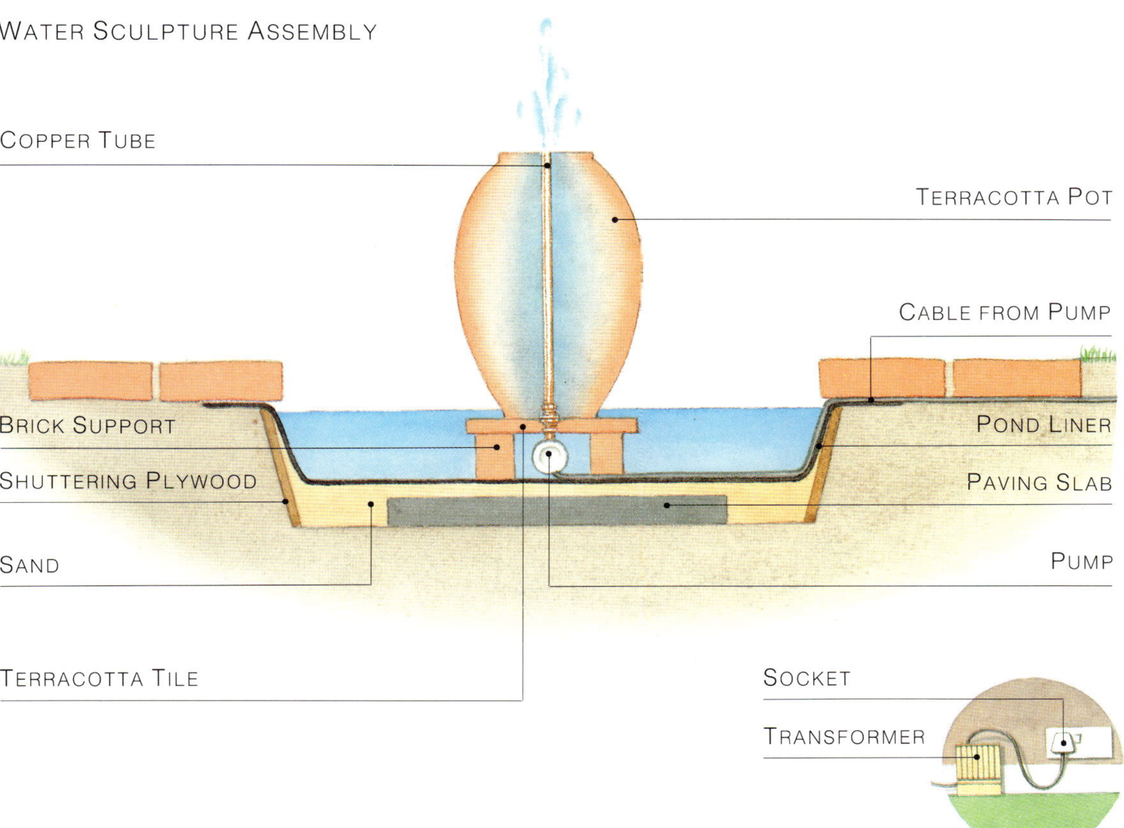

1 Detail of Brick Surround

At each corner of the surround the bricks are laid in pairs perpendicular to the adjoining pair.

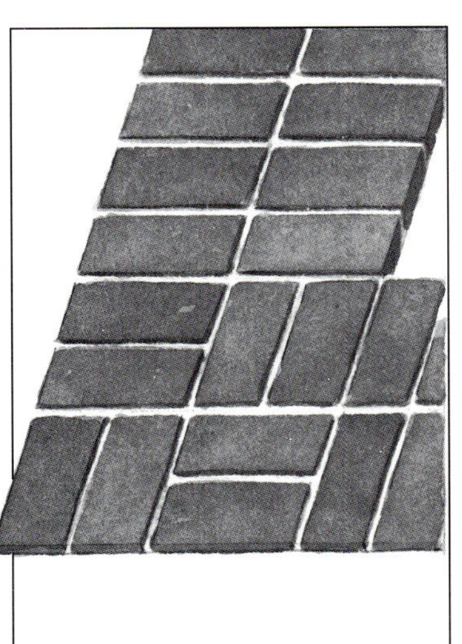

2 Terracotta Pot Support

Pot rests on tile supported by two bricks. Copper tube is connected to pump through holes in pot and tile.

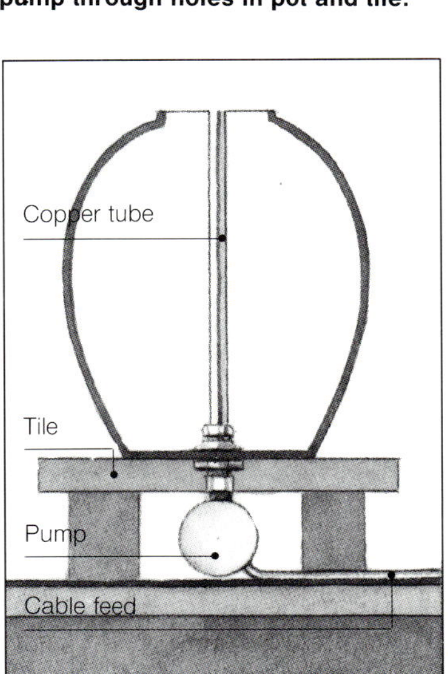

3 Connecting Pump to Pot

Pump pipe is connected to copper tube by compression tank outlet which feeds through pot and tile.

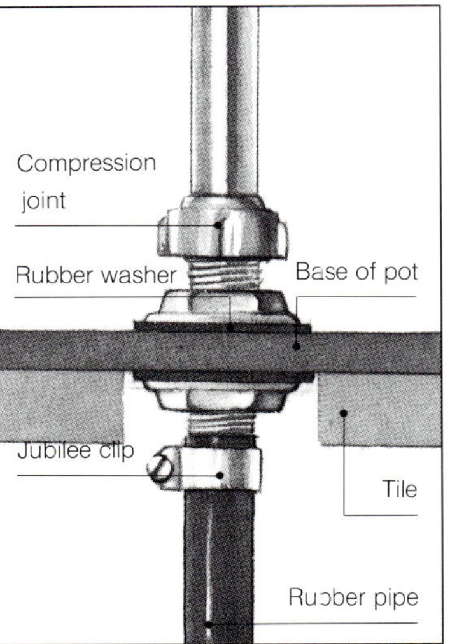

Jardiniere

This elegant, rectilinear jardinière, or plant stand, is inspired by the work of the early twentieth-century designer Josef Hoffmann (1870–1956). He was a Viennese architect, a founder member of the Wiener Werkstätte and a pioneer of functional design. His furniture displays a lack of embellishment and an interest in proportion that was developed further by designers of the Modernist Movement.

Essentially a simple structure, it is made slightly more complicated by the number of right-angled joints. The jardinière incorporates a shallow tray at the top and a shelf at the bottom to hold a collection of plant pots. It is intended for both outdoor and indoor use. The gridded design has been painted a pale 'bone' colour, but other neutral shades would be equally effective.

The idea of grouping elements together to increase their impact is as important in garden design as it is in the design of interiors. Filled with geraniums, the jardinière would brighten up a corner of a patio or seating area, while, positioned near the kitchen door, either outside or in, the stand would also make a convenient home for a collection of herbs grown in containers.

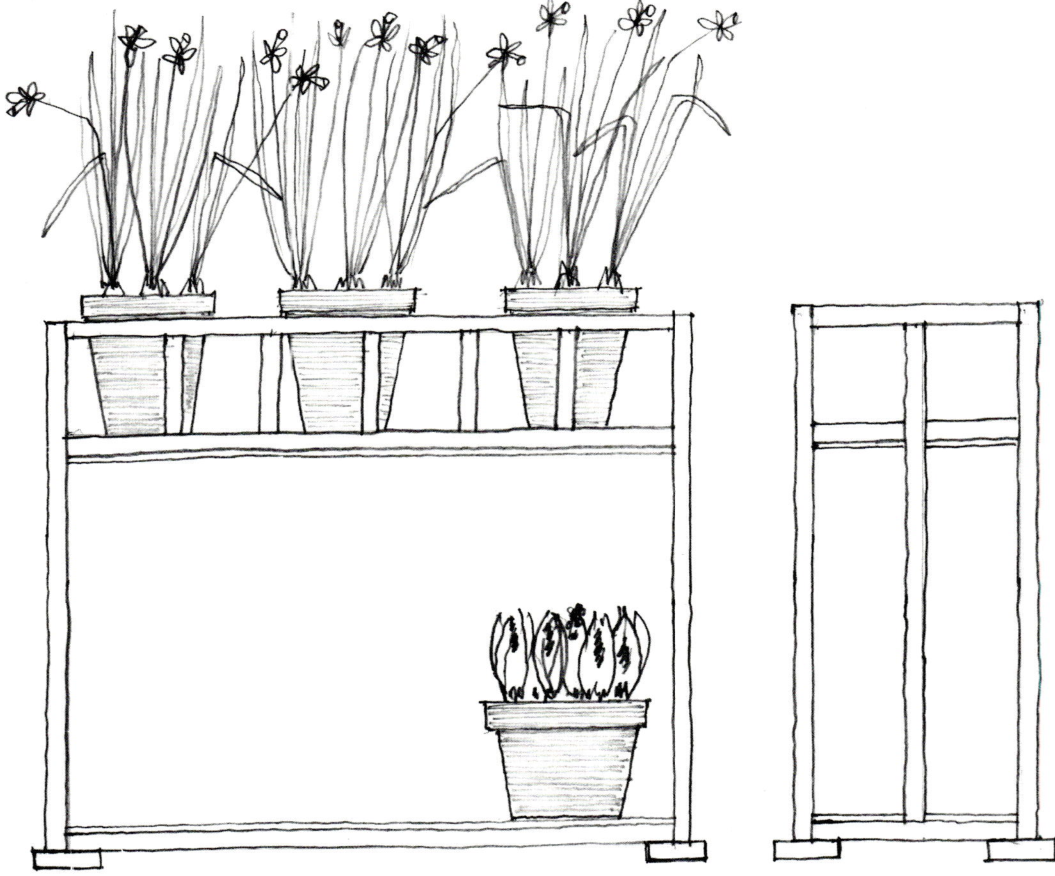

Jardiniere

This simple stand for plants and flowers looks equally good in the garden or the conservatory. The jardinière shown here is made from PAR (planed all round) softwood and then painted. However, if you want to retain the timber finish, then be sure to make it from good-quality softwood or even hardwood, which can then be treated with a water-repellent preservative stain.

The design of the frame uses a number of wood joints, and for ease of assembly we suggest that these are dowelled together. For a stronger job, the joints could be mortised and tenoned, but unless you have a mortising machine it would be too time-consuming to attempt to construct the frame by this method.

Tools

- WORKBENCH (fixed or portable)
- MARKING KNIFE
- STEEL MEASURING TAPE
- STEEL RULE
- TRY SQUARE
- PANEL SAW (or circular power saw)
- TENON SAW (or power jigsaw)
- CHISEL
- MARKING GAUGE
- POWER DRILL
- TWIST DRILL BIT – 3mm ($\frac{1}{8}$in)
- DOWELLING JIG
- DOWEL BIT – 10mm ($\frac{3}{8}$in)
- MALLET
- SCREWDRIVER
- POWER SANDER (or hand sanding block)

Materials

Part	Quantity	Material	Length
CORNER POSTS	4	38 × 38mm ($1\frac{1}{2}$ × $1\frac{1}{2}$in) PAR softwood	779mm ($30\frac{5}{8}$in)
MIDDLE POSTS	2	As above	711mm (28in)
LONG RAILS	6	As above	847mm ($33\frac{3}{8}$in)
END RAILS	6	As above	237mm ($9\frac{5}{16}$in)
VERTICAL PIECES	10	As above	122mm ($4\frac{3}{4}$in)
SHELVES	2	6mm ($\frac{1}{4}$in) WBP plywood	270 × 880mm ($10\frac{5}{8}$ × $34\frac{5}{8}$in)
FEET	4	Offcut of hardwood or softwood	90 × 90 × 30mm ($3\frac{1}{2}$ × $3\frac{1}{2}$ × $1\frac{1}{8}$in)

Also required: 10mm ($\frac{3}{8}$in) diameter dowelling; 50mm (2in) No 8 zinc-plated screws; panel pins

Frame Construction

Cut all the components to length, following the Materials chart.

Making the End Frames

Cut a halving joint to form the intersection of the middle post with the middle end rail *(see* **Techniques, page 152***)*. Mark off on the middle post where the middle end rail will cross it using one of the short vertical pieces as a spacer. The top of the cross halving joint will be this distance down from the top of the middle post.

Mark out and cut the halving joint on the middle post and the middle end rail (fig 1). Repeat for the other end frame.

Strike diagonal lines to mark the centre points for the dowel holes on the ends of all the end rails, on the ends of the middle posts and on the ends of all the short vertical pieces. Using a dowelling jig and a dowel bit (or a drill fitted with a dowel bit and held in a vertical drill stand) drill 10mm ($\frac{3}{8}$in) diameter holes centrally into the marked positions. The hole depths should be slightly over half the lengths of the dowels (ie, 22mm [$\frac{7}{8}$in] deep holes for 40mm [$1\frac{1}{2}$in] long dowels). This gives a small cavity at the end which will accommodate trapped air and glue *(see* **Techniques, Dowel joints, page 154***)*.

1 Fixing Middle End Rail

Mark position of middle end rail on middle post and cut halving joints to fix the two pieces together.

2 Top and Bottom End Rails

Mark dowel hole positions centrally on both ends of middle rail. Dowel to top and bottom end rails to fix.

3 Adding Corner Posts

Dowel posts to end rails: top end rail is flush with top of posts, bottom end rail flush with bottom of posts.

Softwood 146
Drilling 150
Halving joint 152
Dowel joint 154

JARDINIERE ASSEMBLY

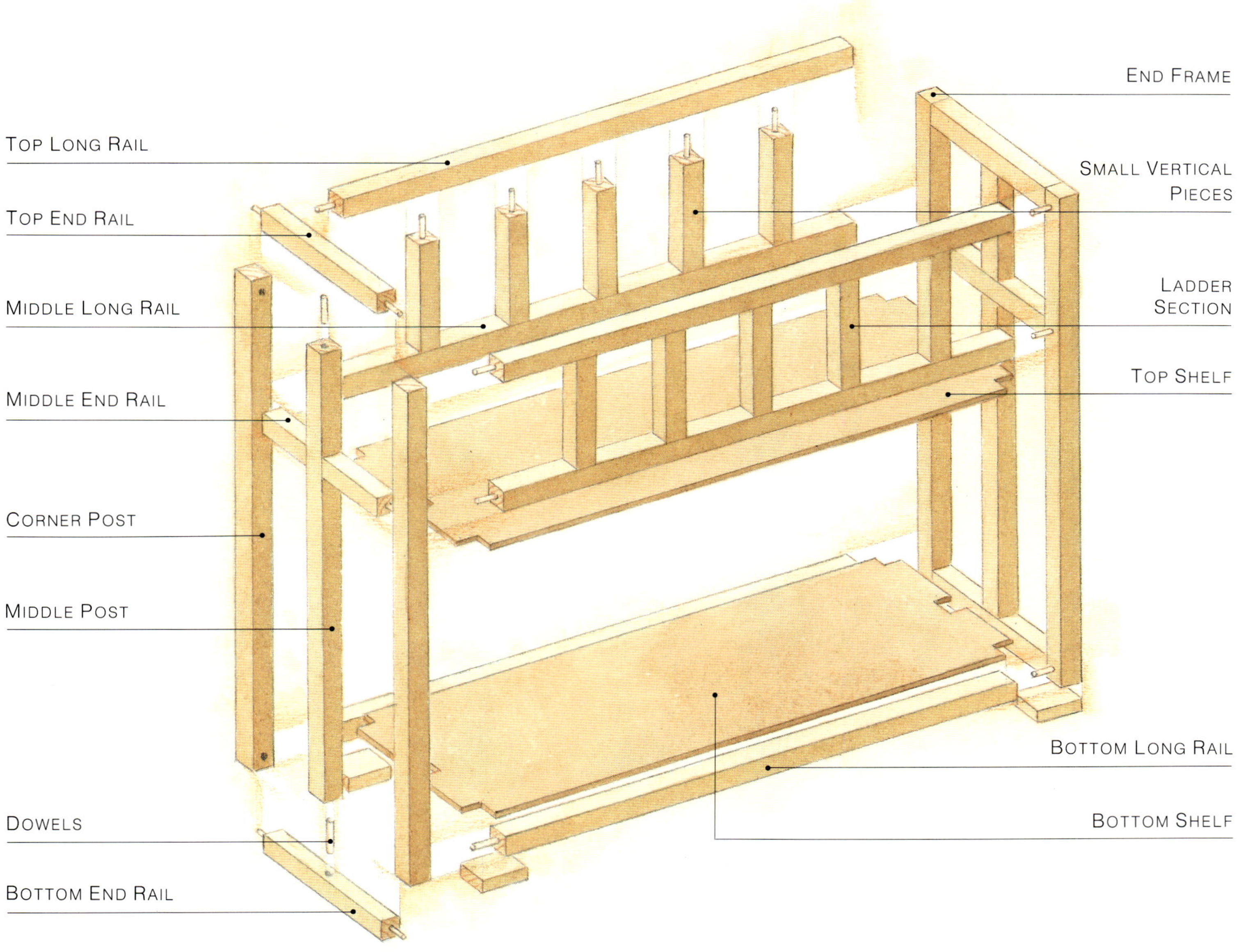

JARDINIERE

Marking square 148

Drilling 150

Screwing 150

Dowel joint 154

Mark out the position of the top and bottom end rails on to the inside faces of the corner posts and strike diagonals again to mark the positions of the dowel holes. Drill the holes as before. Also mark out on each corner post the dowel hole positions for the middle rail, which is the same distance down as the length of a short vertical piece plus the 38mm (1½in) depth of the top end rail. Square round on to the other internal face of each corner post to mark the dowel hole positions to take the top, middle and bottom long rails.

Dry assemble the middle post and the middle end rail together to form a cross, and then dowel on the top and bottom end rails, again without glue (fig 2, page 90). Complete the dry assembly of the end frames by adding the corner posts (fig 3, page 90).

FRONT AND BACK FRAMES

To make up the front and back frames, which look like ladders, mark the positions of the short vertical pieces along one long rail, and mark dowel hole centres regularly and centrally along the rail (fig 1). There is an internal spacing of 110mm (4½in) between each short vertical piece, and also between the end-most vertical pieces and each of the corner posts.

Use this rail as a pattern to transfer the marks on to three of the other long rails. Drill all the dowel holes to the required depth and dry assemble the ladder frame sections.

Drill the dowel holes on the inside of the corner posts, using the marks transferred from the front and back ladder frame construction.

Mark the dowel hole positions centrally on the ends of the bottom long rails, then drill the holes in them and in the bottoms of the corner posts as before.

Dowel and dry assemble each ladder frame section, together with the long bottom rails, into the corner posts of the end frames (fig 2).

Make sure that the assembly is square and fits together perfectly, dismantle in reverse order, then reassemble, this time gluing the joints using waterproof wood adhesive.

SHELVES

The two shelves are cut so that they finish half-way across the thickness of the frame, rather than fitting flush with the outside edges of the frame rails. Notch out the corners and the central part at the ends to fit round the middle and corner posts.

Cut out the bottom shelf to fit on to the bottom rails, and glue and pin it down to the frame (fig 3).

The top shelf is glued and pinned to the underside of the middle rails.

FEET

The feet are fixed underneath each corner and protrude at the sides and ends by the same amount as the 'step' for the bottom shelf (that is, approximately 19mm [¾in]) (fig 4). Any offcut of softwood or hardwood can be used to make them.

Apply waterproof woodworking adhesive, then screw up into the rails using two screws for each foot.

Fill any gaps using an exterior-grade cellulose filler. Finally, paint as required or apply a water-repellent wood preservative stain.

1 Adding Vertical Pieces
Vertical pieces are dowelled in place at equal internal spacings between top and middle long rails.

2 Frame Assembly
Mark dowel positions on corner posts and ends of top, middle and bottom long rails. Drill and join.

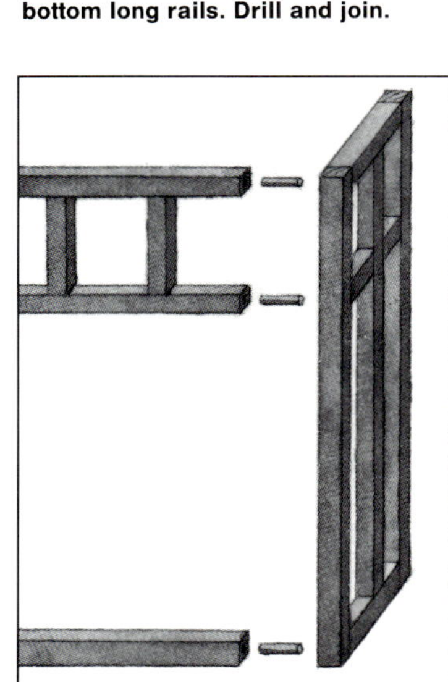

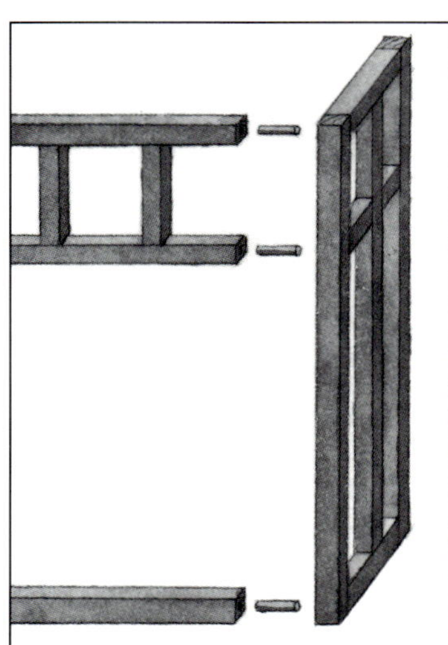

3 Adding Bottom Shelf
Cut shelf to finish half-way across frame rails. Notch ends to fit around posts. Glue and screw in place.

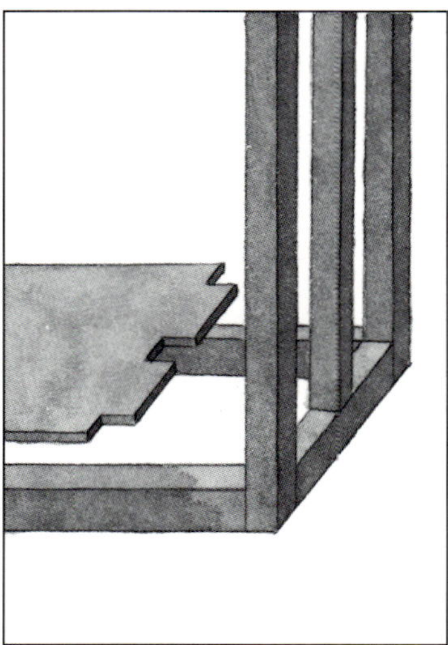

4 Adding the Feet
Cut feet from offcuts of wood. Glue and screw them up into rails so that they protrude by about 19mm (¾in).

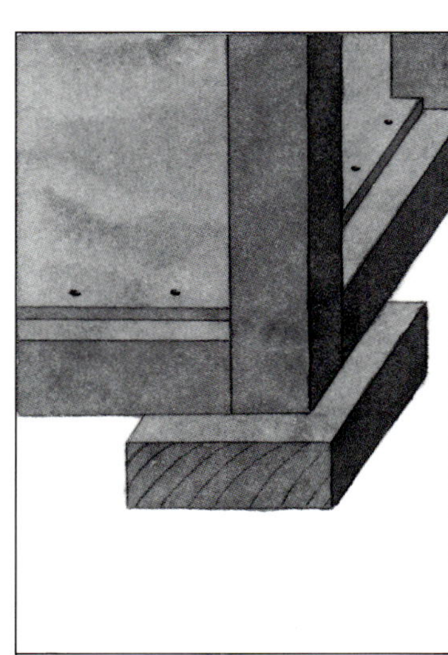

Ponds

An ornamental fish pond will enhance even the smallest garden, providing interest and pleasure with water lilies, reeds and fish mingling with dragonflies, water beetles and small frogs. Ponds are easy to install and require little maintenance.

There are various ways to build a pond, but to ensure success, the whole project needs to be carefully planned in advance, taking into account the way in which the pond will be constructed, its size, shape and location.

First, consider shape and location. The former is purely a matter of taste – a question of whether you want a formal rectangle or would prefer a more natural, curved outline. The main consideration is how you see the whole design blending with your garden, although you should avoid an over-complicated design as this will make the pond more difficult and more expensive to build. The location of the pond is critical, however. Ideally, it should receive sunlight for at least half the day to enable flowering pond plants to thrive. You should try to keep it away from overhanging trees since the shade will not be good for plants and mosquitoes will be encouraged. Deciduous trees pose a particular problem in autumn, when leaves falling into the water can have a harmful effect on pond life if they are left to rot.

A pond at the end of a long garden may sound appealing, but remember that if you want to include a waterfall, underwater lights or a fountain, you face the problem of running an electricity supply a considerable distance. Also, you may not be able to enjoy the sight of the pond from indoors.

The basic factors governing the size are the proportions of the garden and how much time and money you want to spend on the pond. You must ensure that the pond is not 'lost' in the garden, nor must it completely dominate it. Do not make a pond too small since a 'puddle' will not provide the right conditions for water, plants and fish to harmonize. The minimum surface area is really about 3.5 square metres (38 square feet). A smaller pond will not allow the water to be aerated and so it may become cloudy, in which case you would need to install a filtration system.

Water depth should not create major problems. The main hazard is with water that is too shallow, causing the pond to overheat in hot weather (leaving the fish short of oxygen) and to freeze in winter. Anything between 400–750mm (16–30in) will enable an excellent selection of plants to flourish. You should include a 225mm- (9in-) wide planting shelf, about 225mm (9in) below the water surface. The shelf should run around most, if not all, of the perimeter of the pond.

Pond Types

Although a pond can be built using concrete to form the walls and base, few people would attempt this method nowadays since construction can be both tedious and difficult, and the pond may be prone to leaking and cracking. The two most common methods today involve using a pre-formed pond or a liner.

With a pre-formed pond, the size and shape of the pond is governed by the models available, whereas a liner allows you to create whatever shape you want. If you decide on a special shape or a very large pond, then you will have to use a liner, but otherwise both types have advantages and disadvantages when it comes to installation.

The choice of material to line a pond is between butyl rubber and PVC. Although any type of liner can be pierced by sharp objects such as stones or digging implements being thrust into the water, this is less likely to happen with the thicker, better-quality types. Even an economy-grade liner can be expected to enjoy a lifespan of ten years if it is properly installed and respected.

A Pond for a Patio
Not all gardens will have space for a full-sized pond. A half-barrel provides a simple solution that is easy to maintain and will have space for two or three small goldfish and for colourful water lilies.

Colours readily available are black, stone, blue or grey. Although stone, blue and grey are more natural, many people prefer black since it is much less obtrusive in use. However, colour is not vitally important since, after a while, the base of the pond will be covered with a thin layer of mud and its sides will be creamed with algae.

A liner can be used in an above ground pond where the walls are constructed from brick or ornamental stonework. It can also be set into the ground in a level excavation made to the required depth and shape. In this case, sharp objects must be removed from the excavation and a 25mm (1in) layer of sand spread across the bottom. The liner is then placed in the excavation, the edges weighted with bricks, and water then added. The pressure of the water stretches the liner to the shape of the excavation.

Finally, paving slabs are used to make a border around the pond and to conceal the edge of the liner.

Pre-formed ponds are made from plastic or (more expensively) glass-fibre and can also be used above or below ground. In both cases, it is vital to support the sides and to ensure that the rim is exactly level.

The lesser-quality plastic ponds are neither as big nor as strong, but should certainly last for at least ten years and enable you to enjoy a wildlife pond in that time. However, if you really want a stock of outstanding fish and plants then you will need one of the better-quality models, which will last for years if it is properly installed and not damaged by sharp objects.

Whether you plan the pond to be below or above ground, it is vital that the excavation of the framework of bricks or ornamental stonework is lined with sand to provide adequate support for every nook and cranny of the pond's outline as the water exerts pressure on it.

PLANTS

Choose a mixture of types for the best effect; most are grown in plastic containers resting on the base of the pond or on the shelf.

Water lilies are a must, really, while shallow water marginals can be either tall and spikey or ground-carpeting. Deep water aquatics have their roots in containers but their leaves float on the surface, giving interest and shade to the water. Floating plants do not need soil for their roots and some only rise to the surface when flowering. Oxygenating plants, as the name suggests, supply oxygen to the pond and discourage algae. Use four or five for every square metre (yard) of water surface.

Almost inevitably, weed will build up in the pond. Pull up weeds regularly: if the size and location of the pond allow, simply reach in to the water and weed by hand; otherwise, use a rake or a long stick for any parts of the pond that are inaccessible. On no account, however, should you use a chemical algicide. Not only will it kill off the weed, leaving it to decompose in the pond, it may also contaminate your plant and fish stock.

There are many kinds of fish you can use to stock the pond apart from the ubiquitous goldfish, so read a bit about the subject and visit a good local specialist shop or a garden centre with a pond department to see what is available.

BARREL POND

Any water-tight container can be used for a small water garden and a half-barrel is one of the most popular choices. Half-barrels that previously contained beer, wine or vinegar are normally available from large garden centres.

It is important to scrub clean the inside of the barrel first using only clean water, never detergent. A clean barrel is important because otherwise the water will quickly become contaminated, posing a threat to your plants and fish. For this reason do not use a barrel that previously contained either wood preservative or oil.

When you are satisfied that the barrel is thoroughly clean, spread 75–100mm (3–4in) of clean soil in the base of the barrel – keep out weeds or vegetation which will rot and pollute the water. Add enough water to enable you to mix the soil into a slurry of mud.

Planting should be carried out in spring or early summer. Use miniature water lilies and some other small, less vigorous plants. Include oxygenating plants to help keep the water clear.

Next, spread a 50mm (2in) layer of pea shingle over the soil to prevent the fish stirring it up and to help prevent the plants from becoming uprooted. Then fill the barrel with water through a hosepipe with its outlet inside a polythene bag (fig 2); this prevents the jet of water disturbing the soil.

When the barrel is almost full, turn off the water and remove the bag and pipe. Allow about a week for the water to settle and the temperature to stabilize before introducing the fish – two or three small goldfish – and a few snails. The fish will discourage mosquitoes in summer, but do transfer them to a larger pond or to a fishtank indoors for the winter as the small amount of water in a barrel is almost certain to freeze over in a cold winter. In early spring, before returning the fish to the barrel, replace most or all of the water and allow it to settle and the temperature to stabilize as before.

1 Through-section of Pond with Liner

A hole of the required dimensions is dug and lined with sand before the liner is laid in place. Include a planting shelf around the perimeter. The liner is held in place at the edges by bricks, stones or paving slabs.

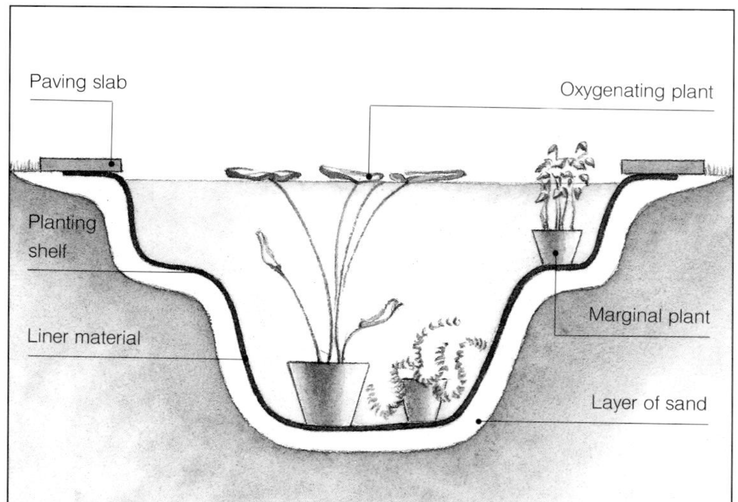

2 Making a Pond from a Half-barrel

Scrub the barrel clean and place a layer of soil at the bottom for planting. A layer of pea shingle prevents soil mixing with water. Fill pond with water through a hosepipe with its nozzle in a polythene bag.

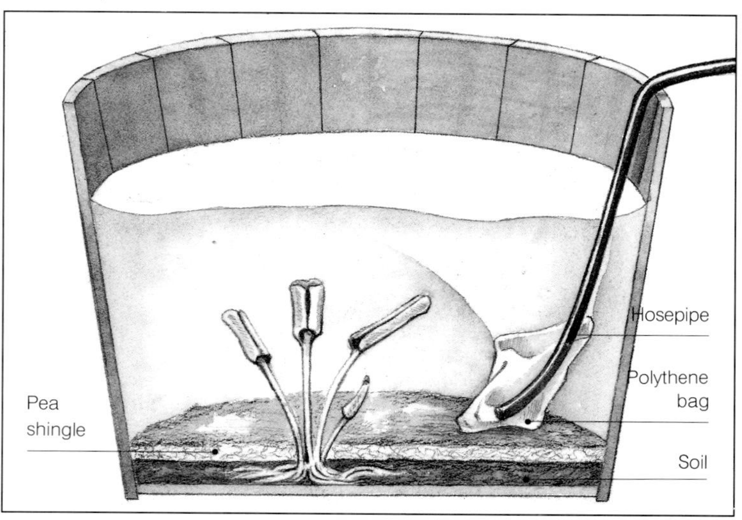

PART 4

SUPPORTS AND DIVIDERS

The opposition of closed and open space is fundamental in garden design. All gardens have boundaries, more or less secure perimeters defined by walls, fences or hedges. But often there is a need to break up space within the garden, dividing one part from another, screening the view of a utility area or vegetable garden, or making a garden 'room', an enclosed area which can create a heightened sense of 'hazard and surprise'. Simple boundaries can be made from living dividers such as hedges, through semi-transparent picket, wattle and beanstick fencing to proper garden walls of brick or stone.

Moving from a rose-covered pergola to an expanse of lawn is far more pleasing than walking along an exposed path. Framing a view with a simple arch, dissolving a boundary wall with climbers trained over a trellis, creating an arbor in a corner of the garden are all design devices which add depth and perspective to what might otherwise be flat and monotonous. By growing plants up pergolas, arbors and other dividers you have the opportunity to add light and shade: the dappled sunlight created by foliage is one of the most appealing sights in the garden.

Supports and Dividers

Trellis is indispensable. Off-the-peg square or diamond wooden mesh is available very cheaply, ready treated, in panels which can be assembled to create a variety of structures or to cover a large surface area. As an extension to a boundary fence, trellis covered with climbing plants filters the wind so that it cannot cut across the garden, and gives a degree of privacy without entirely blocking airflow and light. It is also one of the most economical ways of getting rid of eyesores – ugly sheds, bare blank walls in sour stock brick, concrete blocks, anything which cannot easily be removed can be covered with trellis and plants encouraged to grow. Climbers such as Russian vine (*Fallopia aubertii*) or mile-a-minute (*Polygonum baldschuanicum*), clematis, climbing roses, honeysuckle (*Lonicera* sp) and Virginia creeper (*Parthenocissus quinquefolia*) can materially alter the appearance of any structure. Wisteria will need a greater degree of support and ivy should be avoided at all costs: its aerial roots dig into mortar and damage brickwork. You can also use trellis to make free-standing structures to block unwelcome views.

Trellis can be put to more positive use, to create a whole range of effects. *Treillages*, intricate flat wooden frameworks, were a feature of French formal gardens, traditionally painted green and used against ecru walls. These were often arched, with tapering lines that gave a subtle sense of perspective – a simple *trompe-l'oeil* that enlivened Parisian courtyards. Less elaborate trellis still has this ability to 'dissolve' a flat, dull expanse of wall. Depending on how positive you want the trellis to be, you can stain or paint it to add interest in the winter when the leaves have fallen. Trellis helps to blend and merge the garden with the house, taking greenery up onto walls, the sides of buildings and fences.

A pergola is another type of support for plants, but one which involves some kind of canopy, either as a free-standing arch, a covered walkway or a simple framework projecting out from the side of the house. It is commonplace in Mediterranean countries to attach a plain metal framework and wiring to the house over a rear courtyard or front entrance and allow a vine to create a type of living awning. The leaves of the vine keep the sun off and deflect the heat in the summer; in the winter, the frame and the house are revealed: a cheap, effective solution and one which generates interest by changing from month to month. Plain or painted trellis can also be used overhead; the grid takes the strength out of the sun and makes a lively pattern of light and shade.

In design terms, a pergola acts as a kind of picture frame, intensifying a view. It usually demands some type of focal point – a seat or urn at the end of a walkway, for example. But it also produces a contrast of light and shade which is so attractive in a garden, and it makes an ideal support for plants, since they are freely exposed to sunlight, air and rain.

While there is something especially English about a rose-covered pergola, it is the French who excel at garden ironmongery, including that wonderful green iron which goes to make curved frameworks, such as the one which forms the laburnum avenue in Monet's garden at Giverny. There are different ways of making a pergola, but, generally, if you want the top to curve it must be made of metal, although it is possible to wire beansticks to achieve a curve. A simple version is to attach small sections of curved metal to wooden uprights. Wires for training plants can be passed through holes in the metal frame or trellis attached to the posts to support climbing roses, honeysuckle, and espaliered and cordoned fruit trees.

Walk-through pergola 104
Fences 147
Fixing trellis 152

TRELLISWORK

Trellis is much more than just a support for plants. Trompe-l'oeil *designs add wit and interest to plain expanses of wall (opposite above and opposite centre). Trellis can also be attached to free-standing copper pipes or posts and used to support climbing roses and other plants (opposite below). For a town garden, with little horizontal growing space, trellis provides a vertical extension, acting as a support for container plants (left).*

ALL FENCED IN

Most people need some sort of way to mark boundaries, either with a neighbouring house or between different areas of the garden (overleaf). The style of fencing you choose should reflect and enhance the overall design of your garden: use white painted fencing to contrast with bright flowers, natural rustic poles for a rambling country feel, or strongly geometric panels for a look of urban chic.

Supports and Dividers

Another type of garden enclosure or room is the arbor. Essentially a seat shaded by a canopy of plants, the arbor always adds a certain mysterious, romantic quality to a garden. As well as its visual impact, there is often the added dimension of the perfume of scented flowers growing overhead. The framework itself can be as simple as you like. Trellis is a good component, but special metal arbor frameworks are also available.

There is great diversity in the materials and methods used to create boundaries in a garden. While there is no need to look for an exact match to the design of your house, some styles of fence and wall will be more appropriate than others. Metal railings, of the kind seen in public parks, are generally better in town situations; lapboarding and paddock-style timber fencing are really for the country. Avoid, if you can, building walls in cheap stock bricks which never weather; breeze blocks and concrete posts and wire mesh fencing can also be unappetizing. An existing wall which presents this kind of eyesore can be ameliorated either by covering it with trellis or, in the case of a concrete structure, encouraging the growth of lichens and moss.

Semi-transparent boundaries can be made cheaply with trellis, using standard panels secured to posts. Today you can buy spiked steel socket-type supports which make the job of sinking posts much easier. Inspiration for other types of wooden or panel fencing can be taken from the Japanese, who excel at Mondrian-type arrangements of panels and screens using bamboo uprights and woven rush, roughly equivalent to European traditional wattle fencing.

Wall building is an art in itself. There are many intriguing and inspiring examples: stone inset with flints, shells, pebbles or bottle ends; dry stone walling; brick walls built with spaces to let air and views through; walls made of logs and driftwood. It is a good idea, if you are building a wall from scratch, to leave pockets so that plants can be grown on the vertical face. Alyssum, thrift, aubrieta, campanula and other rock plants will grow in cornices, wall pockets and on tops of dry stone walling.

Hedges are the living boundaries in a garden, easy on the eye, good at creating windbreaks and relatively simple to maintain. As far as types are concerned, there are many alternatives to the ubiquitous privet. Box (although slow-growing), beech, yew, hawthorn and hazel all make excellent and attractive hedges.

Hexagonal Arbor 116
Fences 147

ARBORS

Structures which provide a support for climbing and trailing plants also make ideal locations for garden seats, creating a shady, scented retreat from which to view the garden. Aesthetically, an arbor also provides contrast of light and shade which is so important in giving depth and definition to a layout.

Walk-through Pergola

In a small garden, a pergola, or framework for climbing plants, makes an architectural addition which gives focus to the entire layout, especially when centrally positioned. In a larger garden, a pergola can be extended further to create a proper walkway, a semi-enclosed space to contrast with the open areas of lawn and flowerbed. This particular design can be adapted to vary the length as required, but would not really be effective if made any shorter than three units long.

The structure and the dimensions of the pergola are based around standard trellis panels, which are much cheaper than any you could make for the purpose.

The easiest way to assemble the structure is to construct the top frame first, adding the struts to make the pyramid roof afterwards. Then the position of the posts, or uprights, can be marked out on the ground where you want the pergola to go and metal shoes or spiked steel supports driven in.

The final stage is to cover the outside of the structure with trellis. When viewed from the side, the trellis wall appears to be continuous, but, because the trellis is fixed only to alternate bays, you will get glimpses of the garden as you walk through. As a plain, undressed structure with no covering of plants the pergola has its own attractions, especially when painted a strong positive colour. To support climbing plants over the roof, simply staple wire around the pyramids.

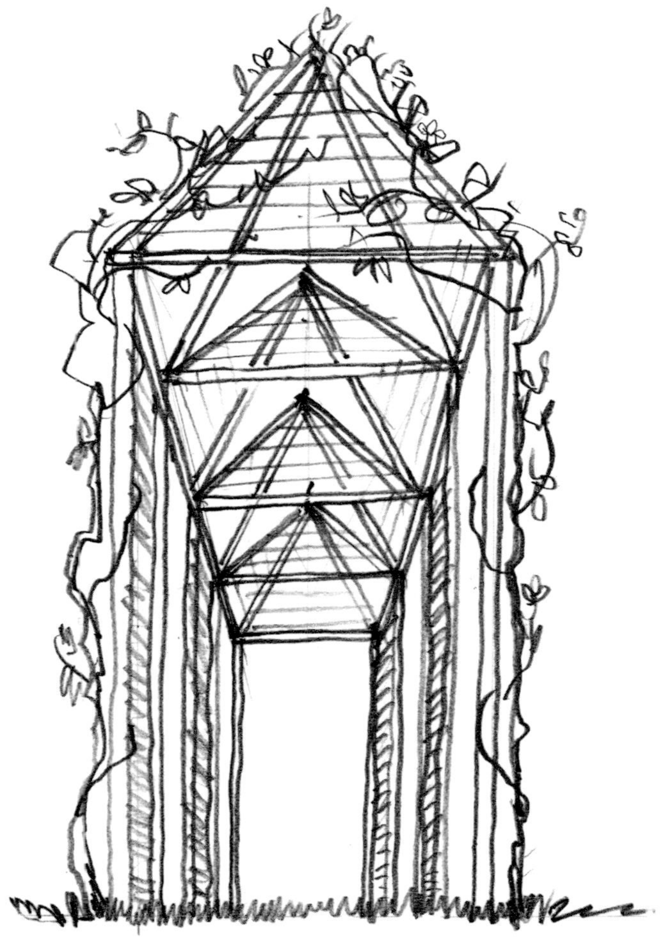

Walk-through Pergola

The light and airy framework of this pergola can be built over a garden path to form a covered walkway of colourful and sweetly-scented climbing plants trained over the easy-to-make, but distinctive, trellis and wire-covered framework. Good plants to use include clematis, especially the small-flowered species such as *C montana* and *C armandii*, climbing hydrangea (*H petiolaris*), sweet-scented plants such as jasmine and honeysuckle, and wisteria. The many varieties of ivy are quickly established, although they can be difficult to contain; instead, you could try ornamental grape vines, the leaves of which turn to spectacular colours in autumn.

The 'roof' is a series of simple pyramids on a timber framework which is fixed on top of fence posts held upright by hammer-in steel fence post supports. Training wires for climbing plants are stapled around the pyramids, and trellis panels are fixed at the sides between the post supports.

Trellis panels usually come in 1830mm (72in) widths, and in heights of 600mm (24in), 900mm (36in) and 1220mm (48in). For this project, the panels are turned to give a height of 1830mm (72in) and a width of 1220mm (48in).

The size of the trellis panels also determines the dimensions of the pergola – ours is 1220mm (48in) wide, and the posts are spaced 1220mm (43in) apart. It is best to keep these measurements the same so that the 'base' to each pyramid is a square, ensuring that the struts are in proportion to the main frame. The height of the posts is 2m (6ft 6in) which means that the trellising is raised off the ground by 170mm (6in). We have only fixed trellising to alternate bays, but this is simply for effect. Our pergola is four bays long, but this is variable and you can have more or fewer bays, according to your requirements.

All timber used is sawn and preservative-treated softwood, as used for fencing.

Pyramid Roof Structure

The series of pyramids that form the 'roof' of the pergola add visual interest and extra height to the design. Training wires are stapled around the struts, enabling plants to grow and thrive and to form a 'living ceiling'.

Materials

Note: All timber is sawn and preservative-treated softwood

Part	Quantity	Material	Length
LONG RAILS	2	75 x 50mm (3 x 2in)	5.25m (17ft 3in)
CROSS RAILS	5	As above	1200mm (48in)
PYRAMID STRUTS	16	75 x 25mm (3 x 1in)	1350mm (53in)*
POSTS	10	75 x 75mm (3 x 3in)	2m (6ft 6in)
TRELLIS PANELS	8		1830mm (72in) high × 1200mm (48in)
HAMMER-IN POST SUPPORTS	10		
TRAINING WIRE	1 large coil		
SCREWS		Zinc-plated steel	50mm (2in) No 8
STAPLES		Galvanized fencing type	19mm (¾in)

* Approximate length only – measure and cut on site for accuracy

Tools

- WORKBENCH (fixed or portable)
- STEEL MEASURING TAPE
- STEEL RULE
- TRY SQUARE
- COMBINATION SQUARE – for marking 45° angles
- PANEL SAW (or circular power saw)
- TENON SAW
- MARKING GAUGE
- POWER DRILL
- DRILL BIT – approximately 3mm (⅛in) diameter to drill pilot holes for screws
- SLEDGE HAMMER
- CARPENTER'S HAMMER
- CHISEL – about 25mm (1in)
- MALLET

Walk-through Pergola Assembly

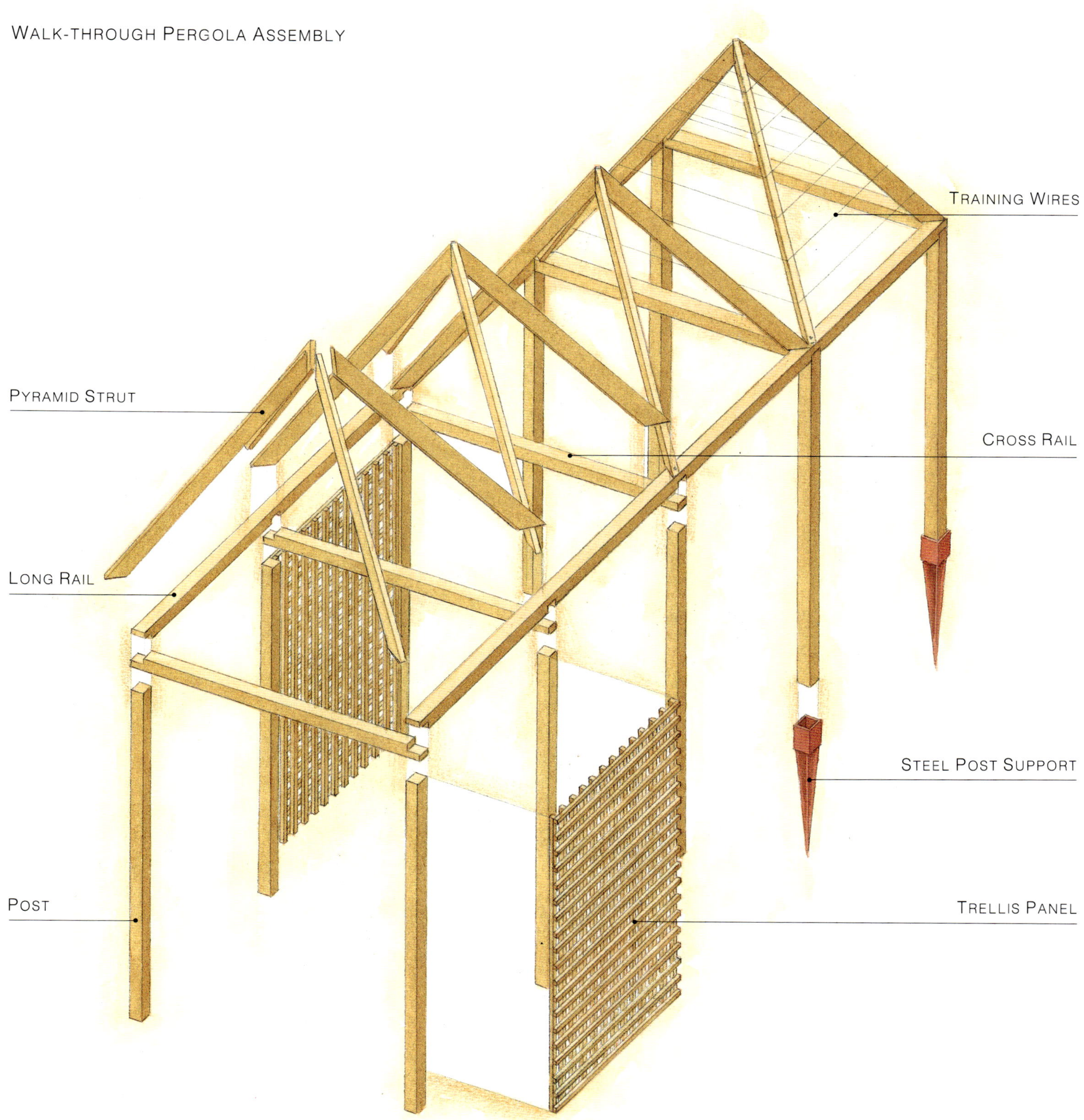

Walk-Through Pergola

Top Frame

Start by making the top frame on which the 'roof' of pyramids is fixed and which will eventually be supported on the vertical posts. The top long rails are made from 75 × 50mm (3 × 2in) sawn and preservative-treated timber, ideally in one full length (that is, if you are making the pergola to the proportions shown in the photograph, the length of four trellis panels plus the five posts of 75mm [3in] width). If it is impossible to buy timber the length required, two shorter lengths can be joined end to end with a simple lap joint or halving joint *(see* **Techniques, Wood Joints, page 152***)*.

Cut the cross rails to the width required, in our case 1370mm (54in) (the spacing between two posts plus the thickness of the posts).

Mark out the positions of the posts on the long rails to suit the width of the trellis panels, in our case at *internal* intervals of 1220mm (48in). Cut halving joints at the appropriate places on the long rails and at the ends of the cross rails, so that they form corner halving joints on the cross rails at either end (fig 1) and T-halving joints on the intermediate rails *(see* **Techniques, page 152***)*. Form the joints so that the long rails are on top.

Screw the joints together through the cross rails from the underside.

'Pyramid' Roof Sections

To work out the exact length of the pyramid struts, measure the diagonal of the base across the frame. Mark this length on a flat floor and strike equal length lines at 45° to this line at either end to give the point of the apex of the pyramid. This gives the lengths of the timber required for the structure forming the pyramid – the measurement should more or less correspond to the length of the cross rails.

Cut the required number of struts slightly overlength and then mitre them all at 45° at both ends in opposite directions and to the correct length required.

To assemble, hold two of the struts in a vice so the mitred faces of one end meet. Screw through from each side using 50mm (2in) No 8 zinc-plated woodscrews (fig 2).

Hold this frame upright in a workbench and lay a third strut against the joint and pilot drill through at approximately 45° into the other frame (fig 3). Repeat for the fourth pyramid strut (fig 4).

Make up the required number of pyramid structures. These are delicate, so handle them carefully.

Place each pyramid on top of the frame already made and fix down into it with a single screw at each corner (fig 5). Once fixed, this is a very strong structure. Repeat for all of the pyramids.

Staple training wires at 150mm (6in) intervals up the pyramids.

Fixing the Posts and Final Assembly

Carry the top structure to its final position and use it to mark on the ground the positions of the fence posts. The posts are spaced at internal intervals of 1220mm (48in) so that they coincide with the cross rail positions.

The easiest way to fix the posts is with steel post supports. These supports are simply hammered into the ground and the posts slot into sockets at the tops of the supports.

Stretch a string line along the line of the posts. This string line will help you to line up the supports and will also give some idea of levels. Push the tip of the support into the ground and use a spirit level to check that it is upright. To drive the support into the ground, a heavy hammer, such as a sledge hammer, will be required. Insert a short length of 75 × 75mm (3 × 3in) timber post into the socket to protect the support from hammer blows, or use a proprietary metal-capped driving tool which should have a tommy-bar handle allowing you to steady the socket and prevent it from twisting as it is hammered in place.

Drive the support into the ground with firm, slow blows of the hammer. At regular intervals, insert a post into the socket and use a spirit level on

❶ Joining Top Frame Rails
Frame rails form corner halving joints at ends and T-halving joints (not shown) at intermediate points.

❷ Joining First Two Struts
Mitre ends of struts at 45° and butt cut faces together. *Inset* Fix with screws at oblique angles.

❸ Adding Remaining Struts
Hold frame in a workbench. Screw through from sides of third strut to face of joint; repeat for fourth strut.

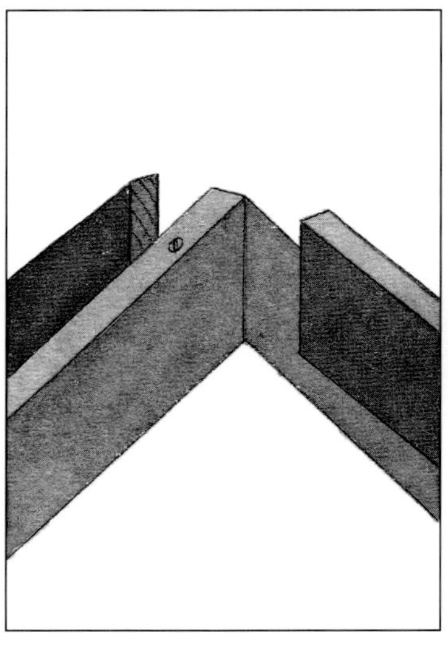

❹ Apex of Finished Pyramid
Finished joints neatly form pyramid apex. *Inset* Angled screws fix third and fourth struts to first two struts.

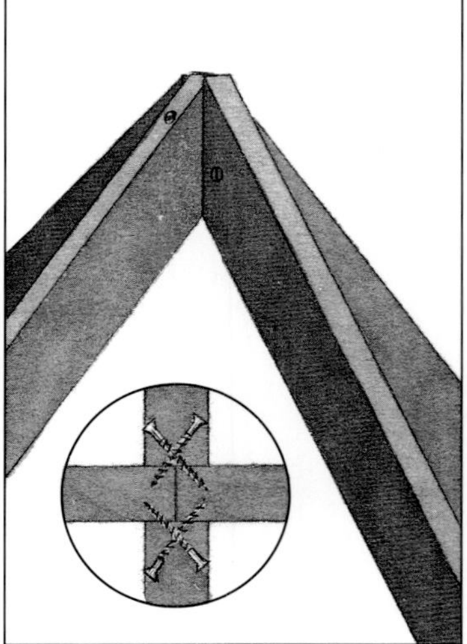

Sawing 148
Drilling 150
Screwing 150
Skew nailing 151
Fixing posts 152
Fixing trellis 152
Halving joint 152
Mitre joint 154

two adjacent faces to check that the spike is going in vertically. Adjustments can be made by pulling or twisting the sockets as necessary.

When the supports have been inserted the posts can be fitted. In some designs of post supports, two bolts have to be tightened to cramp the posts in position, while in others the posts are held with large screws. Double-check that the posts are upright and use a length of straight timber and a spirit level to check that the tops of the posts are level. On flat or slightly sloping ground this will be easy to achieve, but on steeply sloping ground it may be acceptable if the tops of the posts follow the slope of the ground. Use a length of string or a long batten to level the post tops which can be trimmed to an even height, if necessary, using a hand saw.

The next stage is to fix the trellising between the posts (we only fixed it to alternate bays of the pergola). Place bricks or blocks on the ground to support the trellis panels about 150mm (6in) from the ground. We used metal clips to hold the panels of trellis in place and the clips are first nailed to the posts so that they are vertical and inset by the same amount – about 25mm (1in). The panels are then lifted into place and a check is made that the horizontal rails of the trellis panels are level. The panels are then fixed to the clips using zinc-plated screws (*see* **Techniques, page 152**).

If required, the trellis panels can be fixed directly to the posts. Position and level them as above, then drill through the side frames of the panels so that 75mm (3in) long galvanized fencing nails can be driven through the panels, without splitting them, and into the posts. Three fixings will be required on each side of a 1830mm (72in) high trellis panel.

You will need some help to lift the pyramid roof onto the posts. Adjust the roof so that the vertical posts coincide with the corner and cross rail joints, then nail the frame to the tops of the posts using two 100mm (4in) nails skew nailed through the top frame and into each post (*see* **Techniques, page 151**).

5 Fixing Pyramids to Frame
Screw the pyramids to the top frame using a screw through each corner and into the frame rails.

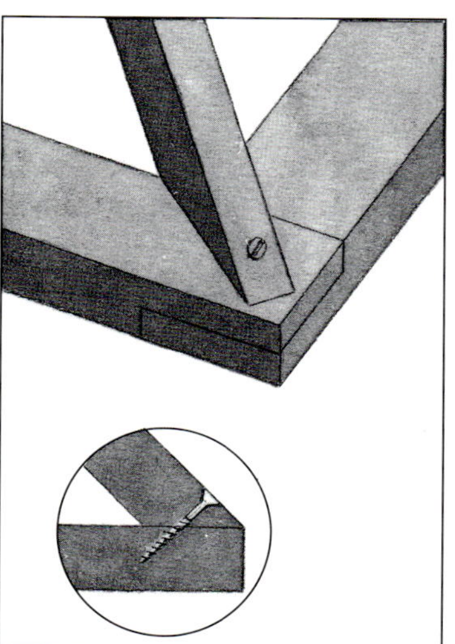

Trellis with False Perspective

Trellising has varied garden applications. This project goes a stage further and follows the French tradition of using trellis to give blank walls a sense of depth and perspective. The result, although simple to construct, is a memorable and effective exercise in *trompe-l'oeil*. You can adapt this idea to cheer up any featureless expanse of wall or disguise unsympathetic stock brick or breeze block.

Perhaps the easiest project in the book to accomplish, this false-perspective trellis could be assembled without too much trouble during the course of a single afternoon once you have established your required dimensions and perspective.

The first step is to draw up a full-size plan: you can adapt the design shown here to fit your space. A false perspective is generally more effective if you arrange it so there is a contrast with a real view. Incorporating a doorway, as here, or any other kind of opening heightens the element of 'hazard and surprise'.

The next stage is to pin together slats of timber to make the required design. Bend the nails over and hammer them flat as they go through the back so they will not pull out. If you want a curved arch, you could make the curve out of exterior-grade plywood cut with a jigsaw.

This trellis design was painted a pale grey to tone with the lichened wall. Trellis looks very effective painted, but the colours should not be too harsh and bright or the illusory effect will be lost.

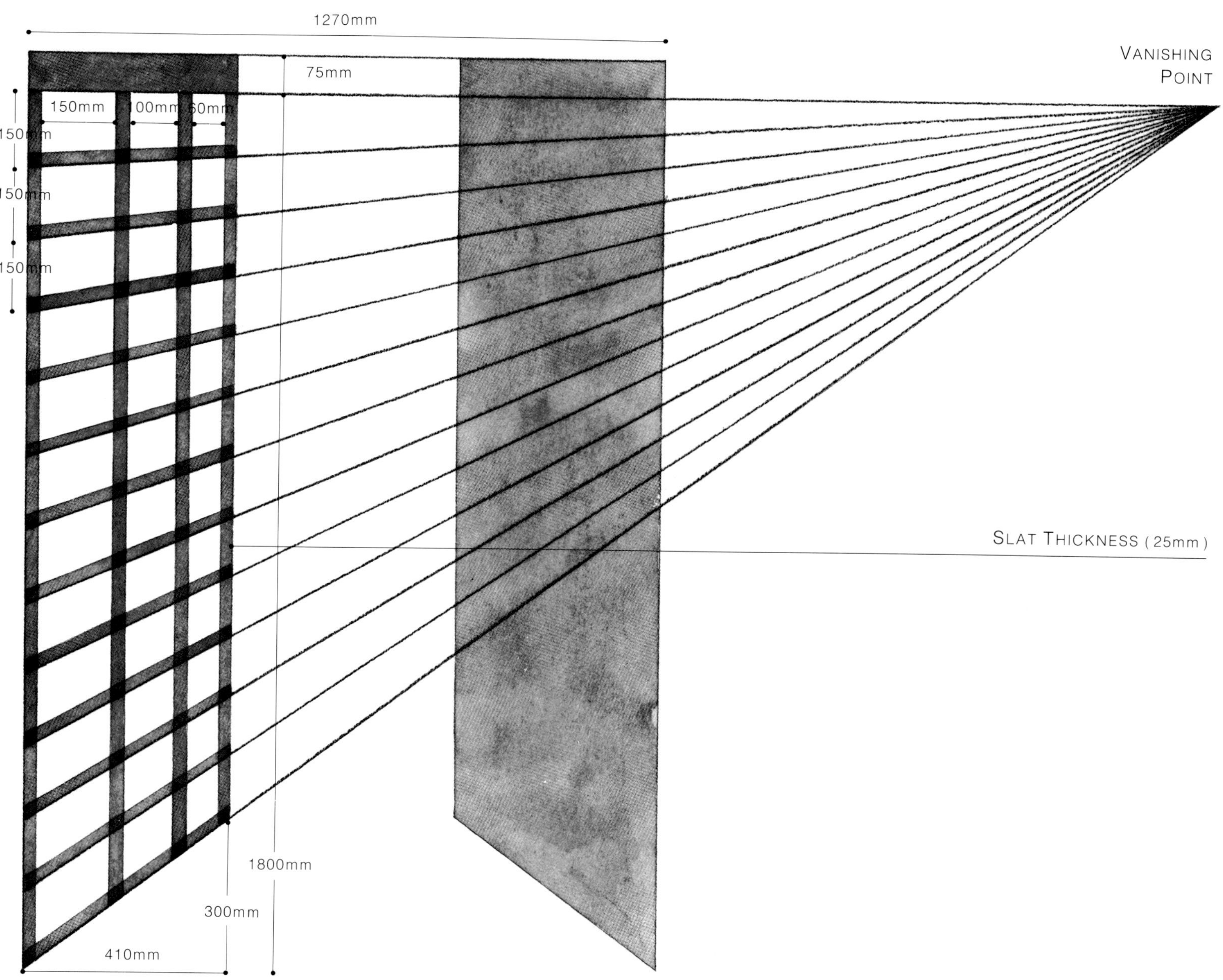

DRAWING UP A PLAN OF THE TRELLIS STRUCTURE

You will need to draw up a full-size plan to calculate the length of the slats and the degree of perspective. The overall height and width shown here are based on the dimensions of the door alongside which we built this project, and can be altered according to the space available.

Trellis with False Perspective

This trellis is constructed so that when it is fixed against a wall, it deceives the eye into believing it is looking at a three-dimensional arch, or a series of three-dimensional arches if several are fixed side by side as shown here.

If you fit the trellis around a door or gateway, sizes are dependent on the dimensions of the door. We used three archways alongside a garden door, which has a matching trellis 'roof' above it. Our arches are separated by 75 x 25mm (3 x 1in) timber 'posts' chamferred at the top. However, the principles of construction are easy to adapt to other sizes and designs according to the size of your garden, the amount of wall space, and personal preference.

A wider batten has also been incorporated at the top to align with the top of the door frame, replacing one of the 'normal size' trellis slats, but again this is optional.

The density of the trellis and the amount of perspective incorporated is entirely down to individual taste, but the dimensions here are a good standard to work from.

Obviously, you will need a wall on which to fix the trellis. This need not be a garden boundary wall: it could be a plain wall of the house, or the wall of a garage or outbuilding.

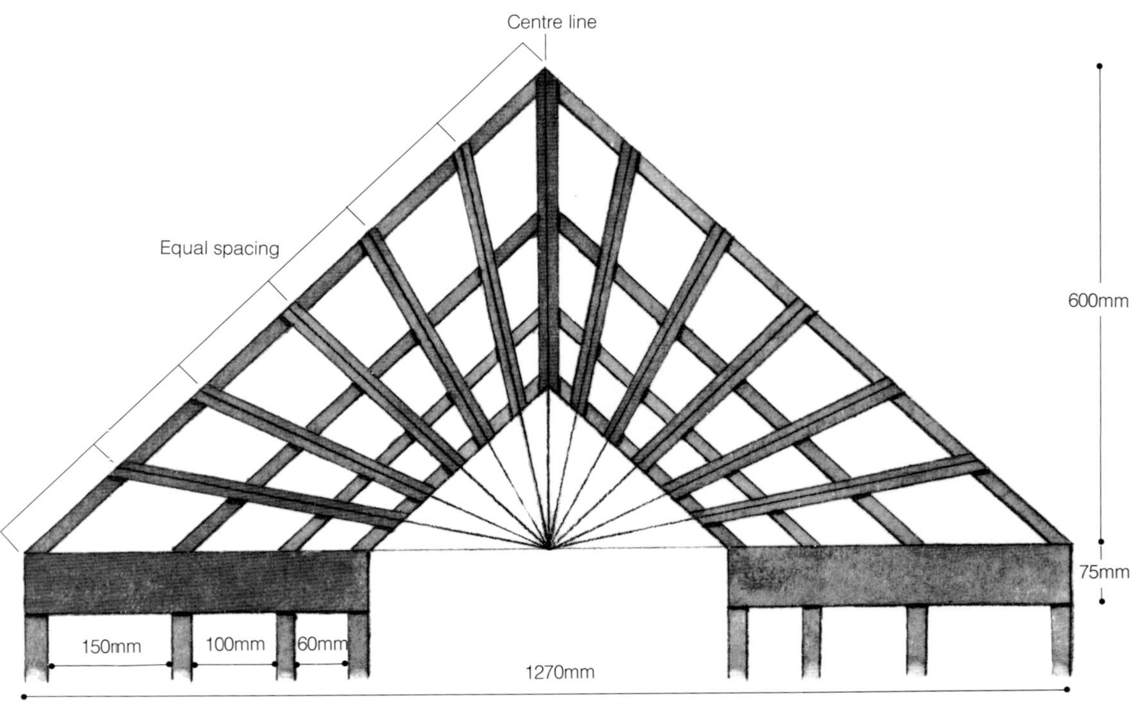

1 Drawing Up a Plan of the Roof Structure

Draw a line to trellis width. Draw a line perpendicular to centre point – top of this line represents apex. Draw in slat thickness, then two sides of triangle. Mark where vertical slats of side panels fall along base and extend lines to centre line, parallel with triangle sides. Mark five equally spaced points on each side and join to centre of base.

Tools

- WORKBENCH (fixed or portable)
- STEEL MEASURING TAPE
- TRY SQUARE
- TENON SAW (or power jigsaw)
- HAMMER
- POWER DRILL
- DRILL BIT – 3mm (⅛in)
- MASONRY DRILL BIT – 6mm (¼in)
- SCREWDRIVER
- SPIRIT LEVEL

Materials

Note: If you experience difficulty buying 25 x 12mm (1 x ½in), you can cut your own slats by ripping down 200 x 25mm (8 x 1in) timber using a circular saw; this will give 16 slats per board if saw blade is not too thick

Part	Quantity	Material	Length
VERTICAL SLATS	8 per trellis arch	25 x 12mm (1 x ½in) sawn softwood	1800mm (72in)*
CROSS SLATS	As required	As above	As required
ROOF SLATS	As required	As above	As required
TOP BATTEN (optional)	1 per arch	75 x 12mm (3 x ½in) sawn softwood	1270mm (50in)**
POST	1 between each arch	75 x 25mm (3 x 1in) sawn softwood	As required

* Finished size – cut overlength and then cut to size after fixing (see text for details)

** Length given is width of each trellis arch; top battens can be cut from two shorter lengths of softwood because centre section is cut away on assembly

Adhesives	**146**
Drilling	**150**
Nailing	**150**
Screwing	**150**

CONSTRUCTION

The easiest way to make this trellis is first to draw up full-size plans on a large, reasonably flat surface such as a garage floor, tables pushed together, or a flat area of concrete, such as a driveway.

You may be able to draw the plan directly on to your flat surface, but it is more likely that you will have to make the drawing on several sheets of paper which can then be taped together to produce a full-size plan. Wherever you construct the trellis, it will be necessary to have enough space for all the pieces to be laid out on this plan and nailed up in place on top of the drawing.

DRAWING UP PLANS

Using our diagrams as a guide, draw up plans for one side of the upright trellis. You need to decide on the height and spaces required. Ours is 1800mm (72in) high, with 12 equal spaces down the outer side, giving 150mm (6in) centres (actually from the base of one slat to the base of the next).

Mark off the width of this one side of trellis; ours is 410mm (16½in) from the outside edge of the outermost vertical slat to the inside edge of the innermost vertical slat. Two more vertical slats are placed between them to give *internal* spacings of 150mm (6in), 100mm (4in), and 60mm (2½in) respectively.

The innermost vertical slat is only 1500mm (60in) long and is placed 300mm (12in) up from the ground. Join the bottom two points and continue this angled line up until it meets a horizontal line drawn across at the very top. This gives you a vanishing point where the two lines cross. All the other cross lines must converge at this point.

Use a slat to mark off the thickness of all the slats across the width and down the length of the trellis.

Draw up the 'roof' section next, starting with the base line of the triangle. Find the centre and draw a vertical line (at exactly 90°) up, 600mm (24in) long, to give the apex of the triangle. Draw in the slat thickness over this centre line. Then draw in the outer lines of the triangle.

If you have made this drawing separate from the main trellis, mark off where the vertical slats of the main trellis will fall along the base line. Draw lines from these positions on to the roof section, parallel with the outer lines of the triangle, joining them all at the centre line.

Equally space five points along each of the upward-sloping sides of the triangle (giving six equal spaces on each side) and join these points to the centre of the base line. Start with the central one, and then space two slats on either side.

Draw in the other slat thicknesses as before, finishing the cross slats at the innermost roof slat (fig 1).

Use the drawings to measure off for the lengths of slats that will be required (remembering to multiply the number of slats in the vertical structure by two), and then multiply the total by the number of arches required. Add on a little extra to each length to allow for trimming the angles at the ends.

When the slats have been obtained, cut them all to length, again allowing a small surplus to allow for trimming at the ends.

MAKING UP ONE SIDE

Start by laying all the cross slats accurately on the drawing, and then place the vertical slats on top.

Apply a dab of waterproof wood glue at every intersection of the slats, then fix by driving a ring-shanked nail through each intersection. If you are nailing up on a workbench, a good way to hold the slats firm while nailing is to drive nails temporarily into the bench at all corners, where the slats cross each other. Make up the required number of trellis frames to this pattern.

MAKING UP OPPOSITE SIDE

Turn over the first side of trellis panel, then draw around it onto the work-surface to give a mirror image of the plan. Make up the required number of trellis frames to this pattern in the same way as before.

MAKING UP THE ROOF

The roof is made in the same way as the side panels. Position the cross slats on the plan, and then place the long parallel slats on top. Glue and nail the intersections.

FINISHING OFF

Saw the protruding ends of the slats flush with the edges of the frames.

Prepare the 'posts' and the top battens. In the latter case, the centre section will be cut out on assembly, so you could use two offcuts for these pieces, rather than a batten the full width of the trellis arch.

Ideally, you should use preservative-treated timber. If not, at this stage treat the whole trellis with a water-repellent preservative. The finished trellis is painted with three coats of microporous paint, or one coat of exterior undercoat and two coats of exterior gloss paint.

FIXING THE TRELLIS

If the trellis is going to support climbing plants, spacers must be inserted between it and the wall so that plants can twine behind the trellis. Otherwise, the trellis can be screwed directly to the wall.

Position a post against the wall, and use a spirit level to check it is vertical. Drill clearance holes for two screws through the post and allow the drill tip to mark the wall. Remove the post and, using a masonry bit, drill the holes to the depth required for the wallplugs. Insert the wall-plugs, then drive zinc-plated screws through the post and into the plugs. The screws should penetrate the wall by about 38mm (1½in).

Fix the adjacent side panel and, using an offcut of top batten as a spacer, fit the roof section, then the next post, then the next roof trellis, then the next post, and so on right across. After this, add the other side trellises, with lengths of top batten, if required, fixed between the top of the side panels and the undersides of the roof panels.

2 Nailing the Trellis
Lay cross slats on plan, then position vertical slats above them. Glue and nail through intersections.

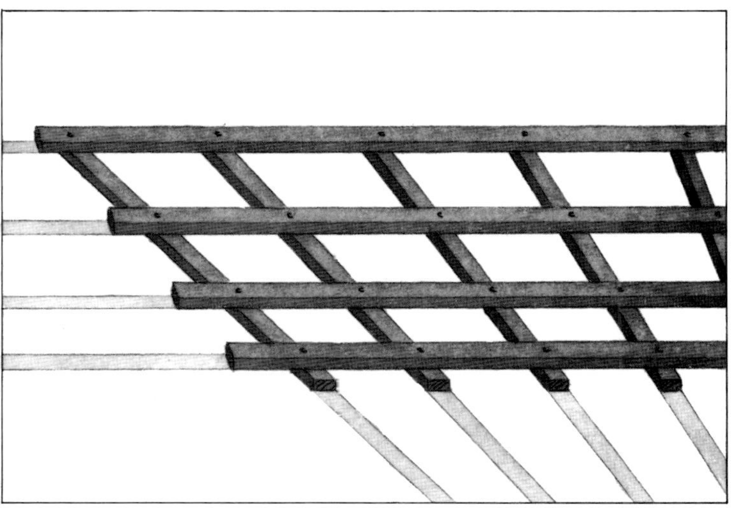

Hexagonal Arbor

An arbor makes a distinctive feature in any garden, displaying climbing plants to great advantage and exposing them to optimum conditions of light and air. Arbors are often all-metal structures, but this simple but elegant framework makes use of ordinary copper tubing and plain wooden rustic posts, readily available from most DIY outlets. The construction process is fairly quick and easy to do.

The three sections of copper tubing (which have been rubbed with plumbers' flux to give them a green colour) are cut to precisely the same length and bent into shape using a curved piece of blockboard or chipboard as a former. Holes are drilled about 100mm (6in) apart along the tubes. Thin green plastic-covered wires are threaded through the holes to make a support for the plants.

As is the case with all posts that need to go into the ground, it is much easier to use spiked steel supports with sockets. The metal spikes are readily driven into the ground and the end of the post can be dropped into the shoe and held in place.

The uprights and cross rails must be treated with a preservative and the resulting dark brown makes a pleasing contrast with the greenish copper.

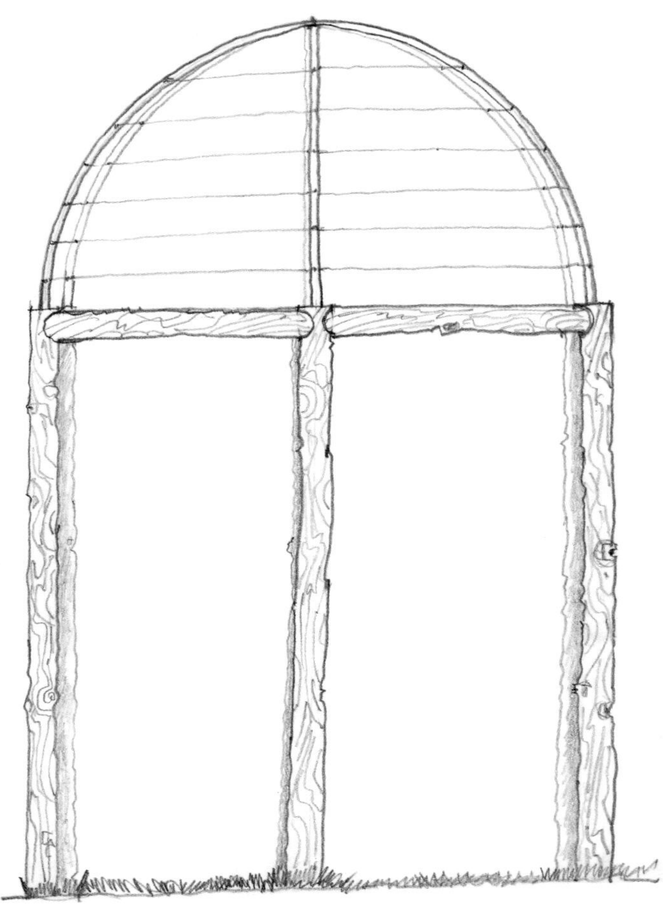

HEXAGONAL ARBOR

This arbor is made from six preservative-treated rustic poles set into the ground at equal intervals and joined by cross rails, with a dome above made from copper tubing. If you brush the tubing with plumbers' flux, a green patina will result. Garden wire is fed around the tubing as a support for climbing plants.

TIMBER FRAME

The height of the frame can be varied slightly. However, the poles should not be less than about 2m (6ft 6in) above ground, otherwise some people may hit their heads on the cross rails; and, for stability, the poles should not be much higher above ground than 2.5m (8ft).

PREPARING THE SITE

Choose a flat site and, using pegs and string lines, mark out the hexagonal shape (fig 1) for the positions. The posts are spaced at 1000mm (39in) centres, with 2m (6ft 6in) between any two opposite posts. It is essential that the post positions are accurately marked.

Dig 600mm (24in) deep holes for the posts. This can be done using a narrow spade or, if available, a post hole borer which is driven into the ground and then removed to deposit excavated earth. Fill the bottom 150mm (6in) of each hole with hardcore to ensure good drainage and prevent the post bottoms rotting.

MAKING THE FRAMEWORK

Make up six L-shapes comprising a post and a cross rail as follows.

Position two posts in neighbouring holes and wedge them vertically. Measure the internal distance between them and add 50mm (2in) to allow for shaping the ends of the cross rails. Remove the posts.

Use a jigsaw to make a curved cut in the ends of the cross rails so that they fit against the sides of the posts. Alternatively, use a hand saw to cut out V-shapes in the cross rails.

At the top of each post, draw 60° angles as a guide to aligning the cross rails (fig 2, below). Continue the lines to the opposite sides of the post as a guide for the dowel fixing positions. Cut the dowelling into 150mm (6in) lengths.

Lay one post on a flat piece of ground. Position a cross rail against the post and drill through the post and into the rail to accept the dowel (fig 3). At least 50mm (2in) of dowel should enter the rail. Fit the dowel using waterproof wood adhesive. Repeat to make five more L-shapes.

ERECTING THE FRAME

Position two posts in their holes and align the cross rail that falls between them with both posts. Use a straight edge and a spirit level to align the posts – if necessary, add or take away a little of the hardcore in the base of the hole. Drill through the 'free' post into the end of the cross rail to align with the angles marked on the top. Join the 'free' post to the cross rail with a dowel as you did before (fig 3).

Continue to join up the L-shaped sections in the same way, checking that the tops of the posts are all at the same height, and then saw off any protruding dowel ends flush with the posts.

MATERIALS

Part	Quantity	Material	Length
POSTS	6	75–100mm (3–4in) diameter treated rustic poles	2.4m (7ft 8in)
CROSS RAILS	6	50–75mm (2–3in) diameter treated rustic poles	As required
DOME BARS	3	22mm ($\frac{7}{8}$in) diameter copper tubing	As required

Also required: Approximately 2m (6ft 6in) of 12mm ($\frac{1}{2}$in) diameter hardwood dowelling

TOOLS

- WORKBENCH (fixed or portable)
- SPADE or POST HOLE BORER
- PANEL SAW
- SPIRIT LEVEL
- STEEL RULE
- JIGSAW
- POWER DRILL
- HAMMER
- SCREWDRIVER
- PLIERS
- HACKSAW
- CRAMPS
- SHOVEL

1 Drawing up a Ground Plan
Posts are spaced 1000mm (39in) apart: mark centre and strike off 1000mm (39in) lines at 60° angles.

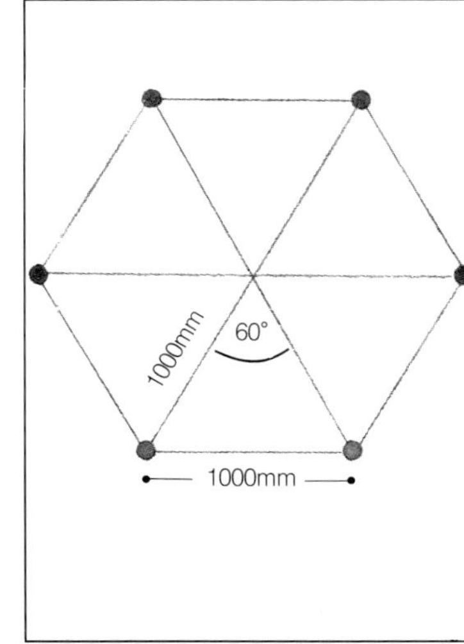

2 Shaping the Cross Rails
Angle ends of cross rails to fit around posts. Use jigsaw for smooth curve or make V-cuts with hand saw.

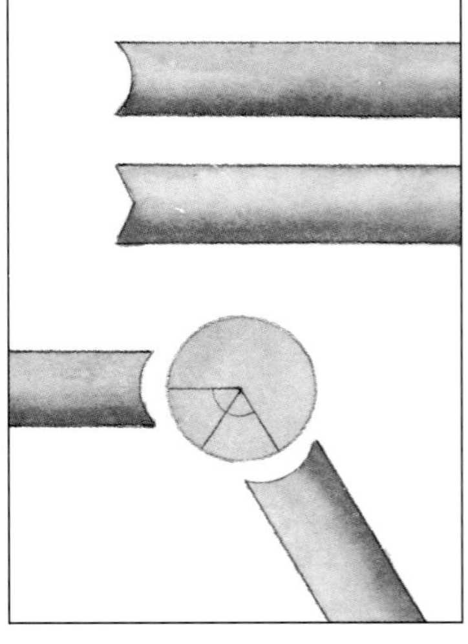

3 Fixing the Cross Rails
Drill holes through posts into cross rails. Insert dowels to fix in place. Angled screw holds dowel in place.

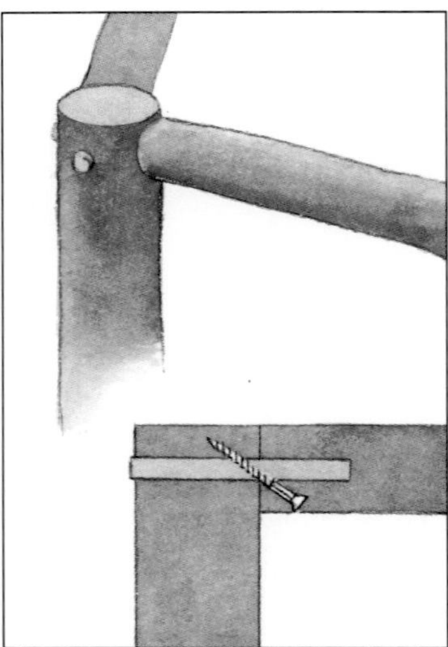

To secure the joints, use a 75mm (3in) screw inserted diagonally through each cross rail (fig 3).

Finally, tie a length of garden wire around the top of the posts, holding it in place on each post using 38mm (1½in) staples. To make the wire taut, twist the two ends together using pliers.

THE DOME

Draw a semi-circle on a large sheet of plywood or chipboard (fig 4) using a pencil and a piece of string to act as a compass. This will describe the section of the dome. When this is done, mark off at 150mm (6in) centres for the positions of holes through which training wires will later be threaded.

Use a piece of 19mm (¾in) chipboard or plywood to make a former for bending the tube to the correct shape. Trace the curve on to the former and cut it out using a jigsaw.

BENDING THE TUBE

Cut the copper tubing to length using a hacksaw. Our tubes were 3.14m (10ft 4in) long. Since the copper will need to be bent a little tighter than the arc, bring it down about 38mm (1½in) at each end.

Cramp the former to a workbench or table and start to bend the piece of tube around it. You will need someone to help you with this: each person should exert a little pressure until the tubing is bent to follow the shape of the former. If you find that the ends lose their shape then you can use a 22mm (⅞in) internal pipe bending spring.

Lay the bent tube on the original dome profile and mark off the 150mm (6in) spacings on to the tube. Drill 3mm (⅛in) diameter holes through the tubing at these marks.

Bend the other two tubes to the shape of the former and then drill the holes as before. Always mark off the spacings on the tubing against the original dome profile.

ASSEMBLING THE DOME

Mark the middle point of each tube, then hammer it flat so that you can drill a 6mm (¼in) diameter hole through each piece (fig 5). Bolt the three pieces together.

Next, drill a 25mm (1in) diameter hole, 50mm (2in) deep in the centre of the top of each post.

The dome can now be lifted on to the top of the posts and the tube ends located in the holes (fig 6). There is sufficient movement in the structure to enable the dome to be positioned.

Thread garden wire through each row of holes, tying each length securely in place.

To fix the dome to the rustic poles, drill straight through the tube horizontally above each post and slip a 50mm (2in) nail through.

Finally make up a dryish concrete mix of five parts sand to one part cement and pour it into each hole along with some small pieces of stone. Tamp it down, then shape it into a convex collar so that rain water will drain away.

HEXAGONAL ARBOR ASSEMBLY

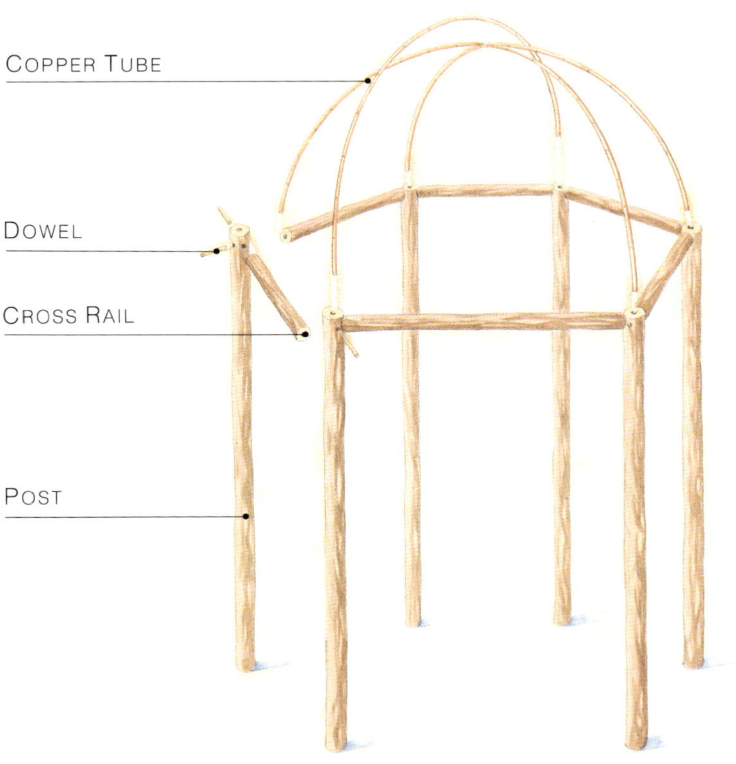

4 Dome Section and Former
Mark off 150mm (6in) spacings on semi-circle. Transfer section of curve to plywood to make former.

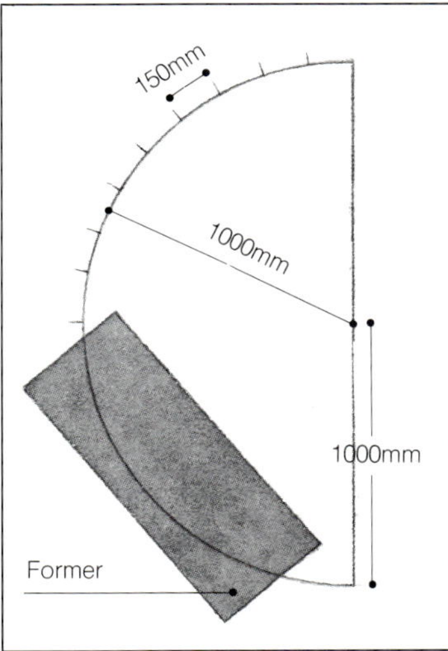

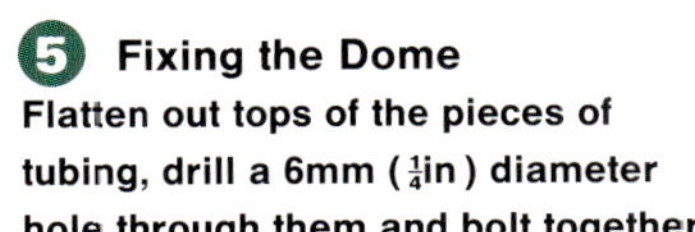
5 Fixing the Dome
Flatten out tops of the pieces of tubing, drill a 6mm (¼in) diameter hole through them and bolt together.

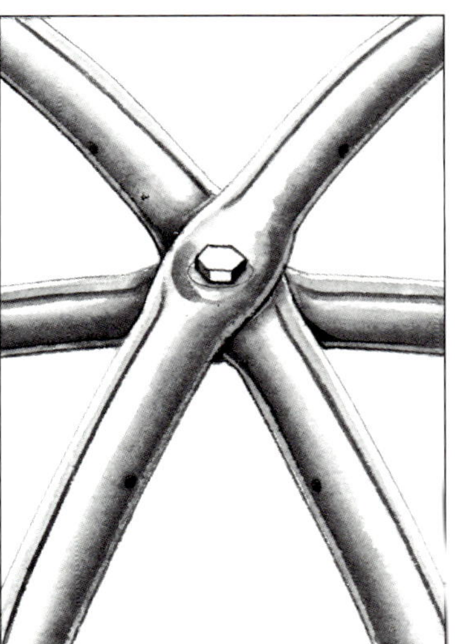

6 Fixing Dome to Posts
Drill a hole centrally in the top of each post. Slot dome into post and drive nail through tubing.

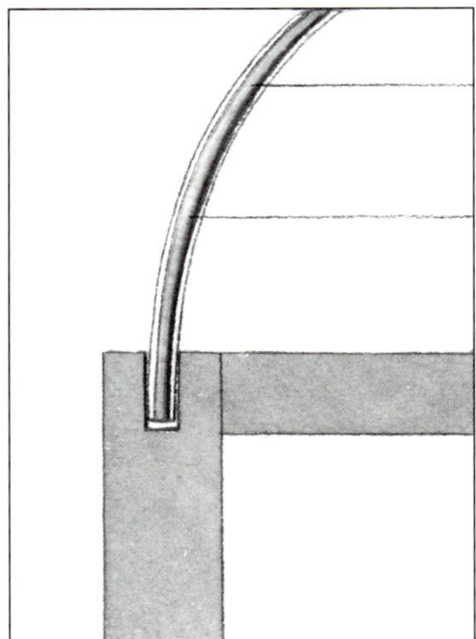

BEANSTICK FENCE

New fencing can look rather harsh and brash and hedges, even when composed of the most quick-growing species, are unfortunately not instant solutions to the problem of garden enclosure. This beanstick fence was designed to provide a more natural-looking boundary than the standard commercial timber fencing; almost, in fact, a 'man-made hedge'. The look is reminiscent of the traditional wattle fence; another source of inspiration was the type of wonderful screens and panels seen in Japanese gardens and walkways. Here the effect is created by combining a strong rectilinear framework with the natural, random texture supplied by the beansticks.

The fence is very easy to make. The beansticks are trapped in the sawn frame, held in place in two grooves made top and bottom between the top rails and a couple of battens between the bottom rails. The sticks are cut to the same length, slotted into the groove and pushed up together.

The sticks themselves do not need to be treated, although the ends could be dipped in preservative to prolong their life. If sticks do become broken or damaged, it is easy to replace them.

This fence, formal enough for a front garden, would also be a good choice for a new house where the planting had not yet had a chance to become established. The beansticks are sufficiently firm and resilient to be animal-proof but chinks of light lend it a lively and varied effect.

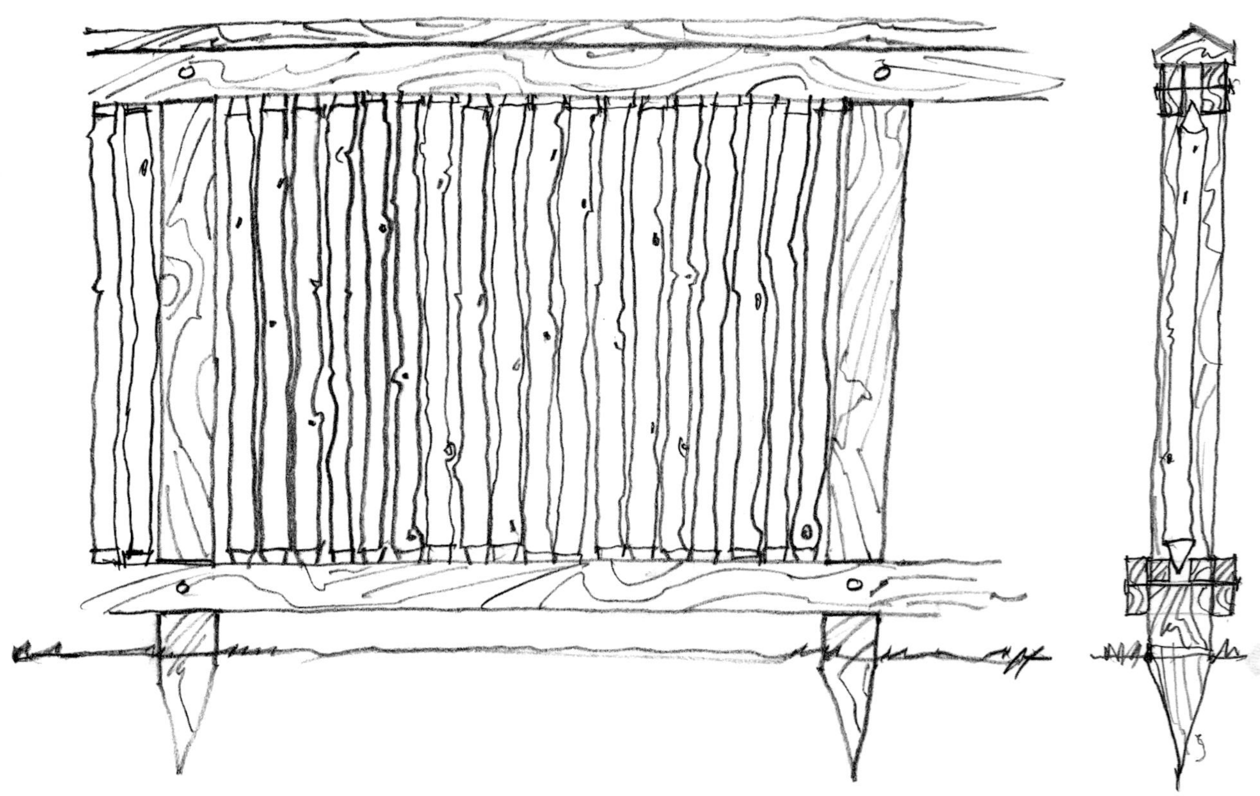

Beanstick Fence

This rustic-looking fence is an ideal project if you want your boundary to look just a bit different from those of your neighbours. It is made from beansticks fixed between a framework of sawn and preservative-treated timber. This can be left in its natural state, it can be stained a darker wood colour, or it can be painted as shown in our example – microporous paint is ideal for treating the timber, being easy to apply without a primer, and easy to re-treat in future as the need arises.

It is unlikely that you will be able to buy the beansticks from a timber merchant. More likely sources are fencing suppliers and garden centres, or directly from the woodmen who cut the sticks.

Cutting is done in winter and early spring, and this is the best time to obtain the sticks. You will need large numbers for this project, and it is a good idea to buy one or two bundles of sticks to start with to see what proportion of the fence they cover. Then you will be able to put in an order to cover the full length of the fence you will be making.

The spacing of the posts depends on the length of the rails you will be using. Rails must be joined at post positions, so if you have 3m (10ft) rails, posts must be spaced 1500mm (60in) apart. For 2.4m (8ft) rails, the post spacing will be 1200mm (48in). Once this is decided, you will be able to work out how many posts (and post supports) are required.

You also need to decide on the height of the posts. Our fence is about 1000mm (40in) high, and in this case the posts are 1500mm (60in) long which allows 500mm (20in) of post to be in the ground. A good rule of thumb is to allow a minimum of 500mm (20in) of post in the ground, or one third of the fence height, whichever is the greater.

Alternatively, you can fit the posts into metal spike post supports which are simply hammered into the ground. The posts fit into sockets in the tops of the spike supports. In this case, 600mm (24in) long spikes are suitable for fences up to 1200mm (48in); for fences up to 1800mm (72in) high use 760mm (30in) long post supports.

The metal post supports are driven into the ground with a scrap of loose-fitting fence post in the socket to protect the socket from sledge hammer blows, keeping a check with a spirit level on all sides of the socket that the spike is going straight into the ground. You will also be able to heave on the spike to correct any tendency for it to go into the ground out of plumb (vertical). Stretch a horizontal string line along the line of the proposed fence to ensure the metal spikes are driven into the ground in line and to the same height.

If you do not use metal post spikes, it is possible on soft ground to sharpen the ends of the posts into spikes and simply hammer them into the ground. However, using this method it is usually difficult to get the posts absolutely in line and vertical, and it is better to take out a hole for each post using a metal post hole borer tool, which can be hired. This hand-operated tool removes a plug of soil to leave a neat circular hole about 225mm (9in) in diameter, and up to 600mm (24in) deep.

Tools

- WORKBENCH (fixed or portable)
- STEEL MEASURING TAPE
- TRY SQUARE
- PANEL SAW (or circular saw)
- TREE-PRUNING SAW
- HAMMER
- DRILL (hand or power)
- DRILL BIT – 6mm (¼in)
- SPANNER
- SPIRIT LEVEL
- CHISEL
- MALLET
- BILLHOOK (or axe or sharp knife)

Materials

Part	Quantity	Material	Length
POSTS	As required	75 × 75mm (3 × 3in) sawn and treated softwood	As required*
RAILS	As required	75 × 25mm (3 × 1in) sawn and treated softwood	As required
BATTENS	As required	32 × 25mm (1¼ × 1in) sawn and treated softwood	As required
CAPPING BOARD	As required	75 × 38mm (3 × 1½in) sawn and treated softwood	As required
BEANSTICKS	As required	Hazel, birch or chestnut	As required

* Post length will depend on the height of the fence and whether you are fixing posts into the ground or into metal spike post supports

Posts can then be stood in the holes, lined up against a string line, and their heights adjusted to bring them all level by packing the holes as necessary. The posts are held upright by ramming hardcore around them, and finally topping off with a collar of concrete around the post at ground level to throw rainwater clear of the post.

Preparing and Fixing Posts

If you decide to point the posts to drive them into the ground (*see* above), the joints can then be cut with the posts in position. In all other cases it is better and easier to cut the joints with the post on a bench.

Hold a side rail flush with the top of the post and mark its depth on the post. Repeat for the other side of the post, and notch out 25mm (1in) wide recesses to the depth of the rails at the top of each post (fig 1).

Position the posts by either dropping them into metal post support sockets or setting them into the ground, adjusting them to the same height. Place a long, straight batten across the post tops or post support sockets and use a spirit level to check that they are level.

If using metal post supports, screw or cramp the post bottoms into the supports. If fixing posts in holes in the ground, pack around them with hardcore and a concrete collar. Double check that all posts are in line, that they are vertical, and that the tops are level.

Fixing Top Rails

Fix the top rails to the posts using two coach screws each side.

If it is necessary to join two rails, cut the rails to coincide with a post position and make a spliced joint (fig 2). To maintain the strength of the fence, you should have only one spliced joint per post, staggering them from side to side.

At the fence ends, cut the rails flush with the edge of the post.

Fixing Bottom Rails

The bottom rails are screwed to the outsides of the posts about 150mm (6in) up from ground level. Fix a coach screw at one end of the rail, and use a spirit level to get the rail level before drilling and screwing at the other end into another post. Use two coach screws per post, and make spliced joints if necessary to coincide with post positions.

Measure the distance between the posts and cut pieces of roofing batten to fit snuggly between them (fig 3). Fit the battens inside the bottom rails, flush with the top edge, with the narrower edge towards the rails. Drive four zinc-plated screws through the bottom rails and into each batten. The battens create a gap about 12mm (½in) wide centrally between the bottom rails.

Repeat all along the fence.

If you plan to paint or stain the frame of the fence, do this now.

Fitting the Beansticks

Measure the distance from the top of the top rail to the bottom of the bottom rail, and cut all the beansticks to this length. They will tend to clog the saw teeth, so use a tree-pruning saw for this job.

Use a billhook, axe or sharp knife to sharpen one end of each of the beansticks so that they wedge into the gap between the battens.

Starting at one end, feed the sticks in through the gap at the top of the frame and wedge them into the gap at the bottom, bunching them tightly until the frame is filled.

Trim all the beansticks flush with the top of the top rails. Use a pruning saw or handsaw, and press each stick down firmly as you cut it.

Finally, nail the capping board along the top of the fence, making sure it covers the edges of the top rails. If you cannot buy a capping board, you can cut one from a length of sawn timber. Paint or stain it to match the fence frame.

Beanstick Fence Assembly

1 Fixing Top Rails
Notch out 25mm (1in) recesses to depth of side rail on sides of post at top. Screw rails to post.

2 Joining Lengths of Rail
Join rails at post positions, if necessary, cutting rails at an angle to form spliced joint.

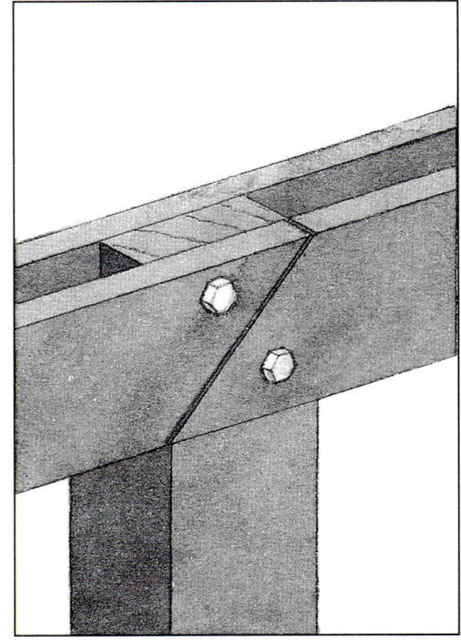

3 Fixing Beansticks
Sharpen one end of stick to a point and feed through top to wedge between bottom rail battens.

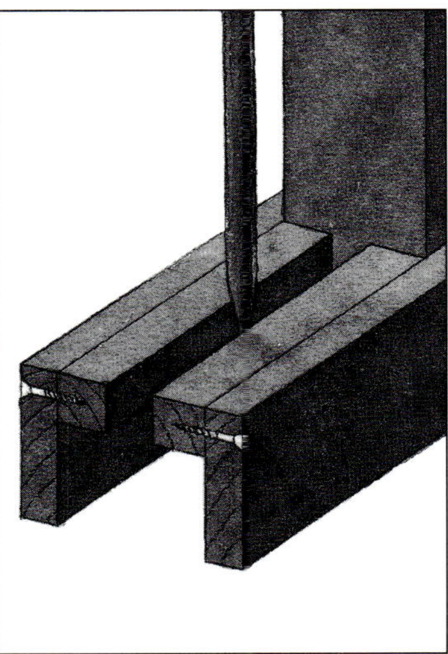

PART 5

CONTAINERS

Every year at Versailles, it takes the army to bring in the lemon and orange trees for the winter, hundreds of planted tubs comprising what must be the ultimate container garden. Container gardening is not usually on such a grand scale, but in every garden there is a place for at least some plants in pots, whether a pair of bay trees in formal tubs flanking an entrance, a collection of simple terracotta bowls tumbling with flowers, or cheerful hanging baskets providing a splash of summer colour.

The versatility of container gardening is one of its main advantages: you can match plants exactly to their soil requirements, and place them where they will look most effective. If the container is not too large, you can move it to a position of prominence when the plant is in bloom. Planters and window boxes are excellent DIY projects, allowing you to tailor-make your containers to suit their location exactly. If you use the same type of containers inside and out, group pots around entrances, on either side of French doors and on window sills you will create views which will help to dissolve the boundary between your house and the garden.

CONTAINERS

POTS OF PLANTS

Container gardening is flexible and provides an instant garden for a small space. Tubs or pots flanking an entrance are a common feature of formal garden designs, but can work well combined with less structured planting (above left). A variety of species can be grown in containers; you can train climbers to grow up purpose-built trellis from a tub (above) and even grow small trees (right).

There are many advantages to gardening in containers. Usually, little or no weeding is required, which saves considerable maintenance time for people with only a few hours to spare. Compost and soil can be tailored to the precise needs of the plant, enabling a far greater range of species to be grown in the same location. Plants can also be arranged to suit the demands of the garden design, or to give shape to a flat landscape. You can also furnish an area with plants which might otherwise be barren, such as in the dry shade under a tree or on a roof.

Some plants positively flourish in containers. Figs, for example, like to be contained; a considerable number of other species can live undisturbed for many years in pots. Growing untidy and invasive herbs, such as mint, in containers also benefits the rest of the garden.

If containers provide a quick and easy way of creating a garden, they are also flexible enough to accommodate and express a whole range of garden styles. Containers are often associated with formal garden designs. Symmetrical arrangements of tubs, clipped box in painted wooden planters and stone urns at the end of walkways or in the centre of radiating beds are all ways of using containers to emphasize the geometry or architectural quality of a garden design.

However, containers can also be delightfully informal. Mediterranean gardens and terraces often feature large terracotta pots carefully positioned to make punctuation points in the overall design. In many Italian and Greek villages, painted and planted oil cans crowd windowsills and balconies, adding a jolt of colour to the elevations of houses. Window boxes or hanging baskets spilling over with vivid geraniums and lobelia also work well in country locations or cottage-style gardens.

CONTAINERS

Whatever the overall style of the garden, containers should be used in a positive way. Place them to create a focal point, in the centre of planting, or arrange a series of pots asymmetrically to lead the eye on through the garden. Containers can also introduce changes of height if they are placed on top of a wall or hung from the side of a house, an important consideration if the rest of the garden is fairly flat. You can also delineate an enclosed area or patio with a row of pots or planters, or make a special feature of an entrance by flanking it with a pair of tubs.

Wherever possible, mass containers in groups for increased effect, rather than dot them about the garden where their impact will be lost. You can group pots on metal garden staging which looks very attractive positioned at either side of a door, or adopt one solution seen on a French roadside, where the entire length of a garden wall was lined in shelves, set about 45cm (18in) apart, on which were ranged dozens and dozens of planted pots.

Plants should be massed in much the same way, although filling a container with a single variety is often more effective than a careful composition of a small amount of different species. Wooden boxes simply planted with box and ivy provide a graphic line of green at the window and require little maintenance to remain attractive and flourishing.

As far as the container itself is concerned, material, size and style vary tremendously. Wherever possible, keep to natural materials – stone, wood and terracotta all look marvellous and age in a sympathetic way. Metal containers, especially when made of lead, zinc or copper, can be attractive and even rubber – in the form of old tractor tyres – can be effective, contributing textural interest. Avoid plastic: it always looks glaringly out of place in a garden; its harshness seems to stem from the fact that, unlike everything else, it does not weather or change, and usually has no texture.

In terms of size, choose containers which are on the generous side. Small pots will be overlooked and tend to have a prissy appearance which is at odds with the robust and striking effects you should be trying to create.

Ready-made containers include a range of plain terracotta shapes from urns to shallow bowls, from traditional flowerpots to troughs. Simple reconstituted stone containers can also look good, particularly if you encourage a little weathering. Wooden planters and tubs available commercially can be customized by staining or painting them to blend in with your house or to make a vivid colour accent. Wooden containers are also, of course, a natural choice for DIY and suit a variety of different applications. A wooden tub is an excellent container home for small trees and shrubs, and half a wooden barrel is a classic. Wooden troughs or planters also make excellent raised beds, a practical and enjoyable way of gardening for older people or those with limited physical strength. Planting does not necessarily have to be at a low level in a container: a pyramid of bamboo sticks tied together and placed in a pot and planted with scarlet-flowering runner beans is a lovely sight!

One of the most appealing features of container gardening is the scope for improvisation and humour in the choice of container. In this area, more than any other, there is great opportunity for creative salvage. Everything from half-barrels to old watering cans can be used as a plant container. Old sinks, wash tubs, chimney pots and stone troughs can all be recycled to great effect, and architectural salvage yards can be a tremendous source of objects in this respect.

THE CONTAINED GARDEN

One of the most important advantages of container gardening is its ability to establish a visual connection between the house and garden. The current popularity of the conservatory bears out the common desire of people to include a sense of the outdoors in their homes. An array of the same type of containers can be used indoors and outside to create views that dissolve the boundary between house and garden.

Compost Bin and Planter

The compost bin and planter are very similar in construction, made from rough-sawn boards fixed to posts. The simple nature of the design and lack of precision required in the finishing mean that these two structures offer a good means of practising your DIY skills and gaining the confidence to move on to more elaborate projects.

A compost bin is an invaluable asset for the gardener, providing a supply of rich organic matter which makes all the difference to the way plants grow. At the same time, recycling your garden and kitchen waste is environmentally beneficial and economically sound.

The front posts of the bin are doubled up, making a slot where boards can be dropped into place as the pile builds up, or easily removed as the compost is taken out. It is worth buying 'pressure preserved' timber – compost is both hot and wet, so the wood needs the maximum degree of protection.

The planter provides a support for young trees, many of which either blow over or suffer from 'windrock', instability of the root structure where growth stops and starts rather than proceeding at an even pace. The cross supports enable the trunk to be fixed firmly in place while the tree becomes established.

The planter is painted with a coat of black tar to preserve the wood. Coach screws are used to bolt the boards to the uprights, giving a smart finishing touch.

Compost Bin

The principle of construction for the compost bin is the same as for the planter (pages 135–7). It is made from fencing-quality sawn and preservative-treated timber which is often sold and cut in imperial as well as metric sizes.

The size of the bin can be varied to suit the site, but it should not be too large, since air will not be able to get to the centre of the heap, hindering the production of good garden compost.

Our bin is about 915mm (36in) square. The height can also be altered according to your own requirements, but you should work in multiples of 150mm (6in) plus an allowance for ventilation gaps between the boards. Our bin is about 990mm (39in) high. Bear in mind that you want a height at which it will be comfortable to tip garden waste into the bin. Also, the heap does not want to be too high or you will not be able to climb onto the heap to tread down the waste material. Opinion varies on the optimum size for the ventilation gaps; we suggest 12–19mm ($\frac{1}{2}$–$\frac{3}{4}$in).

Construction

Cut all of the components to the lengths specified in the Materials chart below. The posts are left long and are cut down to size after the boards have been fixed to allow for the ventilation gaps between the boards. The bin is held together with coach screws, and G-cramps are useful for holding the boards squarely in place while they are being fixed. The coach screw heads are a decorative feature of this compost bin, and it is important that they line up with each other and are the same distance in from the corners.

At the front of the bin, the only fixed board is at the bottom. The other retainer boards slot into the groove between the posts and are built up to the height required. They are therefore easily removed to gain access to the bin contents when the time comes to fork out the rotted compost.

Materials

Note: All timber is sawn and preservative-treated softwood

Part	Quantity	Material	Length
'LONG' BOARDS	9	150 × 25mm (6 × 1in)	915mm (36in)
'MIDDLE' BOARDS	6	As above	890mm (35in)
'SHORT' BOARDS	4	As above	865mm (34in)
RETAINER BOARDS	6*	As above	As above
POSTS	6	50 × 50mm (2 × 2in)	1220mm (48in)
COACH SCREWS	100	Zinc-plated steel	8 × 50mm ($\frac{5}{16}$ × 2in)

* Cut 7 retainer boards if you want the boards at the front to be level with the boards at the side and back

Tools

- WORKBENCH (fixed or portable)
- STEEL MEASURING TAPE
- STEEL RULE
- TRY SQUARE
- PANEL SAW (or circular power saw)
- MARKING GAUGE
- POWER DRILL
- DRILL BIT – approximately 6mm ($\frac{1}{4}$in) diameter to drill pilot holes for coach screws
- SPANNER
- ONE PAIR OF G-CRAMPS

1 Fixing the First Board to the Posts

A 'short' length of board is fixed to the two posts flush and square with the ends to form the bottom row of the back of the bin. Two coach screws at each end hold it in place.

2 Adding the Side Posts and First Retainer Board

A 'long' board at both sides is screwed in place, flush with the ends of the posts. The first retainer board rests against the back of the front posts and is later screwed to the posts from behind.

Sawing	**148**
Drilling	**150**
Screwing	**150**

COMPOST BIN ASSEMBLY

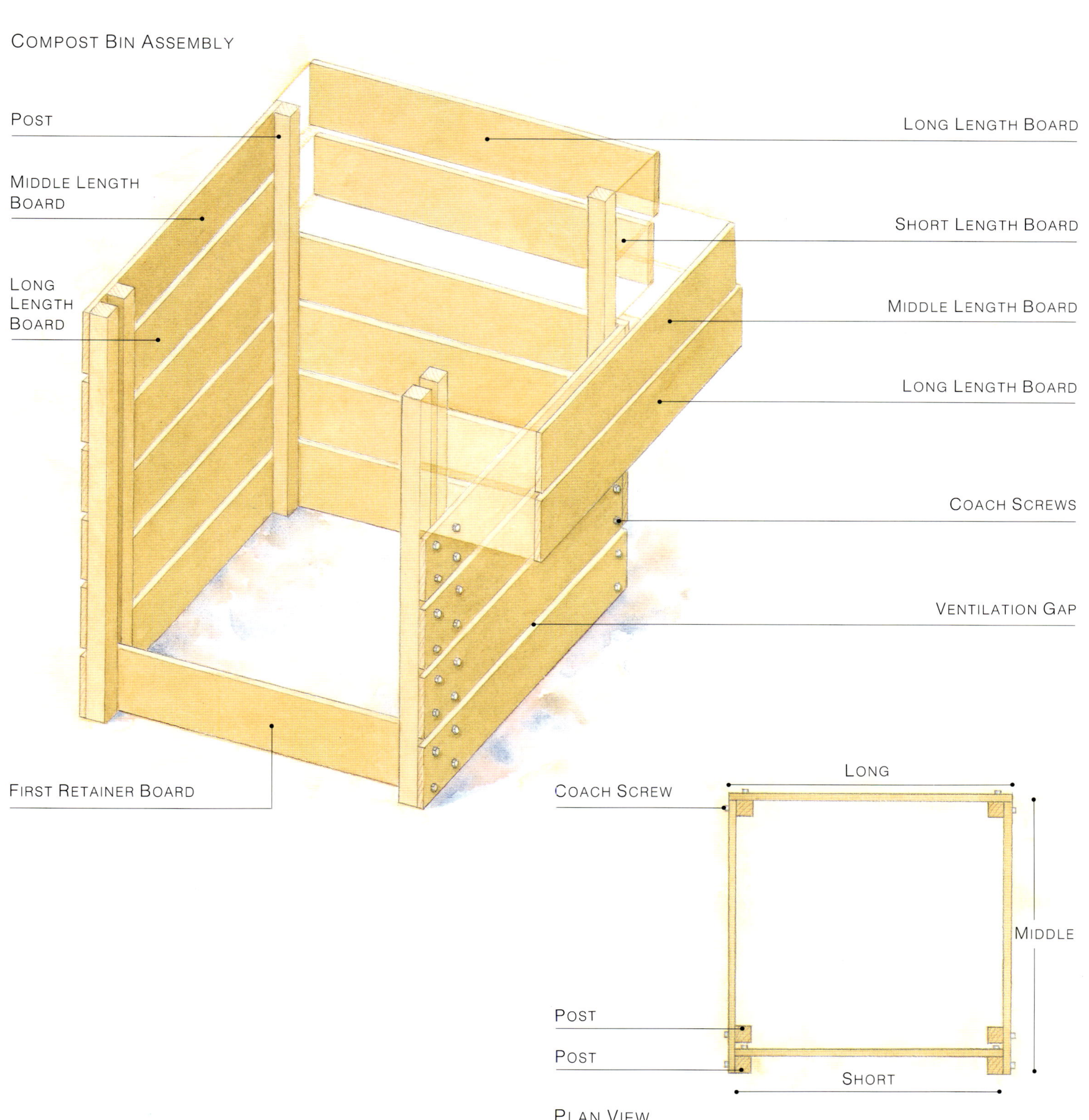

PLAN VIEW

Compost Bin

Squaring the First Row

Start to form the back of the bin by laying two of the posts on a flat surface. Then lay a 'short' length of board across them flush with the bottom ends of the posts, so the outer edges of the posts are 865mm (34in) apart (fig 1, page 132).

Check that the board is square to one of the posts, then cramp it to the post. Drill pilot holes for two coach screws and insert the screws to fix the board to the post.

Use a second board at the other end of the posts to ensure that they are square to the 'short' length of board, then double-check that the post is square to the first board using a try square. Drill pilot holes for the two coach screws to be inserted into the other end of the first board, the same distance in as the coach screws at the other end.

Stand the frame upright and place a 'long' board along the side, flush with the post, and secure it to the post with a G-cramp. Pilot drill and screw it to the post using two coach screws centred on the post.

Repeat for the other side with another 'long' length of board.

Place another post inside this board flush with the end, check that it is square at the top using another 'long' board, and screw into the post through the side board using two coach screws as before.

Take a retainer board and place it on the inside of the front posts (fig 2, page 132).

Building up the Rows of Boards

Place spacing blocks or a spacing batten about 12–19mm (½–¾in) thick on top of the back board, then lay a 'long' length of board across the top (fig 1). Check that it protrudes an equal distance beyond the outside edges of both the posts, then fix it in place with two coach screws at each end as before. For neatness, make sure that the coach screws line up with those on the board in the row below.

Repeat the process with one 'middle' length board on each side; these should both fit flush with the ends of the back board.

Continue working in this way, one row at a time so that the back boards run alternately with 'short'/'long' lengths, and the sides with 'long'/'middle' lengths to the height required. Ours is six boards high plus spaces.

As you work it is important to check that the structure is square by holding a spare board at the top flush with the posts each time a new board is added.

The Front

With the bottom board at the front, screw through into the back of the front posts using two coach screws at each end.

Place the final two posts in position behind the coach screw heads, leaving at least a 12–19mm (½–¾in) gap from the front board to create a slot in which the retainers will be a very loose fit. Hold a post in position on the side boards using a G-cramp, then mark a vertical line on the outside of the boards for the coach screw positions (fig 3).

Screw through each board into the post from the outside using two coach screws per board. Repeat for the post on the other side.

Drop the retainer boards into the slots created by the two posts on each side, building the retainers up to the height required. If you want the retainers to finish level with the boards at the sides and back, rip cut the top one to size.

Finally, cut off the tops of the posts so that they are flush with the top edges of the boards.

Place the bin in an appropriate site away from general view. Almost all types of organic matter can be used for producing compost, although anything too bulky should be avoided because it will slow down the rate at which composting takes place. Similarly, large quantities of leaves also tend to slow the process, and are best kept to decompose separately. Farmyard manure, on the other hand, will accelerate production, and it is a good idea to add a layer of manure or proprietary compost accelerator to your bin every 125–200mm (5–8in). Your compost should be ready after six months or so.

1 Building Up the Rows of Boards

Use spacing blocks or a spacing batten to allow for ventilation gaps when fixing subsequent boards to the back and sides. Alternate 'short' and 'long' boards at the back, 'long' and 'middle' boards at the sides.

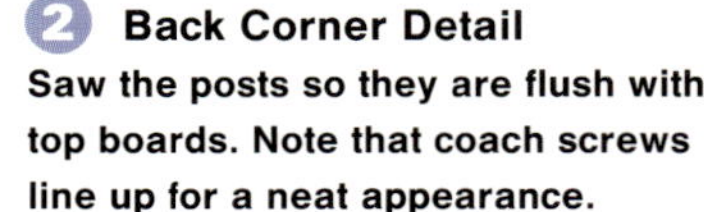

2 Back Corner Detail

Saw the posts so they are flush with top boards. Note that coach screws line up for a neat appearance.

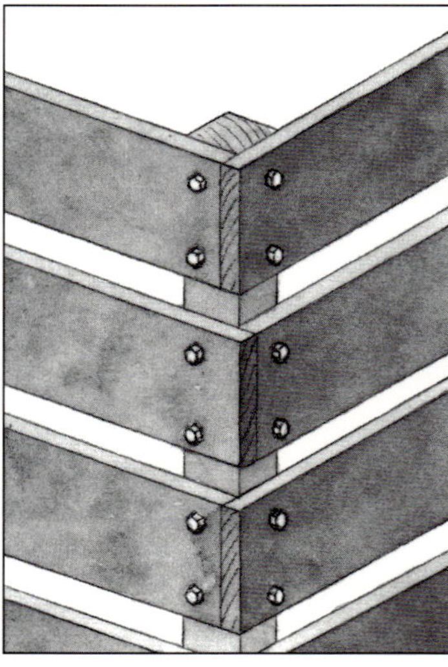

3 Forming the Front Slot

A second post each side is screwed 38mm (1½in) behind front posts and retainer boards drop in place.

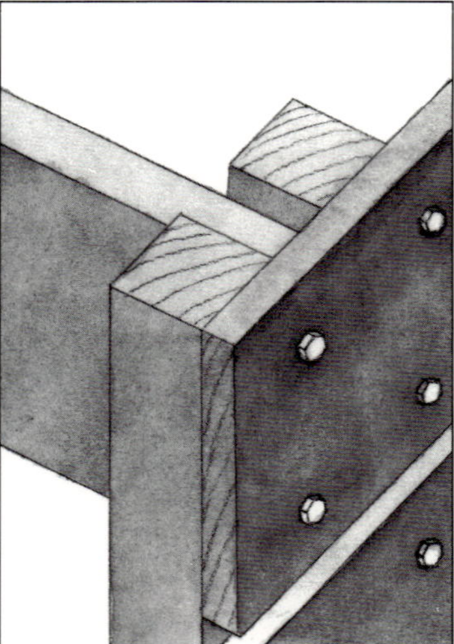

PLANTER

This planter allows you to grow trees, roses, shrubs and other flowers where normally you would not be able to, such as on a paved patio or on a concrete path or driveway. The planter is made from fencing-quality sawn and preservative-treated timber. Much of this is still sold in imperial sizes, although all suppliers will accept orders given in either imperial or metric units. Since the finished planter would be too heavy to lift, there is no need for a floor panel – the planter is placed where required, the planting compost is added and the tree or shrub is planted. There is normally room for other plants around the edge, which will enhance your display.

The size of these planters can be varied according to your specific needs – ours is 760mm (30in) square and 760mm (30in) high, which is a good size for medium-sized trees. For smaller shrubs and flowers you can make smaller planters, and if these are of a size that will still be light enough to move when planted, then it is worth fixing a floor panel in the planter so that you can reposition it at will *(see* **Making a Floor Panel, page 137***)*.

The corner posts are extended upwards and are joined at the top by two cross pieces which form a useful tree support. The planter is held together with coach screws, and it is important that these should neatly align with each other.

POSTS – CUTTING THE TOP JOINTS

Cut the corner posts to length, and then use the clean sawn end of the post to mark out the top joint for housing the cross supports. Place the edge of a length of 75 x 25mm (3 x 1in) timber (cut from 150 x 25mm [6 x 1in]) centrally on the post end at a 45° angle and mark its position (fig 1).

Place the cross support 3mm (⅛in) down from the top of the post, ensure it is at right angles, and mark off the bottom edge. Square round on all four faces, then gauge lines down the sides of the post from those drawn at the top.

Cut down the marked lines on each side of the post with a tenon saw and use a coping saw to remove the centre section.

Repeat for other three posts.

TOOLS

- WORKBENCH (fixed or portable)
- STEEL MEASURING TAPE
- STEEL RULE
- TRY SQUARE
- COMBINATION SQUARE – for marking 45° angles
- PANEL SAW (or circular power saw)
- TENON SAW (or power jigsaw)
- COPING SAW
- MARKING GAUGE
- POWER DRILL
- DRILL BIT – approximately 6mm (¼in) diameter to drill pilot holes for coach screws
- SPANNER
- ONE PAIR OF G-CRAMPS
- HAMMER – if fitting floor panel

MATERIALS

Note: All timber is sawn and preservative-treated softwood

Part	Quantity	Material	Length
'LONG' BOARDS	10	150 x 25mm (6 x 1in)	760mm (30in)
'SHORT' BOARDS	10	As above	710mm (28in)
CORNER POSTS	4	50 x 50mm (2 x 2in)	1350mm (53in)
CROSS SUPPORTS	2	150 x 25mm (6 x 1in) cut to 75 x 25mm (3 x 1in)	1220mm (48in) cut to length as required
COACH SCREWS	80	Zinc-plated steel	8 x 50mm ($\frac{5}{16}$ x 2in)

1 Marking Top Joint on Posts
Mark cross support centrally on post end at 45°. Gauge lines down post to marked position and remove centre.

2 Fixing the Second Frame to Form Main Construction
Fix 'short' boards flush with the ends of two lots of two posts. Screw 'long' boards to the sides of one frame, then place the second frame inside the 'long' boards so that the ends are square and flush.

Planter

Main Construction

Lay two of the corner posts on a flat surface and place a 'short' length of board across them flush with the ends so that the outer edges are 710mm (28in) apart.

Secure the board to the posts by drilling two pilot holes at one end, about 25mm (1in) from the end, and screw in two of the zinc-plated coach screws. For a neat finish try to ensure that each coach screw is the same distance from the edge.

Hold a spare board at the other end to make sure that the post is square, double check using a try square and secure the opposite end of the first board in the same way, drilling the holes the same distance in from the outside edge.

Repeat the process with the other two posts, fixing a 'short' board betweeen them at the base.

Stand one of the frames upright, and place a 'long' length of board along the side flush with the post and secure it in place using a G-cramp. Pilot hole and screw to the corner post with two coach screws centrally on the post. Repeat for the other side of the frame, using a 'long' length of board as before.

Place the other frame inside these 'long' boards, with the corner posts on the inside (fig 2, page 135). Fix the sides to the corner posts with two coach screws at each side.

Building up the Rows of Boards

Take another 'short' length of board and place it on top of the fixed 'long' board so its ends are flush with the posts. Cramp the board to the posts using a pair of G-cramps and fix it in place with two coach screws at each end, aligning them with the screws on the board below.

Take a 'long' length of board and place it on the adjacent side so it overlaps the end of the short board (fig 1). Make sure the end is flush, then screw it into the corner post.

Continue in this way, one row at a time, so that the 'short'/'long' boards run alternately, and ends are visible on each side on alternate rows. Build to five boards high (or whatever height you have decided on). It is most important to check that the structure is square as you work: do this by holding a board at the top flush with the posts each time a board is added.

Fixing the Cross Supports

Measure diagonally across the corner posts at the top of the planter and add 50mm (2in) so that there will be an overhang at each end. Cut two lengths to this measurement from 75 × 25mm (3 × 1in) timber.

At the middle of these two cross supports, cut two cross halving joints (*see* **Techniques, page 152**) and slot together. Fit the cross supports into the slots in the corner posts and glue them in place (fig 3).

Unless you wish to colour the wood there is no need to apply a special finish, as preservative-treated timber is used for this project.

1 Building Up the Sides of the Planter
Build up the rows one at a time, fixing 'short' boards above 'long' boards and vice versa. Always check boards are square with the frame and ends are flush before screwing in place. Align screws with those on the boards below.

2 Joining the Cross Supports
Cut cross halving joints in the middle of the two cross supports so that they slot together.

Preservative 146
Drilling 150
Screwing 150
Halving joint 152

If you do want to change the colour of the wood, apply a water-repellent preservative wood stain of the desired shade. To avoid getting stain onto the coach screw heads, push lengths of plastic or rubber tubing over the heads before staining the planter.

MAKING A FLOOR PANEL

If a floor panel is required, screw 50 × 50mm (2 × 2in) battens to the inside of the planter at the base. Lay 150 × 25mm (6 × 1in) boards across the planter, resting on the battens. Space the boards so that there are narrow gaps about 3mm ($\frac{1}{8}$in) wide between them to allow drainage of excess water. To assist the base in supporting a heavy weight of soil, reinforce it with additional 50 × 50mm (2 × 2in) battens spaced about 225mm (9in) apart under the floor panel and running at right angles to it.

Move the planter to the chosen site before adding the soil and planting the tree or shrub. A layer of small stones at the bottom of the planter will assist drainage.

3 Fixing Supports to Posts

The cross supports fit into the slots cut in top of each post and protrude an equal distance. Glue in place.

PLANTER ASSEMBLY

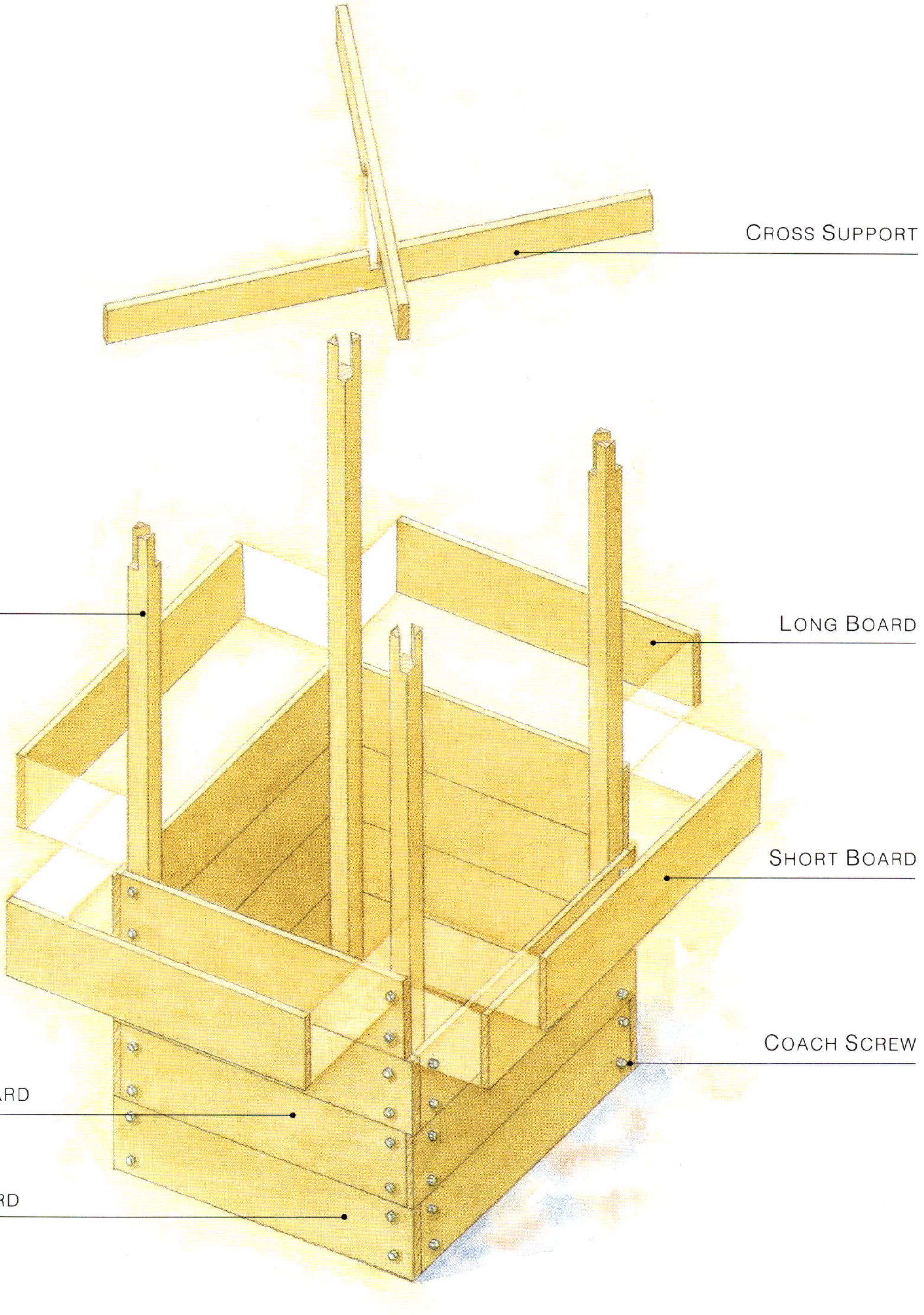

CROSS SUPPORT
POST
LONG BOARD
SHORT BOARD
COACH SCREW
SHORT BOARD
LONG BOARD

Cold Frame

If you can't afford a greenhouse, a cold frame is the next best thing. Most important for raising seedlings or growing early vegetables, it can also be used to provide salad ingredients such as lamb's lettuce, broquette or treviso all through the winter: a year-round usage which makes it an invaluable addition to any garden. If you do have a greenhouse, a cold frame can be used to harden off bedding plants raised in the greenhouse and as a place for overwintering tender biennials.

The design of this cold frame varies little from the traditional version which is such a common garden sight. Extremely versatile and very simple to make, the wooden base is treated with exterior-grade preservative, contrasting with the crisp, white painted 'light' or glazed lid. An important feature of the design is the ability to remove the entire light so that there is free access to the area of ground covered by the cold frame, enabling it to be dug over and planted easily.

Cold frames should be sited in south-facing positions where they will receive maximum sunlight, but, because they are usually portable, the position can be varied from year to year. If there is a danger of scorching at the height of summer, the glass may need to be coated with white 'obscuring paint'.

Unlike traditional cloches or glass bell-jars, a cold frame can be made simply and economically to provide a versatile extension of the growing season.

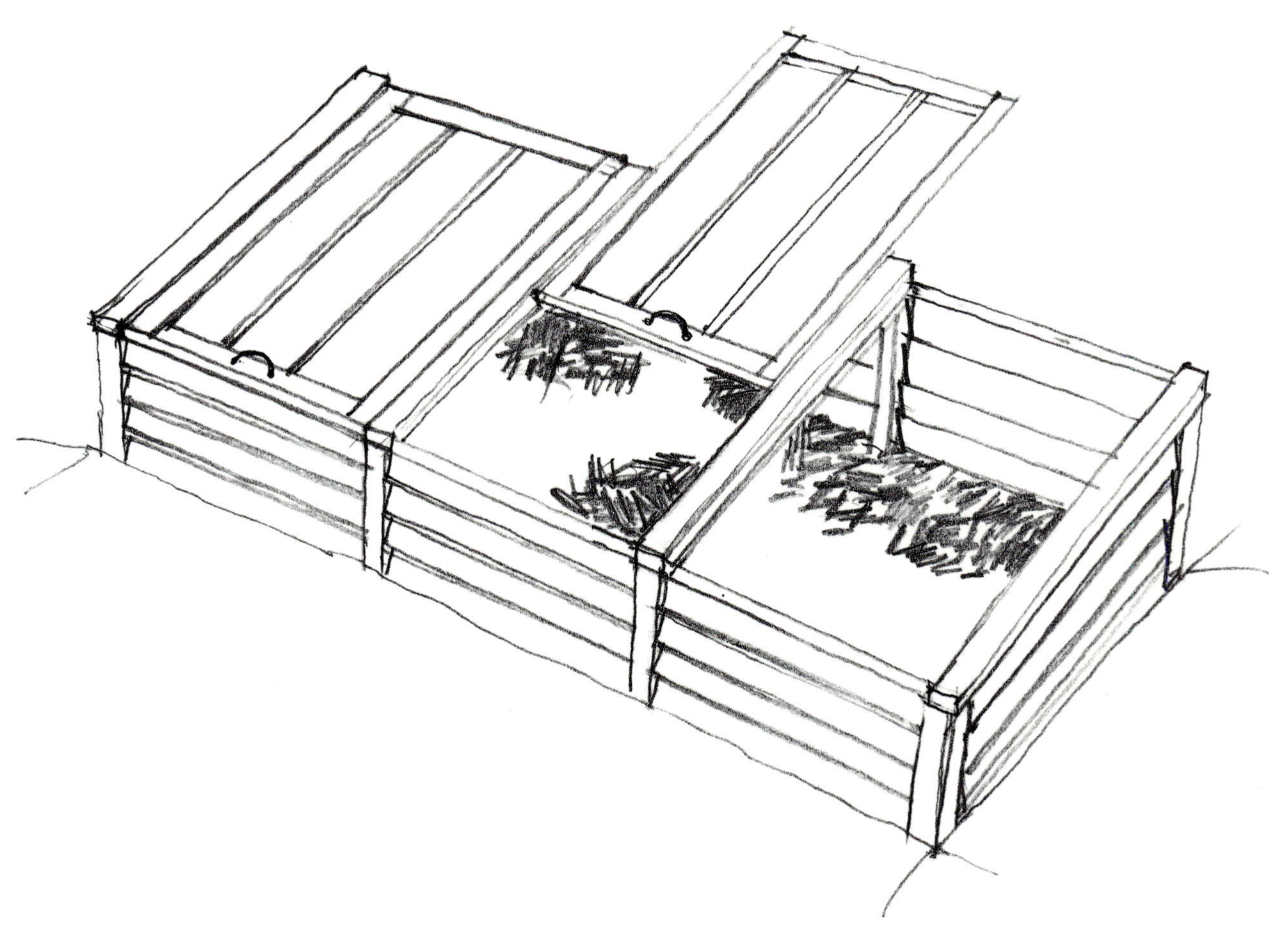

Cold Frame

Tools

- WORKBENCH (fixed or portable)
- STEEL MEASURING TAPE
- STEEL RULE
- TRY SQUARE (or combination square)
- PANEL SAW (or circular power saw)
- TENON SAW
- MARKING GAUGE
- POWER DRILL
- DRILL BIT – approximately 3mm ($\frac{1}{8}$in) diameter
- COUNTERSINK BIT
- SCREWDRIVER
- CLAW HAMMER
- NAIL PUNCH
- PINCERS
- CHISEL – about 25mm (1in)
- MALLET
- SASH CRAMPS (or folding wedges)

Materials

Quantities are for the three-bay frame illustrated

Part	Quantity	Material	Length
Frame Structure			
BOTTOM RAILS	4	50 × 50mm (2 × 2in) sawn and treated softwood	1220mm (48in)*
FRONT POSTS	4	As above	270mm ($10\frac{1}{2}$in)*
BACK POSTS	4	As above	400mm (16in)*
TOP RAILS	4	As above	1230mm ($48\frac{1}{2}$in)*
TOP SUPPORT BATTENS	6	25 × 25mm (1 × 1in) PAR softwood	1230mm ($48\frac{1}{2}$in)
FRONT FIXING BATTENS	6	As above	330mm (13in)*
BACK FIXING BATTENS	6	As above	460mm (18in)*
FRONT & BACK CLADDING	As required	6 × 19 × 150mm ($\frac{1}{4} \times \frac{3}{4}$ × 6in) feather-edge boarding	Width of glazing frame plus clearance
END CLADDING	As required	As above	1120mm (44in)
Glazed Lights			
SIDE RAILS	6	50 × 38mm (2 × $1\frac{1}{2}$in) PAR softwood	1270mm (50in)
TOP RAILS	3	As above	800mm ($31\frac{1}{2}$in)
BOTTOM RAILS	3	75 × 25mm (3 × 1in) PAR softwood	800mm ($31\frac{1}{2}$in)
CENTRAL GLAZING BARS	3	38 × 25mm ($1\frac{1}{2}$ × 1in) PAR softwood	1270mm (50in)
GLASS SUPPORT BATTENS – LONG	12	25 × 12mm (1 × $\frac{1}{2}$in) PAR softwood	1150mm (46in)*
GLASS SUPPORT BATTENS – SHORT	6	As above	400mm (16in)*
GLASS SHEETS	18	Approx. 425 × 400mm (17 × 16in) clear glass	

Also required: 3 D-handles; metal glass clips; mastic for bedding glass; sprigs for holding glass in place; glazed light supports; hinges (optional)

* Leave overlength and then cut to size after fixing – see text

A cold frame will be appreciated by all keen gardeners, whether their speciality is flowers, fruit or vegetables. The frame will be useful for seedlings, propagation and for growing tender and/or early plants.

Our frame has been developed from the tried and tested standard cold frame that has evolved over the years. The main frame is made from sawn and preservative-treated (tanalized) softwood, put together in a series of inset 'bays' clad with feather-edge boarding fixed between the main frames. This gives the frame a distinctive style and avoids the bland appearance of a conventional cold frame. However, you may prefer to run the cladding along the whole length of the frame, which is quicker and easier.

The size of the frame from front to back and end to end is optional and can be varied as you wish according to what you want to grow. Our frame is a good average size, being 370mm ($14\frac{1}{2}$in) high at the front, 500mm (20in) high at the back and 1220mm (48in) from front to back. The beauty of this design is that you can have a single section, or make a block of two, three or more. We have built a three-section frame, and quantities in the Materials chart are for a frame of this size.

The glazed lights in our design are loose, giving flexibility in use. You have the option of sliding them back a little way for ventilation, farther back to tend for plants within the frame, or they can be lifted at the front and propped open a little way for ventilation. Alternatively, they are easy to slide off, either from the front or the back, allowing them to be removed completely. However, you could glaze the lights with sheets of clear plastic, which is also a safer option if young children play in the garden. In this case, you would fix the lights at the back with hinges; you will need a 75 × 50mm (3 × 2in) timber rail along the back, level with the support battens.

Drilling 150
Screwing 150
Skew nailing 151
Butt joint 152

COLD FRAME ASSEMBLY

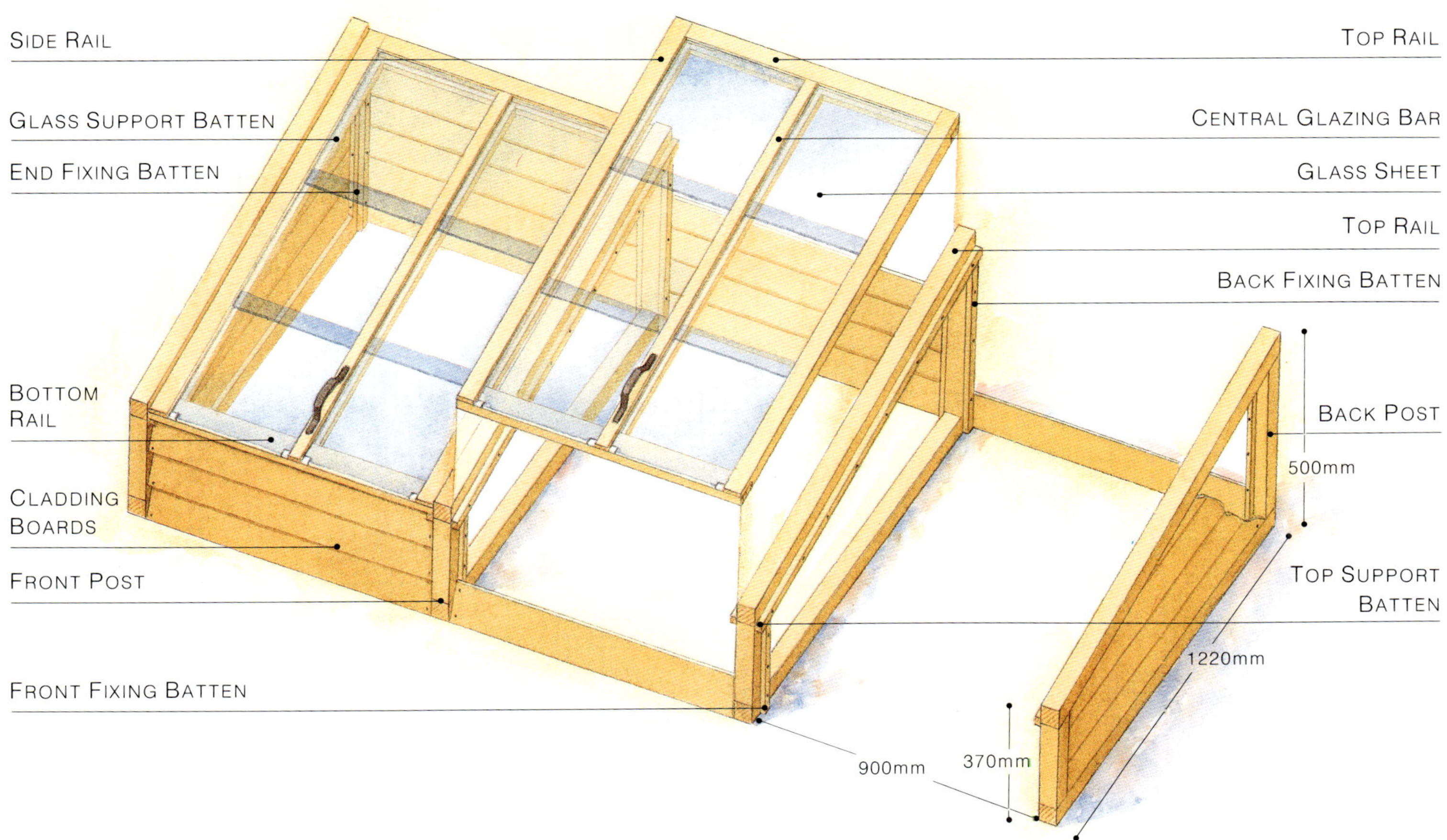

FRAME STRUCTURE

MAKING THE DIVIDERS

The ground frame structure is built around four dividers (if you are making a three-bay cold frame), and construction starts with these. Start by cutting out the four components of the dividers – the top and bottom rails, and the front and back posts – from 50 x 50mm (2 x 2in) sawn softwood all at least 50mm (2in) overlength.

Lay the bottom rail down and mark off its final length centrally on one side. Place the front and back posts in position alongside.

Mark off the final heights of the front and back posts, and then lay the top rail alongside these top marks (with the correct post heights on the outer edges of each) so that the correct angles to cut the tops of the posts can be marked. Cut the posts to length.

Nail up the frame by skew nailing through the bottom and top rails into the posts.

Once the frame has been finished, check it for square, then cut off the 'horns' (protruding ends) of the top and bottom rails so they are flush with the posts. Make up the required number of frames – four in our example.

SUPPORT AND FIXING BATTENS

Place an offcut of the 50 x 38mm (2 x 1½in) glazing frame side rail, 2mm ($\frac{1}{16}$in) down from the upper edge of the top rail to position the top support battens. You will need one on each side of the central dividing frames and on the inner sides of the end frames. Nail them in place, then saw the ends flush with the front and back posts.

Unless you are nailing the cladding in continuous lengths to the front and back of the dividing frames, you will need to nail fixing battens to the front and back posts.

Hold the battens in place so that the tops can be marked at the angle of the top support batten. Cut the battens to this angle, then screw them in place so that they are flush with the inside edges of the front and back posts (fig 1, page 142). Saw the ends of the battens flush with the bottom edge of the bottom rail. Fix side battens on both sides of the dividing frames, and on the inner sides of the end frames.

To support the cladding at the ends, measure internal heights of the front and back posts on the end frame. Cut battens to these lengths and fix to the inside edges of the end frames (fig 2, page 142).

Cold Frame

Glazed Lights

Cut out all the components. Each glazed light frame will require two sides, one top rail, one bottom rail and one central glazing bar (fig 3).

Mark out all the joints as shown (fig 3). The sides are jointed to the top rail using corner halving joints *(see* **Techniques, Halving joint, page 152** *).* The bottom rail is lapped on to the sides so that the bottom rail is on the underside.

The glazing bar is joined to the top rail with a T-halving joint and to the bottom rail with a lap joint on the *opposite* side (the underside) so that it laps on to the bottom rail as shown (fig 3).

Letter all the joints clearly to identify them for assembly, and then cut them all out.

Making up the Glazed Light Frames

Glue all the joints to the top and bottom rails, starting with the central glazing bar. Use a waterproof woodworking adhesive such as Cascamite Turn the frame over so that it can be screwed together from the underside. Use a try square to make sure that the frame is square, and hold it with cramps to keep the joints tight while drilling two pilot holes and a countersink for each of the three top joints. Screw the top joints together.

Drill and screw the bottom corner joints with three screws each. Measure to check that the central glazing bar is central on the bottom rail, then drill two holes and screw the bar to the bottom rail.

Lay the frame on a flat surface and check it is square by measuring the diagonals. Then nail on a bracing batten to keep the frame square while the glue is drying. Clean off any excess glue with a damp cloth and leave the joints to dry.

Repeat the process for the required number of frames – in this case three.

Glass Support Battens

Cut four lengths of 25 x 12mm (1 x $\frac{1}{2}$in) batten to the internal length of the glazing frame and nail them so that they are flush with the underside of the frame.

Then cut two lengths to the internal widths between the side battens at the top. Nail the battens at the top between the two pairs of side battens, with the lower edge flush with the underside of the frame.

Repeat for the other frames.

Cladding

Although we used feather-edge boarding for cladding the frame, other cladding boards could equally well be used – for example, shiplap, tongued-and-grooved, or V-jointed.

For the sides, cut the cladding to the internal dimensions of the end frames. Fix the cladding, working up from the bottom board, nailing into the fixing battens. When using feather-edge boards, the cladding boards should overlap by about 12mm ($\frac{1}{2}$in), and the nails holding the lower edge of each board should pass through the top edge of the board beneath to hold it securely. Use galvanized round head nails. When fixing the end cladding, the top boards must be shaped to the slope of the top rail.

The front and back cladding boards are cut to fit between the dividing frames so that the glazed frames, when fitted, will be a loose fit. You will need to leave enough clearance to allow for the timber to swell when it gets wet. Check that the main dividers are spaced so that there is about 2mm ($\frac{1}{16}$in) clearance between the dividers and the sides of the glazing frames so that they will slide easily.

Nail the cladding boards to the front and back fixing battens, working up from the bottom boards as before. The upper corners at each end of the top boards will have to be notched out so that the cladding boards will fit tightly around the top support battens.

If you are fixing the front and back cladding in a continuous strip, dispense with the front and back fixing battens, and nail the cladding boards directly to the front and back posts of the dividing frames. If the boards are of insufficient length to

1 Fitting the Top Support Batten and Side Fixing Battens

Left **Detail shows spacing block held 2mm ($\frac{1}{16}$in) down from top rail to position top support batten.** ***Below*** **Top support batten runs length of top rail; side fixing battens fit flush with inside edges of front and back posts and are angled at top to fit beneath top support battens.**

2 Fixing End Battens

Cut end panel fixing battens to internal heights of posts, and fit flush to inside edges of frame.

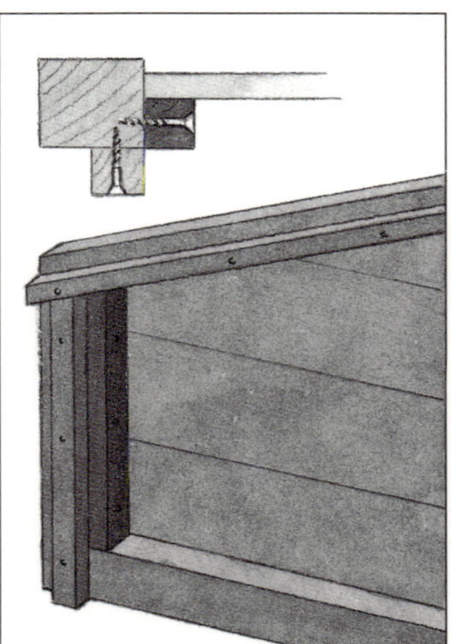

Drilling 150
Nailing 150
Screwing 150
Expanding wall bolt 151
Fixing cladding 151
Butt joint 152
Fitting hinges 152
Halving joint 152

3 Making the Frames for the Glazed Lights
Top **Corner halving joints fit side rails to top rail; T-halving joint fits glazing bar to top rail; lap bottom rail to underside of side rails and glazing bar.** ***Below*** **Glue and screw from underside; bracing batten holds frame square.**

clad the frame in continuous strips, shorter lengths of cladding boards can be used: simply butt joint them together so that the joint coincides with the mid-point of a front or back post. Stagger these joints so they do not line up with joints in boards directly above or below.

Preserving And Finishing Off

It is most important to treat the whole of the frame assembly with at least two coats of clear or green grade wood preservative. When dry, this can then be painted with a micro-porous or exterior gloss paint, or it can be treated with a water-repellent preservative stain if a natural wood colour is required. You must not use creosote or any wood preserver that is harmful to plants.

Fitting the Glass, Handles and Hinges

Have the glass cut to fit the glazed frames. We had ours cut in three sheets on each side, with the bottom sheet feeding first and subsequent sheets overlapping the previously fixed sheet. The bottom sheet is held by small aluminium clips, nailed to the bottom glazing frame rail and bent back over the edge of the glass to prevent it from slipping out. All the sheets are bedded into mastic on the glazing support battens. The glass sheets are held with small nails, called glazing sprigs nailed into the side rails so that they are horizontal and hold the glass down. The bottom edges of the overlapping sheets of glass rest against two glazing sprigs which prevent the sheets from sliding down.

As an alternative to glass, the lights can be glazed with clear plastic sheeting, which is cheaper and much safer. Make sure that you buy purpose-made horticultural plastic which will encourage the plants to thrive and will also prevent premature yellowing and cracking of the plastic. Do *not* buy plastic containing an ultra-violet (UV) inhibitor as nothing will be able to grow in the cold frame.

To make it easier to lift the glazed lights for ventilation and access to the plants, screw a D-handle into the bottom end of the glazing bar.

If the glazed lights are left loose, they can be lifted at the front edge and wedged open with a wooden block for ventilation; the lights can also be slid backwards or forwards to gain access to inside the frame.

Alternatively, the glazed lights can be hinged at the back, and this is a particularly good option when the lights are glazed with plastic and are therefore lighter. In this case, cut a 75 x 50mm (3 x 2in) batten to the total length of the frame and bevel the top edge to allow the glazed light to fold back beyond 90° (so that it will rest open against a wall or fence behind the frame). With the batten level with the top support battens, screw it to the back posts. Then screw hinges into the back edges of the glazing frames, and into the top edge of the bevelled batten (*see* **Techniques, page 152**).

A simple ventilation prop can be made from a 150 x 100 x 50mm (6 x 4 x 2in) timber block with 25mm (1in) steps cut along one edge to allow variable ventilation up to 150mm (6in). Another method is to fix a swing-down prop to hold the glazed light partially open. The prop can be fixed to the underside of the central glazing bar and held out of the way in a spring tool clip when not in use.

If the frame is glazed with plastic lights and hinged at the back, fix hooks and eyes to the front edge of the frame to hold the lights firmly closed in windy conditions.

The frame should be positioned in a sunny place, and can simply be rested on the soil. Alternatively, you could place it on a partially buried row of bricks which will help to keep the timber dry. If the frame is to be permanently sited, it should be placed on a strip of damp-proof course placed on two rows of bricks over a concrete foundation. Fix the frame using expanding wall bolts inserted into the brick foundation through the bottom rails, or you could use metal strips screwed to the foundation and to the inside of the frame structure.

4 Glass Support Battens
Cut side battens to internal lengths of frame and top battens to internal length between side battens.

TOOLS, MATERIALS AND TECHNIQUES: TOOLS

TOOLS FOR PREPARATION

Bench stop and vice A vice is fitted to the underside of a bench, the jaws level with the bench top. The jaws are lined and topped with hardwood to protect the work and any tools being used. Some vices incorporate a small steel peg (a 'dog') that can be raised above the main jaw level. This allows awkward pieces of wood to be cramped in position when used with a bench stop fixed at the opposite end of the bench.

Drill stand Enables a power drill to be used with extreme accuracy when, for example, dowel jointing. The hole will be perpendicular to the surface and its depth can be carefully controlled. The drill is lowered on to the work with a spring-loaded lever which gives good control.

Sliding bevel This is a type of square used to mark out timber at any required angle.

Marking gauge This is used to mark both widths and thicknesses with only a light scratch. The gauge comprises a handle, on which slides a stock bearing a steel marking pin which can be fixed at a precise point.

Mortise gauge Similar to a marking gauge, it has two pins, one fixed, one adjustable, to mark out both sides of a mortise at the same time.

Marking knife Used to score a thin line for a saw or chisel to follow, ensuring a precise cut.

Mitre box A simple open-topped wooden box which is used to guide saws into materials at a fixed 45° or 90° angle, to ensure an accurate cut.

Plumb bob and chalk Used to check or mark accurate vertical lines on walls. A plumb bob is simply a pointed weight attached to a long length of string. The string can be rubbed with a stick of coloured chalk to leave a line on the wall.

Portable workbench A collapsible, portable workbench is vital for woodworking. It is lightweight and can be carried to the job, where it provides sturdy support. A portable bench is like a giant vice – the worksurface comprises two sections which can be opened wide or closed tightly according to the dimensions of the work and the nature of the task.

Spirit level Used for checking that surfaces are horizontal or vertical. A 1000mm (39in) long level is the most useful all-round size. An aluminium or steel level will withstand knocks and it can be either I-girder or box-shaped in section. A 250mm (10in) 'torpedo' spirit level is useful for working in confined spaces and can be used with a straight-edge over longer surfaces.

Steel measuring tape A 3m (3yd) or 5m (5yd) long, lockable tape (metal or plastic) is best, and one with a top window in the casing makes it easier to read measurements.

Steel rule Since the rule is made of steel, the graduations are indelible and very precise. A rule graduated on both sides in metric and imperial is the most useful. The rule also serves as a precise straight-edge for marking cutting lines.

Straight-edge Can be made from a length of 50 × 25mm (2 × 1in) scrap wood. It is used in combination with a spirit level to tell whether a surface is flat and also for checking whether two points are aligned with each other.

Try square An L-shaped precision tool comprising a steel blade and stock (or handle) set at a perfect right angle to each other on both the inside and outside edges. Used for marking right angles and for checking a square.

Combination square A versatile measuring and marking tool comprising a steel rule, try square, mitre square and spirit level.

TOOLS FOR SHARPENING AND CUTTING

Chisels Used to cut slots in wood or to pare off thin slivers. Some chisels may be used with a mallet when cutting slots. When new, a chisel's cutting edge is ground and must be honed with an oilstone to sharpen it before use.
Mortise chisel Used for cutting deep slots.
Firmer chisel For general DIY use.
Bevel-edge chisel Used for undercutting in confined spaces.
Paring chisel Has a long blade for cutting deep joints or long housings.

Dowelling jig Cramps on to a piece of work, ensuring that the drill is aligned over the centre of the dowel hole to be drilled.

DRILLS

Hand drill For drilling holes for screws or for making large holes, particularly in wood. It will make holes in metal and is useful where there is no power source. A handle attached to a toothed wheel is used to turn the drill in its chuck.
Power drill These range from a simple, single-speed model (which will drill holes only in soft materials) to a multi-speed drill with electric control. Most jobs call for something in between, such as a two-speed drill with hammer action.

DRILL BITS

You will need a selection of drill bits in various sizes and of different types for use with a drill.

Auger bit Has a tapered, square shank that fits into a carpenter's brace. It is used to make deep holes in wood, the usual lengths being up to 250mm (10in). Diameters range from 6mm ($\frac{1}{4}$in) to 38mm ($1\frac{1}{2}$in). The tip has a screw thread to draw the bit into the wood.
Countersink bit After a hole is drilled in wood, a countersink bit is used to cut a recess for the screwhead to sit in, so ensuring that it lies below the surface. Different types are available for use with a carpenter's brace or a power drill.
Dowel bit Used to make dowel holes. The top has two cutting spurs on the side and a centre point to prevent the bit from wandering off centre.
End-mill/Hinge-sinker bit Primarily used for boring flat-bottomed holes to accept the hinge bosses on concealed hinges. End-mills are used in electric drills, ideally fitted in drill stands, and should be set to drill no deeper than 12mm ($\frac{1}{2}$in).
Flat bit Is used with a power drill. For maximum efficiency the bit must be turned at high speed from about 1000 to 2000 r.p.m. It drills into cross grain, end grain and man-made boards.
Masonry bit Has a specially hardened tungsten-carbide tip for drilling into masonry to the exact size required for a wallplug. Special percussion drill bits are available for use with a hammer drill when boring into concrete.
Twist drill bit Used with a power drill for drilling small holes in wood and metal.

Power router This portable electric tool is used to cut grooves, recesses, and many types of joints in timber, and to shape the edge of long timber battens. A range of cutting bits in different shapes and sizes is available and when fitted into the router the bits revolve at very high speed.

SAWS

Circular saw For cutting large pieces of timber or sheets of board, as well as grooves and angles. The most popular size has a diameter of 184mm ($7\frac{1}{4}$in). Circular saws can be extremely dangerous and must be used carefully. The piece of work must be held securely, supported on scrap battens, and the blade depth set so that it will not cut into anything below the work. The tool should be fitted with an upper and a lower blade guard.
Coping saw Used to make curved or circular cuts. It has a narrow blade, which can be swivelled. When cutting, the blade can be angled so that the frame clears the edge of the work.
Hacksaw For cutting metal. A traditional hacksaw has a wooden handle and a solid metal frame. The blade is tensioned by a wing-nut. Modern hacksaws have a tubular frame which is adjustable for different lengths of blade.
Jigsaw More versatile than a circular saw, although not as quick or powerful. It cuts curves, intricate shapes, angles and holes in a variety of materials. The best models offer variable speeds.
Padsaw Has a narrow, tapered blade to cut holes and shapes in wood. A hole is drilled and the saw blade is inserted to make the cut.
Panel saw A hand saw used for rough cutting rather than fine carpentry. It has a flexible blade of 510–660mm (20–26in).
Tenon saw For cutting the tenon part of a mortise and tenon joint, and for other delicate work. It has a stiffened back and the blade is about 250–300mm (10–12in) long.

Rasp A coarse file, available with flat or half-round surfaces, used to shape wood.

Surforms Available in a range of lengths from approximately 150–250mm (6–10in), these rasps are useful for the initial shaping of wood. The steel blade has a pattern of alternating small teeth and holes through which waste wood passes, so that the teeth do not get clogged up.

HAND TOOLS

Abrasive paper *see* **Sanding block**

CRAMPS

For securing glued pieces of work while they are setting. There are many types of cramp, but the G-cramp is the most commonly used and is available in a wide range of jaw sizes.

G-cramp Also called a C-cramp or fast-action cramp, it is important for our projects that the jaws of the cramp open at least 200mm (8in). The timber to be held in the cramp is placed between the jaws which are then tightened by turning a thumb-screw, tommy bar or other type of handle. With a fast-action cramp, one jaw is free to slide on a bar, and after sliding this jaw up to the workpiece, final tightening is achieved by turning the handle. To protect the work, scraps of wood are placed between it and the jaws of the cramp.
Sash cramps These employ a long metal bar, and are indispensable for holding together large frameworks, although you can improvise in some cases by making a rope tourniquet. This consists of a piece of rope which is tied around the object, and a length of stick to twist the rope and so cramp the frame tightly.
Webbing cramp The webbing, like narrow seat-belt type material, is looped around the frame, pulled as tight as possible by hand, and then finally tightened by means of a screw mechanism or ratchet winder.

HAMMERS

Claw hammer The claw side of the head of the hammer is used to extract nails from a piece of work, quickly and cleanly.
Cross-pein hammer The pein is the tapered section opposite the flat hammer head, and it is used for starting off small pins and tacks.
Pin hammer A smaller version of the cross-pein; this is useful for light work.

Hand staple gun A trigger-operated tool which fires a staple straight into a surface, usually fabric, fibreboard or thin wood over a wooden batten. Its advantage over conventional pinning with a hammer is that it is used one-handed.

Mallet Most commonly used to strike mortise chisels, although if a chisel has an impact-resistant handle then a hammer may also be used. The tapered wooden head ensures square contact with the object being struck.

Nail and pin punches Used with a hammer to drive nails and pins below the surface so that they are hidden and the holes can be filled.

Orbital sander This gives a fine, smooth surface finish to wood. A gritted sanding sheet is fitted to the sander's base plate. Sheets are graded from coarse to fine, and the grade used depends on the roughness of the surface to be sanded. Orbital sanders produce a great deal of dust, so always wear a mask when using one.

Paintbrushes A set of paintbrushes for painting and varnishing should ideally comprise three sizes – 25mm (1in), 50mm (2in) and 75mm (3in). A better finish is always achieved by matching the size of the brush to the surface – a small brush for narrow surfaces, a large brush for wide areas.

PLANES

Block plane Held in the palm of the hand, it is easy to use for small work and chamfering edges. Also useful for planing end grain.
Jack plane A good all-purpose tool with a long blade used for straightening long edges.
Power plane Finishes timber to precise dimensions. A one-hand model is lightweight and can be used anywhere, whereas the heavier two-hander is intended for workbench use. A power plane will also cut bevels and rebates.
Smoothing plane A general-purpose, hand-held plane for smoothing and straightening surfaces and edges. The plane is about 250mm (10in) long and its blade 50–60mm (2–$2\frac{1}{2}$in) wide. The wider the blade the better the finish on wide timber. There is a fine adjustment for depth of cut and a lever for lateral adjustment.

Sanding block and abrasive paper A sanding block is used with abrasive paper to finish and smooth flat surfaces. The block is made of cork, rubber or softwood and the abrasive paper is wrapped around it. Make sure in doing so that the paper is not wrinkled. Coarse paper is used for a rough surface and fine paper for finishing.

Screwdrivers Come in many shapes and sizes, the main differences being the type of tip (for slotted or cross-point screws), the length, and the shape of the handle, which varies from straight or fluted to bulb-shaped.

Ideally, you should have a range of screwdrivers for dealing with all sizes of screws. Ratchet models, which return the handle to its starting point, are easy to operate since your hand grip does not need to change.

Spanner A spanner is required for tightening coach-bolts, and any type that fits the head of the bolt is suitable. If the correct-size open-ended or ring spanner is not available, any type of adjustable spanner may be used.

Materials

Timber and Boards

Timber This is classified into two groups – softwoods and hardwoods. Softwoods come from evergreen trees and hardwoods from deciduous trees. Check your timber for defects before buying it. Avoid wood which is badly cracked or split, although you need not be concerned about fine, surface cracks since these can be planed, sanded or filled. Do not buy warped wood, as it will be impossible to work with Check for warping by looking along the length of a board to see if there is any bowing or twisting

Wood for outdoor projects must be protected from rot and insect attack. It can be bought pre-treated with preservative, but this is expensive and not always readily available. Alternatively, you can buy untreated wood and treat it, as soon as possible, with one of the finishes described here. Pay special attention to end grain and to posts which will be buried below ground – a double coating is a good idea here.

Softwood Although usually referred to as 'deal' or 'pine', it comes from many different sources. Softwood is much less expensive than hardwood and is used in general building work. It is sold in a range of standard sizes. After 1.8m (6ft), lengths rise in 300mm (12in) increments up to 6.3m (20ft 8in). Standard thicknesses are from 12mm (½in) up to 75mm (3in) and widths range from 25mm (1in) to 225mm (9in).

It is important to remember that standard softwood sizes refer to sawn sizes – that is, how it is sawn at a mill. Sawn timber is suitable for most of the projects in this book. However, where a smooth finish is specified, where appearance and accuracy are important, it will need to be planed. Such wood is referred to as PAR (planed all round), and, since planing takes a little off each face, it is approximately 5mm (3/16in) smaller in width and thickness than stated.

Hardwood Expensive and not as easy to obtain as softwoods, hardwoods often have to be ordered or bought from a specialist timber merchant. Many timber yards will machine hardwood to your exact specification.

Boards Mechanically made from wood and other fibres, they are versatile, relatively inexpensive, made to uniform quality and available in large sheets. You need to know the advantages of each type of board before making your choice.

Plywood Made by gluing thin wood veneers together in plies (layers) with the grain in each ply running at right angles to that of its neighbours. This gives it strength and helps prevent warping. The most common boards have three, five or seven plies. Plywood is graded for quality: A is perfect; B is average; and BB is for rough work only. Usual thicknesses of plywood are 3mm, 6mm, 12mm and 19mm (⅛in, ¼in, ½in and ¾in). WBP (weather and boil proof) grade board must be used for exterior work.

Blockboard Made by sandwiching natural timber strips between wood veneers, the latter usually of Far Eastern redwood or plain birch. Although plain birch is a little more expensive than redwood it is of a much better quality. Blockboard is very strong, but can leave an ugly edge when sawn, making edge fixings difficult. Blockboard is graded in the same way as plywood and common thicknesses are 12mm, 19mm and 25mm (½in, ¾in and 1in).

Tongued-and-grooved boarding Also called match boarding, or matching, this is widely used for cladding frameworks. The boarding has a tongue on one side and a slot on the other side. The tongue fits into the slot of the adjacent board; this join expands and contracts according to temperature and humidity without cracks opening up between boards. Make sure you use exterior grade boarding for outdoor projects.

Feather-edge boards These taper from a thick edge across to a thin edge. When fixed in place, the thick edge of one board overlaps the thin edge of the next board.

Adhesives and Fillers

Adhesives Modern adhesives are strong and efficient. If they fail, it is because the wrong adhesive is being used or the manufacturer's instructions are not being followed carefully. For outdoor woodworking, you must always use either a synthetic resin adhesive that is mixed with water (this has gap-filling properties, so is useful where joints are not cut perfectly) or a two-part epoxy resin adhesive where the parts are applied separately to the surfaces being joined.

Fillers For outside work, always use an exterior grade filler which has been specially formulated to withstand the natural movement of cracks and holes caused by weather changes.

If the wood is to be painted over, use an exterior cellulose filler. This dries white and will be evident if used under any other kind of finish. When a clear finish is needed, fill cracks and holes with a proprietary wood filler or stopping. These are thick pastes and come in a range of wood colours. You can mix them together or add a wood stain if the colour you want is not available. Choose a colour slightly paler than the surrounding wood, since fillers tend to darken when the finish is applied. Some experimentation may be needed on a waste piece of matching wood.

Finishes

The choice of finish is determined by whether the wood or board is to be hidden, painted or enhanced by a protective clear finish.

Paint A liquid gloss (oil-based) paint is suitable for wood, and is applied after undercoat. Generally, two thin coats of gloss are better than one thick coat. Non-drip gloss is an alternative. It has a jelly-like consistency and does not require an undercoat, although a second coat may be needed for a quality finish. If you intend to spray the paint, you must use a liquid gloss.

Microporous paint This is applied directly to the wood – neither primer nor undercoat is needed. The coating will not flake or blister as the special formulation allows trapped moisture to evaporate. If applied over old gloss paint, it will lose the quality that prevents flaking or blistering.

Preservative Unless timber has been pre-treated with preservative and it is not to receive an alternative decorative finish, you must use a coat of preservative. Modern water-based preservatives are harmless to plant life. They are available in clear, green and a number of natural wood colours. The preservative sinks well into the wood, preventing rot and insect attack.

Varnish For outdoor use, you must always use an exterior grade varnish – stated on the container – or a yacht varnish. It is available as a gloss, satin or matt finish, all clear. Varnish also comes in a range of colours, so that you can change the colour of the wood and protect it simultaneously. The colour does not sink into the wood, so if the surface becomes scratched or marked then its original colour will show through. A wood stain or dye can be used to change the colour of wood. It sinks into the wood, but offers no protection, so varnish is also needed.

CONCRETE

Concrete Made by mixing Portland cement and ballast (a mixture of sand and aggregates) with water. The usual mix for paths, bases and foundations is one part cement to four parts ballast. Although concrete mix is available dry-mixed in bags, it is only economically viable for small jobs. Concrete can be mixed by hand, but it is an arduous task, and it is advisable to hire a small electric mixer.

Precast concrete paving slabs These come in a range of shapes and sizes with 450mm square (18in square) being the most popular, since anything larger is difficult to handle. There is a limited range of colours, and surface finishes are smooth, patterned or textured. Thicknesses are usually 35–40mm (about 1½in).

Bricks and **Mortar** *see* **Techniques: Bricklaying, pages 156–7**

DIVIDERS

Fences Required principally to mark boundaries and to create privacy and security. Among the most popular types are:
Vertical closeboard A solid, secure fence which can be of any height. Feather-edge boards are nailed to horizontal arris rails which, in turn, are fixed to timber or solid concrete posts.
Waney-edged panels Pre-fabricated panels made from larch or pine planks which overlap horizontally. The panels are normally 1800mm (72in) wide and 600–1800mm (24–72in) high, and are fixed to timber or concrete support posts.
Palisade Vertical timber pales (stakes) nailed to arris rails at 50mm (2in) intervals and in turn fixed to timber posts. Pales can have ornate or square tops. Heights vary, but 900mm (36in) is the most popular. Usually used for front gardens.
Ranch-style Horizontal timber rails nailed at intervals to timber posts. A two-rail fence is usually about 1000mm (39in) high; a four-rail fence is about 1300mm (51in) high.
Chain link A secure fence, 900–3600mm (36–144in) high. The metal mesh can be galvanized or plastic-coated. Posts are iron or concrete.
Plastic wire Ornamental fencing commonly used to mark a boundary or surround a fish pond or herbaceous border. The fencing can be fixed directly into the ground, but it should be fixed to posts if it is over 600mm (24in) high. It is sold in rolls and cut to the required length.

Rustic poles Hazel, birch or chestnut poles are available from garden centres. Diameters generally range from 50–125mm (2–5in). You will need the larger sizes for main uprights and bearers and the thinner ones for cross beams. The poles have bark attached; this will peel off in own time.

Trellising Square trellis is available in panel heights from 600–1220mm (24–48in) and in 1800mm (72in) long sections. The squares are each about 150mm (6in) and the trellis is made from hardwood battens. Diamond trellis comes in heights from 300–1220mm (12–48in) and lengths of 1800mm (72in).

FIXINGS

The choice of fixing depends on the size and weight of the materials being fixed.

Nails For general-purpose frame construction.
Round wire nails With large, flat, circular heads, these are used for strong joins where frames will be covered, so that the ugly appearance of the nails does not matter.
Annular ring-shank nails Used where really strong fixings are required.
Round lost-head nails or **oval brads** (*oval wire nails*) Used when the finished appearance is important.
Panel pins For fixing thin panels, these have unobtrusive heads that can be driven in flush with the wood's surface or punched below it.
Masonry nails For fixing timber battens to walls as an alternative to screws and wallplugs.

Screws All types of screws are available with conventional slotted heads or cross-point heads. The latter are the best type to use if you are inserting screws with an electric screwdriver.

For most purposes, screws with countersunk heads are ideal as the head lies flush with the surface after insertion. Round-head screws are for fixing metal fittings such as door bolts, which have punched-out rather than countersunk screw holes. Raised-countersunk head screws are used where a neat appearance is important.
Wood screws These have a length of smooth shank just below the head. This produces a strong cramping effect, but there is a possibility of the unthreaded shank splitting the wood.
Twin-thread screws Less likely to split wood than wood screws. Except for larger sizes, they are threaded along their entire length, giving an excellent grip in timber and boards.

Coach screws For heavy-duty fixings when making frameworks requiring a strong construction. The screws have square or hexagonal heads and are turned with a spanner. A washer is used to prevent the head cutting into the timber.

Wallplugs Use a masonry drill bit to drill a hole which matches the size of screw being used (a No 10 bit with a No 10 screw, for example). Insert the plug in the hole, then insert the screw through the object being fixed and into the plug.

Wall anchor bolt Similar to a wallplug, but with its own heavy-duty machine screw. You need to make a much larger hole in the wall, typically 10mm (⅜in) in diameter. The anchor sleeve expands in the hole as the bolt is tightened.

Expanding wall bolt This comprises a segmented body which expands as the bolt inside it is tightened. The body grips concrete, brick or stone securely. There are various lengths and diameters and there are also versions containing a hook or an eye. Most bolts are zinc-plated, but aluminium bronze versions are available where greater resistance to corrosion is required.

Corrugated fasteners For strengthening glued joints in frameworks. Sizes are 6–22mm (¼–⅞in) deep and 22–30mm (⅞–1¼in) long.

Staples A useful means for quickly anchoring plastic mesh fencing to timber posts.

Battens A general term used to describe a narrow strip of wood. The usual sizes are 25 × 25mm (1 × 1in) or 50 × 25mm (2 × 1in).

Battens can be screwed to a wall to serve as bearers for shelves or they can be fixed in a framework on a wall, with sheet material or boards mounted over them to form a new 'wall'.

Dowels Used to make framework joints or to join boards edge-to-edge or edge-to-face.

Hardwood dowels are sold in diameters ranging from 6–10mm (¼–⅜in). Generally speaking, dowel lengths should be about one-and-a-half times the thickness of the boards being joined.

Dowels are used with adhesive and, when the joint is complete, it is important to let excess adhesive escape from the joint. Dowels with fluted (finely grooved) sides and chamfered ends will help this process. If you have plain dowels, make fine sawcuts along the length yourself.

Techniques: Sawing and Cutting

Measuring and Marking Square

Mark the cutting lines lightly with a hard pencil first, and then use a marking knife, straight–edge or try square along a steel rule to create a sharp, splinter-free line.

To mark timber square, use a try square with the stock (handle) pressed against a flat side of the timber, called the face side or face edge. Mark a line along the square, using a knife in preference to a pencil, then use the square to mark lines down the edges from the face mark. Finally square the other face side, checking that the lines join up right around the timber.

If you are measuring and marking a number of pieces of the same length, then cramp them together and mark across several of them at the same time.

Spacing Batten

This is simply an offcut of wood, about 19mm or 25mm square ($\frac{3}{4}$in or 1in square), which is used to ensure that any slats to be fixed across a frame are spaced an equal distance apart. To ascertain the length to cut the spacing batten, simply bunch all the slats at one end of the frame. Measure to the other end of the frame and divide by the number of spaces (which you can count while you have the slats laid side by side). The resulting measure is the length to cut the spacing batten, which is used to position each slat exactly.

Bracing

When making a frame, it is vital that it should be square, with corners at perfect right angles. You can ensure this by using one of two bracing methods.

3-4-5-method Measure three units along one rail, four units down the adjacent rail, then nail a bracing batten accurately to one of the unit marks. Pull into square so that the bracing batten measures five units at the other unit mark, forming the hypotenuse of the triangle. Saw off the batten ends flush with the frame, but do not remove the batten until the frame is fitted in place.

Try square method Nail a batten into one rail, pull into square by using a try square, and then nail the batten into the adjacent rail.

Making Folding Wedges

Folding wedges are very useful for cramping large frames on a bench top during assembly. The wedges are always used in pairs, but more than one pair may be used to hold a large framework.

Make each pair of wedges from a piece of timber (hardwood is an ideal material for this) measuring 38 × 38 × 330mm ($1\frac{1}{2} \times 1\frac{1}{2} \times 13$in). Make the wedges by sawing the timber diagonally into two pieces.

To use the wedges, a wooden batten is first nailed to the bench and the item to be cramped is placed against the batten. Another batten is nailed to the bench, parallel with the first, and about 45mm ($1\frac{3}{4}$in) away from the item. The wedges are now placed between the item and the second batten. Next, the ends of the wedges are knocked inwards with two hammers, thereby cramping the frame.

Sawing and Cutting

Cross-cutting to length by hand Hold the timber firmly with the cutting line (*see* **Measuring and Marking Square,** above) overhanging the right-hand side of the bench (if you are right-handed). With the saw blade vertical and the teeth on the waste side of the line, draw the handle back to start the cut. To prevent the saw jumping out of place, as you start hold the thumb joint of the other hand against the side of the saw blade.

Rip-cutting by hand With the timber or board supported at about knee height, start the cut as described above, then saw down the waste side of the line, exerting pressure on the down cut only. If the saw blade wanders from the line, cramp the edge of a timber batten exactly above the cutting line on the side to be retained, and saw along it.

Using a portable power saw If the cutting line is only a short distance from a straight edge, adjust

1 Marking Timber to Length and Square All Round
Mark across the face of the timber with a trimming knife held against a try square blade. Move knife around corners and mark sides, and finally mark other side to join up the lines.

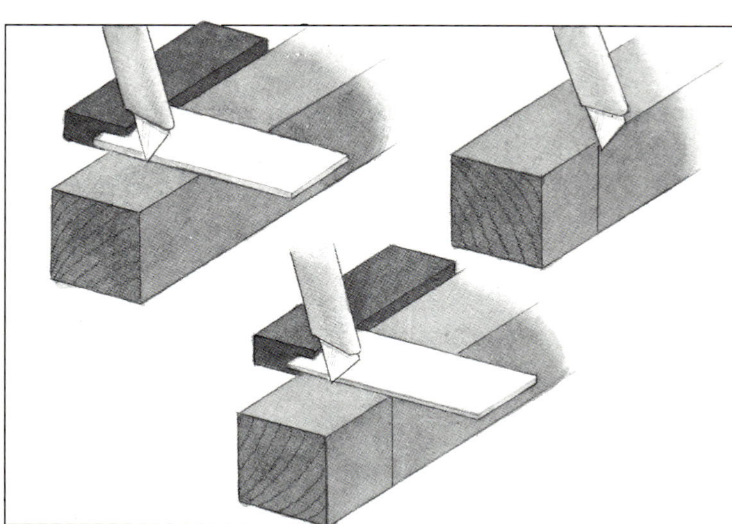

2 Using Spacing Battens
Measure distance from bunched slats to frame end. Divide by number of spaces to get spacing batten size.

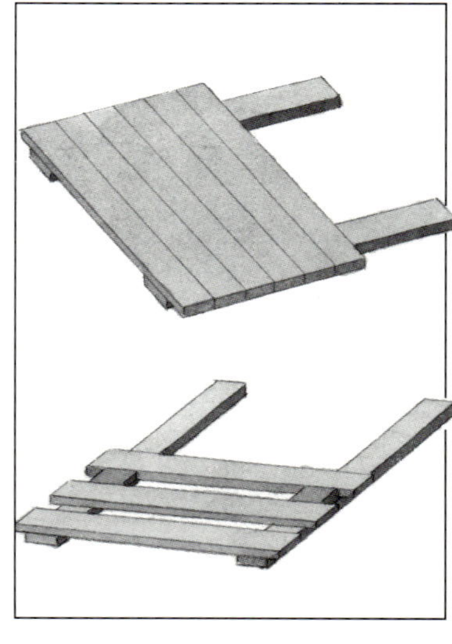

3 Making Folding Wedges
Saw wood diagonally. Nail batten to bench; wedges fit between batten and item being cramped.

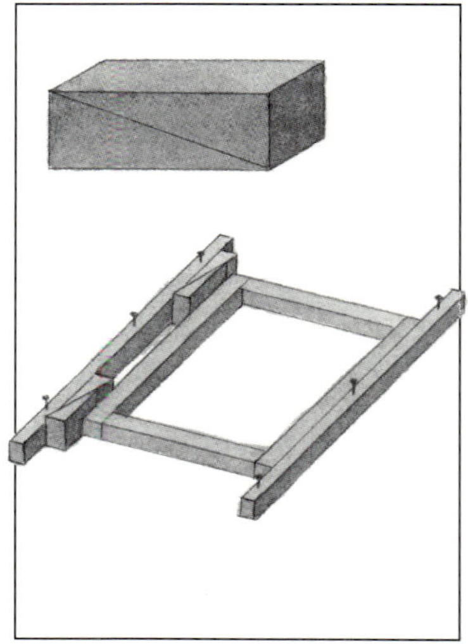

the saw's fence so that when it is run along the edge of the timber, the blade will cut on the waste side of the cutting line. If the timber is wide, or the edge is not straight, cramp a batten to the surface so that the saw blade will cut on the waste side of the line when run along the batten.

Ensuring a straight cut When cutting panels or boards using a power circular saw or jigsaw, the best way to ensure a straight cut is to cramp a guide batten to the surface of the work, parallel with the cutting line, so the edge of the saw sole plate can be run along the batten. The batten position is carefully adjusted so that the saw blade cuts on the waste side of the cutting line. Depending on which side of the cutting line the batten is cramped, when using a circular saw, it is possible the motor housing will foul the batten or G-cramps used to hold it in place. In this case, replace the batten with a wide strip of straight-edged plywood cramped to the work far enough back for the motor to clear the cramps.

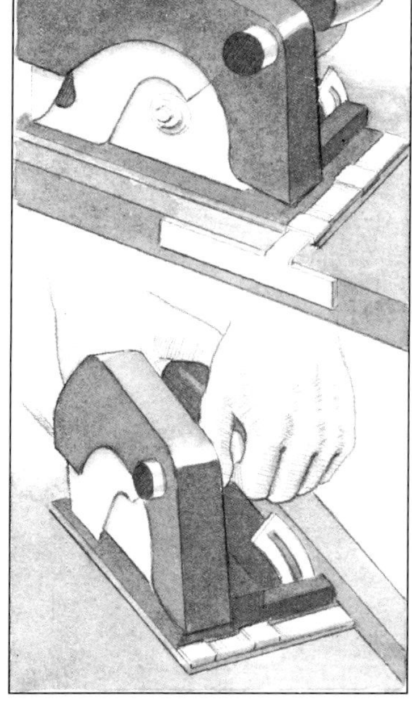

5 Straight Power-Saw Cutting
Top **Use the rip fence of the saw if cutting near the edge.** ***Above*** **Cutting alongside the batten as a guide for obtaining a straight cut.**

CUTTING A CIRCLE

With a coping saw Mark out the circle, score the cutting line, and drill a hole about 10mm ($\frac{3}{8}$in) in diameter just on the inside of the circle. Disconnect the blade from one end of the frame, pass the blade through the hole, and re-connect it to the frame. It will be best to cramp the piece of work vertically when cutting the circle. The blade can be turned in the frame to help the frame clear the piece of work, but even so, with a coping saw you will be restricted in exactly how far you are able to reach away from the piece of work. If the circle is some way from the edge, use a padsaw to cut it.

With a padsaw A padsaw, also called a keyhole saw, has a stiff, triangular pointed saw blade attached to a simple handle. A very useful padsaw blade is available for fitting in a regular knife handle.

Because this saw has no frame, it is ideal for cutting circles and other apertures, like keyholes, anywhere in a panel.

Preparation of the circle for cutting is the same as for a coping saw. When cutting with a padsaw, keep the blade vertical and make a series of rapid, short strokes without exerting too much pressure.

CUTTING GROOVES

By hand Start by marking out the groove with a marking knife. Hold the piece of work on a bench and, with a tenon saw, make vertical cuts just inside the marked lines to the depth of the groove. If the groove is wide, make a series of other vertical cuts in the waste wood. Now chisel out the waste, working from each side to the middle. Finally, with the flat side of the chisel downwards, pare the bottom of the groove so that it is perfectly flat.

With a router Use a straight-sided router bit set to the depth required for the groove. Ideally, the bit should be the exact width of the groove. Make the cut along the waste side of the line with a batten cramped in place to guide the base of the router.

4 Cross-cutting to Length
Hold the timber firmly. Steady the saw blade with the thumb joint as you start to saw.

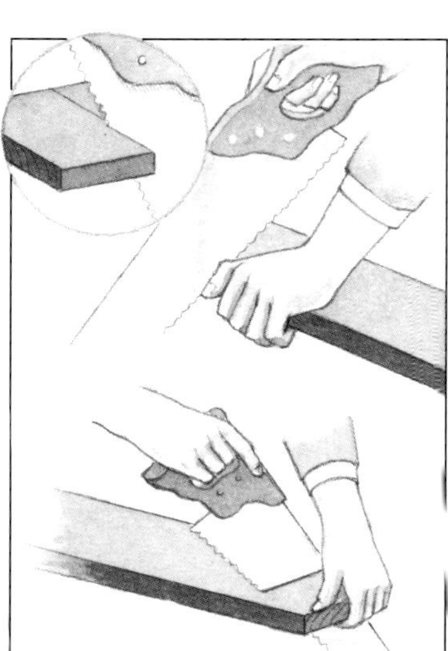

6 Cutting with a Tenon Saw
Start the cut as for a hand saw. As the cut progresses keep the blade horizontal.

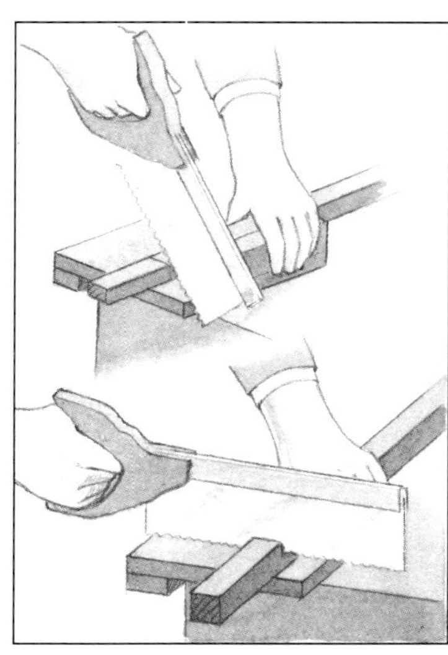

7 Straight Rip-cutting
Cramp a straight batten alongside the cutting line and saw beside the batten. A wedge holds the cut open.

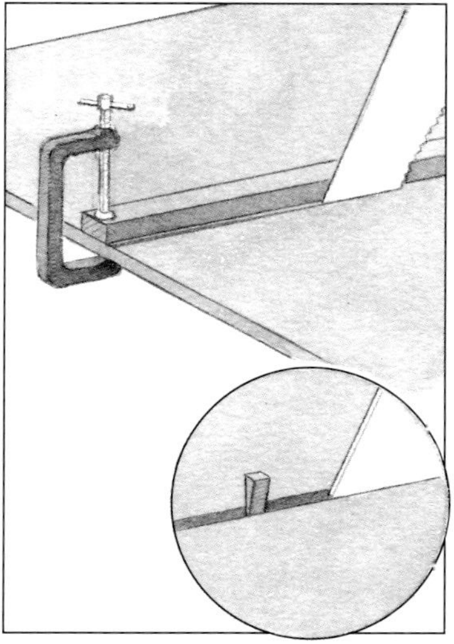

8 Cutting Circles by Hand
1 **Drill a small hole and cut circle using a padsaw.** ***2*** **Making cut with a coping saw.**

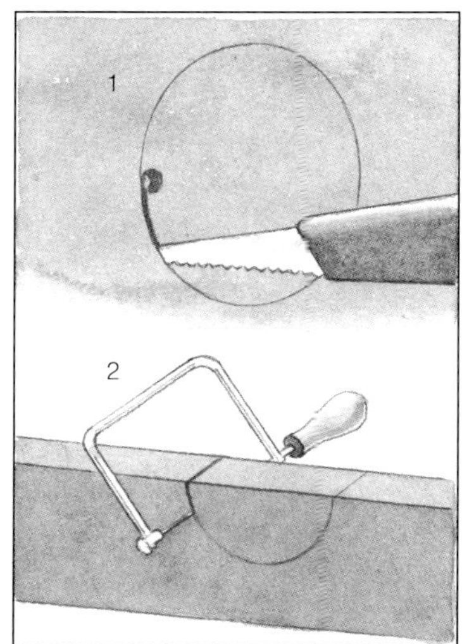

TECHNIQUES: DRILLING AND FIXINGS

CUTTING REBATES

A rebate is an L-shaped step in the edge of a piece of timber.

By hand Use a marking gauge to mark the rebate width across the top face of the piece of work and down both sides. Mark the depth of the rebate across the end and sides.

Hold the timber flat and saw down on the waste side of the marked line to the depth of the rebate. Chisel out the waste one bit at a time along the end grain.

With a router It is not necessary to mark out the rebate unless you want a guide to work to. However, do practise on scrap wood to be sure of setting the router correctly.

If using a straight cutter, adjust the guide fence on the router so that the correct width is cut, then plunge and adjust the cutting depth so that the router will cut to the correct depth. When the router is correctly set up, simply hold it flat on the piece of work and move it against the direction of the cutter's rotation.

If you are using a cutter with a guide pin, simply adjust the depth of cut and then run the cutter along the edge of the wood to form the rebate. The cutter will follow irregularities in the wood, so make sure your wood is perfectly straight.

PLANING

By hand Make sure that the plane blade is sharp and properly adjusted. Stand to one side of the work with feet slightly apart so you are facing the work. Plane from one end of the work to the other, starting the cut with firm pressure on the leading hand, transferring it to both hands, and finally to the rear hand as the cut is almost complete. Holding the plane at a slight angle to the direction of the grain may improve the cutting action.

With a power plane Remove loose clothing, and wear goggles and a dust mask. Cramp the work in place. Start the plane and turn the adjuster knob to set the depth. Start with a shallow cut and increase the depth if necessary.

Stand comfortably to one side of the work and, holding the plane with two hands, set it into the work at one end and pass it over the surface to the other end. When you have finished, switch off and make sure the blades stop spinning before resting the plane down with the cutting depth at zero.

DRILLING

To minimize the risk of splitting timber, drill pilot and clearance holes for screws.

The **clearance hole** in the timber should be fractionally smaller in diameter than the screw shank.

The **pilot hole** to receive the screw should be about half the diameter of the clearance hole. The hole depth should be slightly less than the length of the screw.

To ensure that screwheads lie level with the surface of plywood, chipboard and hardwood use a **countersink drill bit**.

Drilling vertical holes To ensure vertical holes mount the drill in a stand. If this is not possible, stand a try square on edge so that its stock is resting on the work alongside the drilling position, and the blade is pointing up in the air. Use this as a siting guide and line up the drill as close as possible with the square to ensure the drill is vertical. It is also helpful if an assistant can stand back and sight along the drill and square from two sides to ensure the drill is straight.

SCREWING

When screwing one piece of wood to another ensure that half of the screw penetrates through the bottom piece of wood. Its thickness should not exceed one-tenth of the width of the wood into which it has to be inserted. Keep screws at a distance of five times their shank diameter from the side edge of the wood, and ten times the shank diameter from its end.

NAILING

The correct length of nail to use is two-and-a-half to three times the thickness of the timber being fixed. However, check that the nail will not

1 Chiselling a Groove
After making saw cuts at side, chisel out waste from each side. Finally pare base flat.

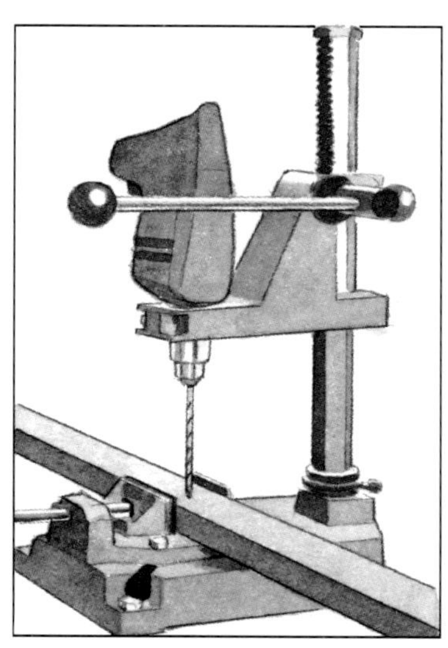

2 Drilling Vertical Holes
With a drill stand, not only will the drill bit be held vertical, but depth is controlled.

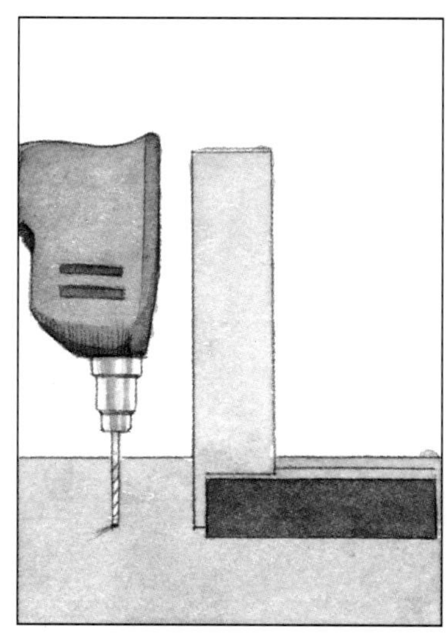

3 Freehand Drilling Guide
When drilling it can be helpful to stand a try square alongside the drill to ensure accuracy.

4 Drilling Depth Guide
There are various guides to control drilling depths, such as rings for drills and sticky tape.

pierce right through two pieces being fixed. Wherever possible nail through the thinner piece of wood into the thicker piece.

Nails grip best if driven in at an angle ('skew nailing'). A row of nails should be driven in at opposing angles to each other. Framework joints are usually held in by skew nailing. Cramp or nail a block of wood temporarily against one side of the vertical piece to stop it sliding as the first nail is started.

To prevent wood from splitting, particularly if nailing near an edge, blunt the points of the nails by hitting them with a hammer before driving them home. Blunt nails will cut through timber fibres neatly, while pointed nails are more likely to push the fibres apart like a wedge.

FIXINGS

Solid wall The normal fixing for a solid wall is a woodscrew and plastic or fibre wallplug. Before drilling the fixing hole, check with a metal detector that there are no pipes or cables hidden below the surface. Drill the holes for the wallplug with a **masonry drill bit** in an electric drill. The wallplug packing will indicate the drill size to use. Switch to hammer action if the wall is hard. The screw should be long enough to go through the fitting and into the wall by about 25mm (1in) if the masonry is exposed, and by about 35mm (1$\frac{3}{8}$in) if fixing into a rendered wall.

6 Skew Nailing for Strength
Hold the frames together in a cramp and join them by skew nailing (driving nails at an angle). The joint will not then pull apart.

If the wall crumbles when you drill into it, mix up a cement-based plugging compound (available from DIY stores). Turn back the screw by about half a turn before the compound sets (in about five minutes). When it is hard (in about one hour) the screw is removed and a heavy fixing made.

If your drill sinks easily into the wall once it has penetrated the rendering, and a light grey dust is produced from the hole, you are fixing into lightweight building blocks. In this case, special winged wallplugs should be used.

To make a quick, light-to-medium weight fixing in a solid wall, a masonry nail can be used. Choose a length that will penetrate the material to be fixed, and pierce an exposed masonry wall by 15mm ($\frac{5}{8}$in) or a rendered wall by about 25mm (1in). Wear goggles in case the nail snaps when you strike it; hammer it gently through the material to be fixed and into the wall.

Expanding wall bolts In rugged construction work, wall fixings are made with expanding bolts. The hole drilled in the wall must be deep enough to accept the segmented body of the bolt. Check the manufacturer's instructions for the exact diameter of the hole. The body of the bolt is placed in the hole, the bolt passed through the fixture to locate in the body, and then the nut of the bolt turned with a spanner, expanding the segmented body and causing it to grip tightly.

Fixing cladding Always fix cladding boards from the bottom upwards. Use a spirit level to check that the first board is horizontal – if it is not exactly level, the boards above will start to run out of true, making it impossible to fix them.

5 Drilling Holes for Screws in Timber
Drill a clearance hole in the thinner piece. Countersink this hole, then drill a pilot hole to slightly less than screw length. *Inset* To counterbore, drill to the diameter of the screw head to required depth, then as above.

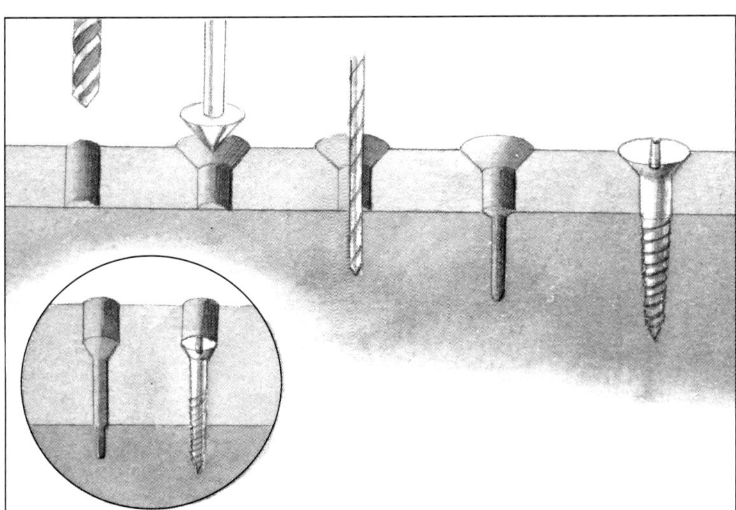

7 Techniques for Joining Wood by Nailing
Nails should be two-and-a-half to three times the thickness of the timber being fixed. Assemble frames on bench by nailing against batten. *Inset* Blunt nail points to avoid splitting timber.

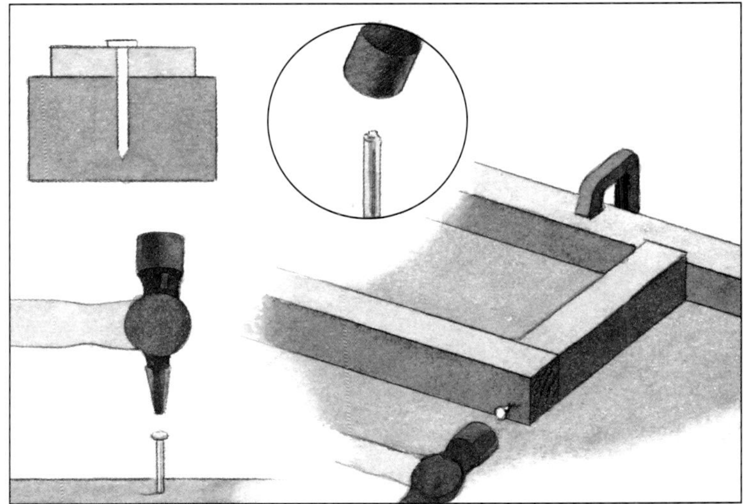

TECHNIQUES: FIXINGS AND WOOD JOINTS

Nail through the centre of the first board into each of the vertical support battens behind, using 25mm (1in) galvanized round head nails. If boards have to be joined to span the full width of the structure, then butt the edges closely and ensure that joints are always made against a vertical support batten.

If you are fixing feather-edge boards, it is important that they overlap uniformly and you will need to use a spacing block cut from a spare piece of wood. If the boards are 112mm (4½in) wide and the spacer is 100mm (4in) wide then, by aligning the spacer with the bottom edge of the previously fixed board and resting the overlapping board on top, you will get a consistent overlap of 12mm (½in). Nail through the lower edge of each board, into the top edge of the board it overlaps and through into the batten.

Tongued-and-grooved boards are fixed by driving the nail at an angle through the tongue and tapping the head below the surface. The groove of the next board slides over the tongue to conceal the nail.

Shiplap cladding is fixed in the same way except that the boards do not interlock, but simply overlap.

Fixing trellis Trellis should be fixed about 150mm (6in) clear of the ground so that it will not rot at the base. Stand the trellis on blocks of the correct height while it is being secured to timber uprights or a wall. Use a spirit level to check that the horizontal rails are true, then drill holes into the side uprights of the trellis through which galvanized nails are inserted and then driven into the posts behind. If you nail directly into the trellis there is a chance the wood will split. Three fixings either side of an 1800mm (72in) high trellis panel will suffice. Alternatively, use purpose-made clips screwed to support posts. The trellis panel slots into clips.

When fixing to a wall, use 25mm (1in) thick wood blocks behind each fixing point to keep the trellis clear. Pre-drill the holes and use about 75mm (3in) long No 8 or 10 zinc-plated screws and wallplugs to secure the trellis.

Fixing posts and poles On concrete paths and paving slabs laid on mortar you can use a steel base as a fixing point for posts. The base is a square plate with a projecting cup into which the post is located. The base is bolted in place.

Metal post spikes are driven into the earth. Again, the post fits into a square cup and is cramped in place. As the post is above ground it is far less susceptible to rotting at the base.

Posts and poles can be fixed directly into soil. In firm soil and where shorter posts are used, then well-compacted hardcore is usually adequate support. In loose soil and for longer posts and poles, a combination of stones and concrete should be used. For a post 1800mm (72in) high, at least 600mm (24in) should be buried below ground.

Fitting Hinges

Butt hinges These are conventional flapped hinges and are available in steel (commonly) or in brass, which is better for high-quality work. They are relatively simple to fix in place, except that the hinge flaps have to be recessed into the timber using a chisel or router.

Mark out the hinge positions on the frame of the item to be hung, making sure that the hinges are not positioned so that the fixing screws will go into the end grain of cross members and be likely to pull out.

The length of the hinges is marked out first, using a marking knife, then the width of the hinge and the thickness of the flap are marked using a marking gauge. With a chisel held vertical, and a mallet, cut down around the waste side of the recess, then make a series of vertical cuts across the full width of the recess. Remove the waste by careful chiselling, then finally pare the bottom of the recess flat using the chisel held flat side downwards (fig 4).

If you are careful, you can remove the bulk of the waste from a hinge recess using a straight bit fitted in a router. The bit is set to cut to the depth of the recess required, and afterwards the corners can be finished off using a chisel.

1 Fixing Cladding
Above **Nail tongue, then slot groove of next board over.** ***Below*** **Use spacing block for feather-edge boards.**

2 Fixing Posts
Left and top right **Post spikes fix posts in place.** ***Below right*** **Post hole borer digs hole in which to fix post.**

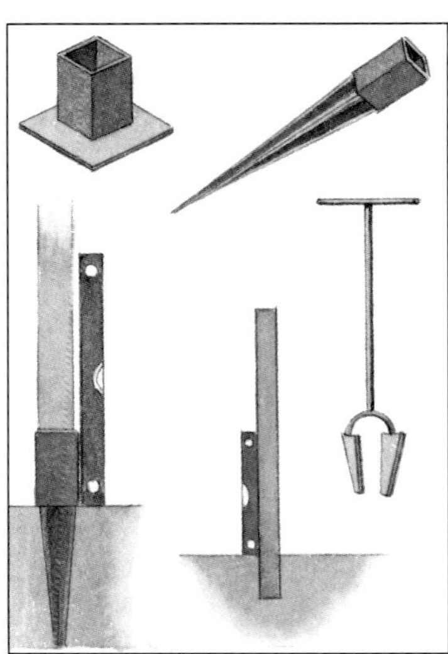

3 Fixing Trellis Panels
Panel clips are screwed to vertical support posts. Trellis panels slot into clips and are screwed in place.

Wood Joints

Butt joint This is the simplest frame joint of all. The ends of the timbers to be joined must be cut square so that they butt together neatly. Corner and T joints can be formed, which are glued and nailed for strength. Corrugated fasteners can also be used to hold these joints, especially where the sides of the frames will be covered to hide the fasteners. When T joints are being formed from inside a frame, they can be skew nailed.

Halving joint Also known as a half-lap joint, these may be used to join wood of similar thickness at corners or to T or X joints. The joint is formed by cutting each piece to half its thickness. Use a **try square** to mark the width of the cut-outs and a **marking gauge** set to half the thick-

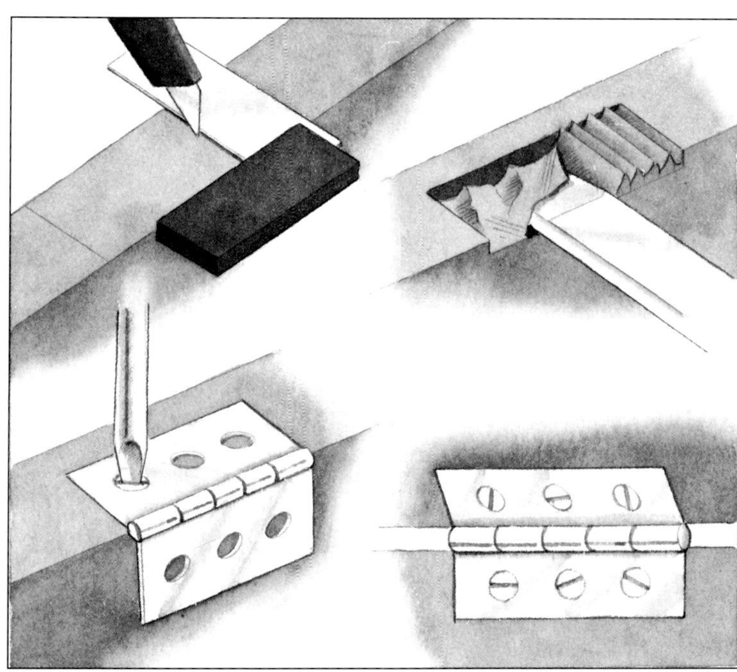

ness of the wood to mark their depth. Be sure to cross-hatch the waste wood with a pencil so that the correct side is removed. To form a corner half-lap, saw down as for making a tenon joint (*see* **page 154**). To form a 'T' or 'X' half-lap, saw down each side of the 'T' cut-out to the depth of the central gauge line, then chisel out the waste.

Housing joint Used mainly for shelving, this is basically a slot into which a shelf fits. The 'through' housing joint goes to the full width of the shelf, while a 'stopped' housing joint is taken only part of the way across the board. Chisel the waste away from each side. In the case of a stopped housing, chisel the waste from the stopped end first. If you have a router, it is easier to cut a housing joint by running the router across the board against a batten which is cramped at right angles to the board.

A rebate joint is similar to a housing joint, but positioned at the top of a piece of board; it can be cut in a similar way.

4 The Stages in Fitting a Butt Hinge
Using a try square and a trimming knife, mark out the length of hinge. With a marking gauge mark width and thickness of hinge flap. With chisel vertical, cut round outline of hinge. Make series of cuts across width of recess. Pare out the waste then check that flap lies flush. Screw the butt hinge in place.

8 Types of Housing Joints
***Top* A through housing joint; *Middle* Through housing joints on the side of a central support; *Bottom* A corner housing joint.**

5 Simple Butt Joints
***Top* Corner and *Below* T joints can be formed by skew nailing or by using corrugated fasteners.**

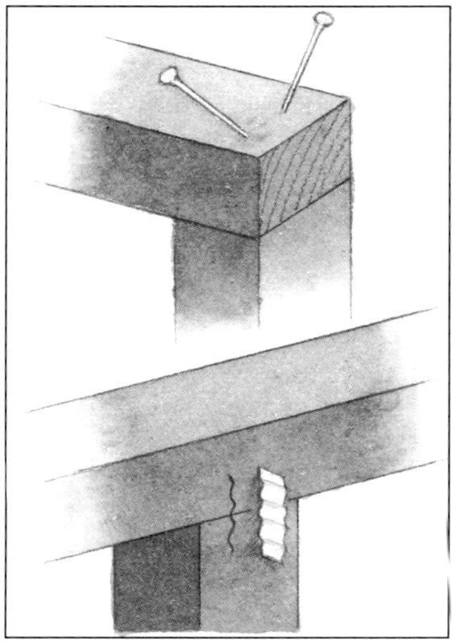

6 Types of Halving Joints
***Top* A corner halving joint. *Bottom left* A T-halving joint. *Bottom right* A cross halving joint.**

7 Forming a Halving Joint in Timber Battens
Mark width of the cut-out. Mark half the thickness of the wood with a marking gauge. Cross hatch area to be removed. Saw down sides with a tenon saw, then chisel out the waste.

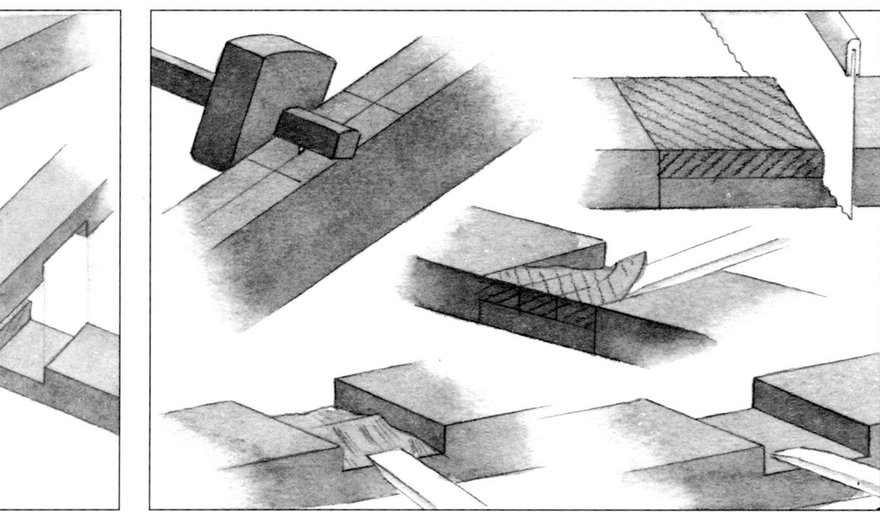

TECHNIQUES: WOOD JOINTS

Dowel joint Dowels are a strong, simple and hidden means of joining wood together.

Use pre-cut grooved dowels with bevelled ends (*see* **Materials, page 147**). These range from 6mm ($\frac{1}{4}$in) diameter by 25mm (1in) long to 10mm ($\frac{3}{8}$in) by 50mm (2in). The dowel length should be about one-and-a-half times the thickness of the wood being jointed. When making your own dowels, their length can be twice the thickness of the wood. Cut grooves down the length of dowel to allow glue and air to escape, and chamfer the ends.

On both pieces of wood, use a marking gauge to find the centre line, and mark with a pencil. Drill the dowel holes to half the dowel length with the drill held in a **drill stand**, or aligned with a **try square** stood on end. Drill the dowel holes in one of the pieces to be joined, insert centre points in the holes, then bring the two pieces of the joint together so they are carefully aligned. The centre points will make marks in the second piece of wood where the dowel holes should be drilled. Drill the holes to half of the length of the dowels, plus a little extra for glue. Where dowels are used for location rather than strength, set the dowels three-quarters into one edge and a quarter into the other.

Put adhesive in the hole and tap dowels into the holes in the first piece with a mallet. Apply adhesive to both parts of the joint; bring the pieces together and cramp them in position until the adhesive has set.

1 Dowels to Join Panels
Right **Mark dowel positions. Drill holes, insert centre points. Mark second piece.**

2 Types of Dowel Joint
Dowels can join panels edge to edge and join frames at corners. They can be hidden or have ends exposed.

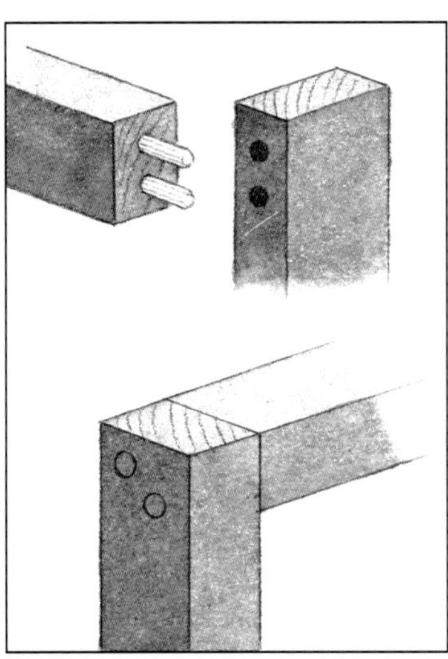

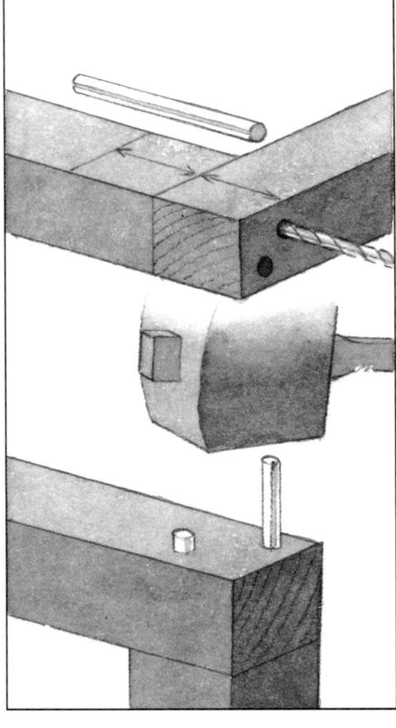

3 Making a Dowelled Frame
If edge of frame will not be seen, drill holes for dowels after making frame. Hammer dowels home; cut ends flush after glue dries.

4 Using a Dowelling Jig
If dowels are to be hidden, a dowelling jig makes it easy to drill holes that align in both pieces.

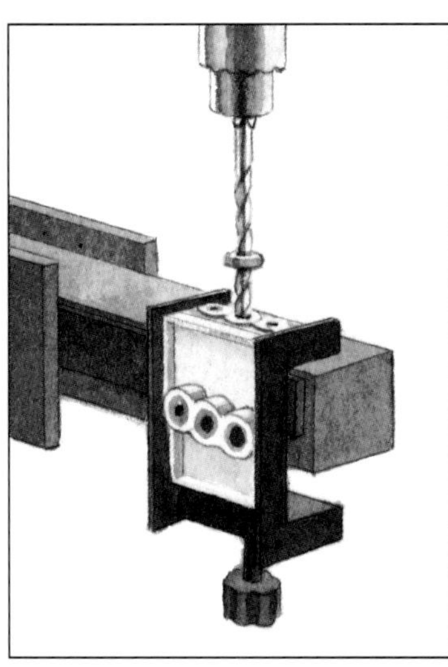

Using a dowelling jig A dowelling jig enables accurate dowel holes to be drilled. It is cramped over the workpiece above the pre-marked hole centres. A bush of the same diameter as the drill bit is selected and fitted on the jig. The bush holds the drill vertically as the hole is made. A depth gauge ensures that the hole is the required depth. The jig is then set up on the mating piece of wood and the process repeated.

Mitre joint A simple mitre joint is glued and pinned; a stronger one is made using dowels, or by sawing oblique cuts into which wood veneers are glued. Cut the joints at 45° using a mitre box as a guide.

Mortise and tenon joint A mortise and tenon joint can be marked out with a mortise gauge. Mark out the tenon (the tongue) so that it is one-third of the thickness of the piece of wood. The mortise (the slot) is marked at the same width in the other piece. The length of the mortise should match the width of the tenon being fitted. Drill out most of the waste with a series of holes using a bit slightly smaller than the mortise width. Working from the centre, chop out the mortise with a chisel to the depth required. If making a through joint (in which the end of the tenon is visible), turn the wood over and finish chiselling out the mortise from the other side.

Hold the tenon piece upright, but sloping away from yourself, secure in a vice, and use a tenon saw carefully to cut down to the shoulder. Then swivel the wood around to point the other way, and saw down to the other side of the shoulder. Next, position the wood vertically and cut down to the shoulder. Finally, place the wood flat and saw across the shoulder to remove the waste. Repeat for the waste on the other side of the tongue. Check that the two pieces fit well before gluing and assembling the joint. For added strength, cut small additional shoulders at each end of the tenon.

Bare-faced mortise and tenon joint If the tongue of a tenon joint is offset to one side, this produces a bare-faced tenon as shown (fig 8). This produces a strong joint where narrow rails meet thicker frame rails.

A bare-faced tenon is cut in the same way as a halving joint.

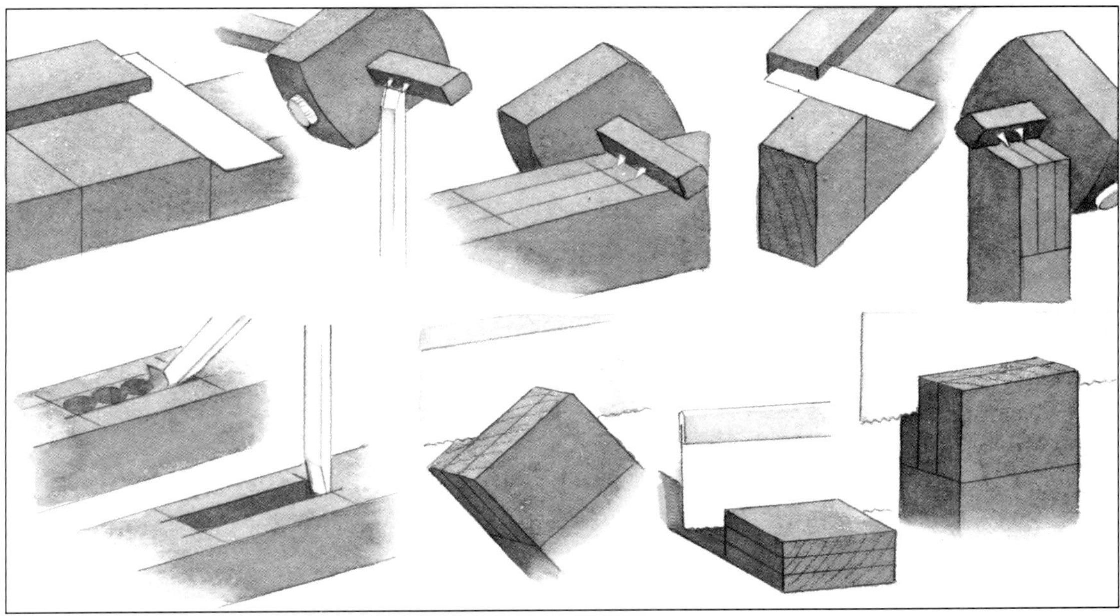

6 Marking and Cutting a Mortise and Tenon Joint
Mark the length of the mortise slot to match the size of the rail being joined. Set the mortise gauge to the width of the chisel being used to cut out the mortise slot. (Chisel should be about one-third the width of wood being joined.) Use the mortise gauge to mark the mortise, and also the tenon, on the rail. Drill out the mortise and complete the cut with a chisel. Use a tenon saw to cut out the tenon.

5 Cutting Mitre Joints
Mitres make right-angled joints. Use a mitre box to ensure a 45° angle and cut joint with a tenon saw.

7 Mortise and Tenon Joints
***Top* A common or stopped mortise and tenon joint. *Below* Through mortise and tenon joint.**

8 Making a Bare-Faced Mortise and Tenon Joint
Tenon is offset to one side. Mark and cut as shown here.

9 Shouldered Tenon Joint
For enhanced strength, saw down small additional shoulders at each end of the tenon.

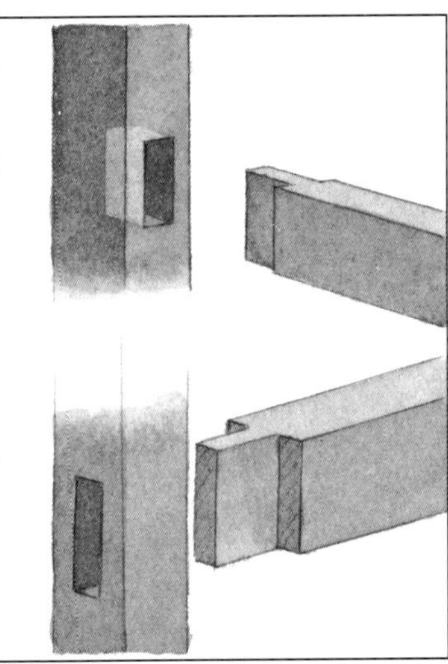

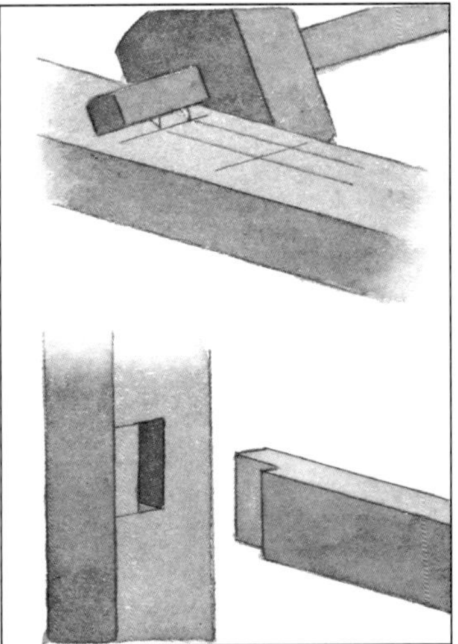

TECHNIQUES: BRICKLAYING

TOOLS

Bolster chisel and club hammer For cutting bricks.

Buckets You will need two of the same size, one for measuring mortar ingredients, the other for cement.

Builder's square Three battens in the proportions 3:4:5 nailed to form a right-angled triangle. Used to check that each course is vertical.

Gauge rod This is a 25 × 25mm (1 × 1in) batten marked off in 75mm (3in) increments. It is used to check that courses of bricks are vertical. It should be slightly longer than the intended wall height.

Laying trowel Used to spread mortar on bricks.

Mortar board For holding small amounts of mortar.

Pointing trowel Small trowel for shaping mortar joints.

Profile board Made from a piece of scrap wood about 500mm (20in) long, nailed across two battens which are driven into the ground. You will need two – one for either end of the wall. The top of each board is notched at appropriate intervals to represent the edges of the foundation strips and the wall. The notches then hold the string line taut for accurate bricklaying.

Shovels You will need two of these, one for mixing and one for lifting cement from its bag.

Spirit level For checking brickwork horizontally and vertically.

String line Needed as a guide to laying the brick courses horizontally.

Watering can For adding water to the mortar mix.

MATERIALS

Bricks Bricks are made to a uniform size of 215 × 102.5 × 65mm ($8\frac{5}{8} \times 4\frac{1}{8} \times 2\frac{5}{8}$in). Since allowance has to be made for 10mm ($\frac{3}{8}$in) thick horizontal and vertical mortar joints, they are regarded as being 225 × 112.5 × 75mm ($9 \times 4\frac{1}{2} \times 3$in).

Bricks come in many colours and textures, and it is important to choose a type that will harmonize with your garden and house. Second-hand bricks are popular for garden projects since they blend well with any environment. Builders' merchants stock a selection of bricks; local demolition sites or architectural salvage yards are good hunting grounds for second-hand bricks.

Mortar This is needed to bond the bricks together. It is made by mixing cement, soft builders' sand, and lime or plasticizer in the proportions of 1:5:1 with water. Bags of ready-mixed mortar are available, but they are really only economical for very small jobs such as repair work.

Ordinary Portland cement (sold in 50kg [110lb] bags) is usually used although white Portland cement is available if you want pale joints to match pale bricks.

Builders' sand is sold by the cubic metre (yard). Most builders' merchants will sell smaller quantities in bags – larger quantities are tipped from a lorry into a loose pile.

Lime is sold in bags, liquid plasticizer in containers.

When calculating how much to buy, a good rule of thumb is to allow one bag of cement and 0.2 cubic metres (yards) of damp sand for every 400 bricks.

Should you need to store cement before use, then keep it under cover and raised off the ground. A pile of sand will attract children and animals so cover this, too.

Mix mortar on a clean surface. In hot weather, only mix as much as you can use in an hour, since the mortar will start to stiffen. Never try to reactivate mortar by adding more water: it will crack up. On a hot day, it is worth dipping each brick in water before laying it.

First, mix the dry ingredients until the pile is a uniform grey colour. Make a crater in the top and pour in some water, then turn the pile over continuously, adding a little more water from time to time until the mix is buttery. A good test for the right consistency is to chop the mixing shovel through the pile until the ridges remain intact.

TECHNIQUES

Laying foundations Unless the brickwork is built on a firm base it will soon start to subside. Judging foundations is a matter of common sense, although always err on the side of caution if in any doubt.

Whereas a low brick planter or barbecue can be built on a sound existing patio or drive, more ambitious projects require tailor-made solid concrete foundations. For a garden wall up to 1000mm (39in) high (two brick thickness), dig a trench 500mm (20in) wide and deep, and lay a levelled bed of concrete in the trench to a depth of 230mm (9in). For a single brick thickness wall, you will need to dig a

1 Single Brick Foundation
Dig trench and lay concrete bed as indicated. Lay bricks and backfill with soil once mortar has hardened.

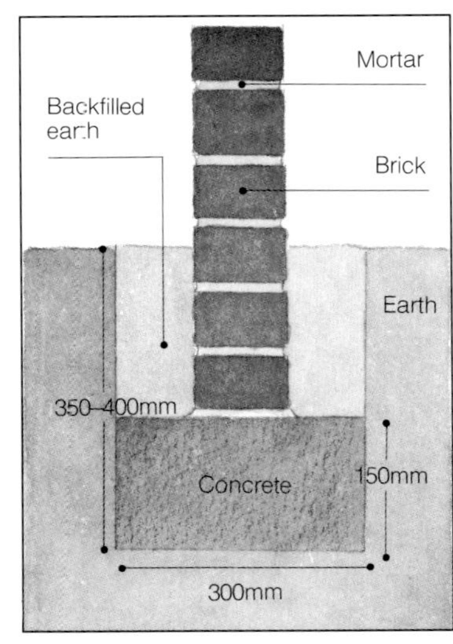

2 Laying First Two Bricks
Lay first brick using profile board as guide. Lay second brick 1500mm (60in) away; check it is level with first.

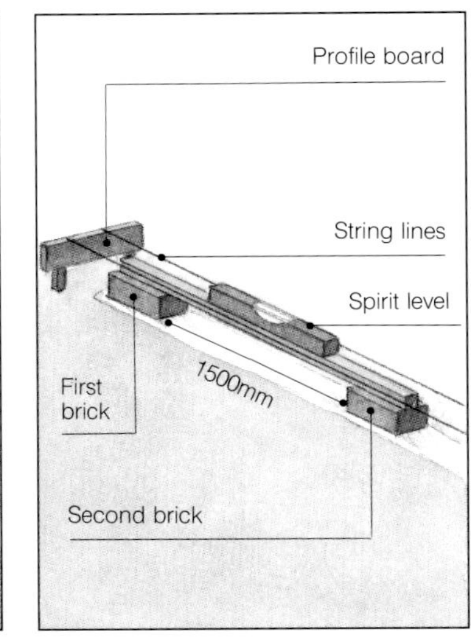

3 Laying the Second Course
Begin with a half brick to stagger courses, then continue along. Always check bricks are vertical and level.

trench 300mm (12in) wide and 350–400mm (14–16in) deep, and lay a 150mm (6in) deep bed of concrete in the trench.

The concrete mix should be one part cement to four parts of ballast. Allow it to harden for four days and keep it covered with polythene in wet weather. In hot weather, cover the concrete with damp sacking, spraying it occasionally with water.

Cutting bricks To cut a brick, score a continuous line around all four faces using a bolster chisel and a club hammer. Place the brick on a pile of sand, put the blade of the chisel in the groove and tap sharply with the hammer for a clean cut.

Brickwork bonds For stability, a wall must be built in a definite bond formation such as one of the examples illustrated (fig 7). Stretcher and open bond formations are suitable for single brick thickness walls up to a height of 1000mm (39in). Piers (support columns), as indicated (fig 5), are essential at both ends and at 1800mm (72in) centres.

A double brick thickness wall requires bricks to be cut near the corners to ensure that the vertical joints are staggered.

Laying bricks Set up string lines at either side of the foundation trench as a guide to laying the first course of bricks. Make profile boards from pieces of scrap wood notched as appropriate for a single or double brick wall – the notches trap the string, pulling it taut.

Spread a layer of mortar about 1500mm (60in) long and lay the first brick in place with the indentation facing upwards. Lay a second brick 1500mm (60in) or so away. Place a spirit level on a straight-edge piece of wood spanning the two bricks and tap the higher brick down using the trowel handle until both are level.

Mortar should always be a little thicker than 10mm (⅜in) since the bricks will compress it slightly.

As each brick is laid, spread a 10mm (⅜in) layer of mortar on the end to form a vertical joint between it and the preceding brick. Use the spirit level and trowel to level each brick. Complete the first course.

Cut a brick in half to start the second course. Build up the ends of the wall as shown (fig 4), so that you are always working three or four courses above the course being filled. The course being completed must be laid to a taut string line which should be anchored into the course above using bradpoint nails.

Check continually with the gauge rod that the courses are accurate. Also check the face of the brickwork to ensure it is plumb.

The top course of bricks (the coping course) protects the wall from the weather. On a single brick wall, stand half bricks on edge. Whole bricks on edge complete a double thickness wall.

Joint finishes It is best to finish the joints as each course of bricks is completed. The simplest joints to make are flush joints, made by scraping away excess mortar using the edge of a trowel.

Rounded joints are more decorative and are made by drawing a steel rod through the mortar.

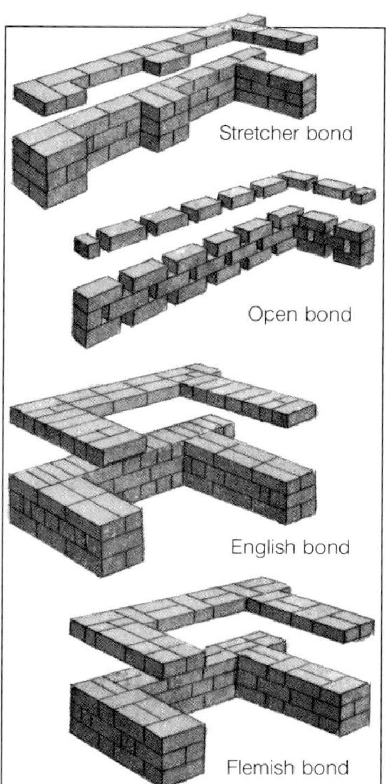

7 Brickwork Bonds
Each course must be laid to stagger with the course above and below. Four popular bonds are shown here.

4 Laying Additional Courses
Build up the ends of the wall first, then fill in the intervening bricks, completing one course at a time.

5 Forming Piers
For long walls, stagger the brick formations as shown to form piers at 1800mm (72in) centres.

½ brick
¾ brick
¾ brick
Whole brick
Whole brick

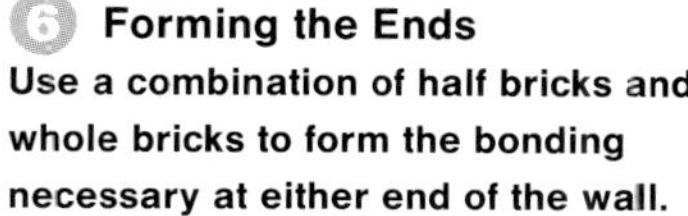

6 Forming the Ends
Use a combination of half bricks and whole bricks to form the bonding necessary at either end of the wall.

8 Cutting a Brick
Score line around faces of brick. Lay it on bed of sand, insert chisel in groove, tap sharply with hammer.

INDEX

Page numbers in *italic* refer to illustrations

Acknowledgments

The publisher thanks the following photographers and organizations for their kind permission to reproduce the photographs in this book:

8 left Brigitte Thomas; **8** right Gary Chowanetz/ Elizabeth Whiting & Associates; **9** Lamontagne; **10** left Brigitte Thomas; **10** right Jerry Harpur/Conran Octopus (designer Tim Du Val); **11** left Marijke Heuff (designer K Noordhuis); **11** above right Brigitte Thomas; **11** below right Marijke Heuff (The Coach House – Little Haseley); **12** above left Lamontagne; **12** above right Ron Sutherland/Garden Picture Library (designer Rick Eckersley); **12** centre left René Stoeltie; **12** centre right Georges Lévêque; **12** below left Brigitte Thomas; **12** below right Arnaud Descat/Agence Bamboo; **13** above left Bent Rej; **13** above right John Glover/Garden Picture Library; **13** centre left Lamontagne; **13** centre right Lars Hallen; **13** below left Tim Street-Porter/Elizabeth Whiting & Associates; **13** below right Georges Lévêque; **14** left Gilles de Chabaneix for Terence Conran; **14** centre Lamontagne; **14** right Gary Rogers/Garden Picture Library; **15** Brigitte Thomas; **16** Marijke Heuff (designer Mien Ruys, Dedemsvaart); **17** Georges Lévêque; **18** above left Lamontagne; **18** above right Georges Lévêque; **18** centre left Ron Sutherland/Garden Picture Library; **18** centre right Gary Rogers; **18** below left Brigitte Thomas; **18** below right Ron Sutherland/Garden Picture Library; **19** above left Brigitte Thomas; **19** above right Steven Wooster/Garden Picture Library; **19** centre left Anthony Paul/Garden Picture Library; **19** centre right Lamontagne; **19** below left Lamontagne; **19** below right Ron Sutherland/Garden Picture Library; **20** above Georges Lévêque; **20** below left Belle (Geoff Lung); **20** below right Georges Lévêque; **21** above Tim Street-Porter/Elizabeth Whiting & Associates; **21** below left Bent Rej; **21** below right Rodney Hyett/Elizabeth Whiting & Associates; **43** Neil Lorimer/ Elizabeth Whiting & Associates; **45** Lars Hallen (M-L Rosenbroijer); **46** left Andrew Payne/Garden Picture Library; **46** centre René Stoeltie; **46** right Gary Rogers/ Garden Picture Library; **47** Brigitte Thomas; **48** Lamontagne; **49** left Gillian Darley/Edifice; **49** right S & O Mathews; **50** left Marijke Heuff (designer K Noordhuis); **50** centre Andrew Lawson; **50** right Brigitte Thomas; **51** above Oliver Gregory; **51** below left Andrew Lawson; **51** below right Marijke Heuff (Mr & Mrs Brinkworth); **70** Boys Syndication; **74** Marijke Heuff (Mr F Tiebout and Mr F de Greeuw); **76** Marijke Heuff (Mr & Mrs Adriaanse-Quint); **78** left Brigitte Thomas; **78** centre Lamontagne; **78** right Brigitte Thomas; **79** Ron Sutherland/Garden Picture Library; **80** Nexus Designs, Melbourne, Australia; **81** above left Christian Sarramon; **81** above right Lamontagne; **81** below Georges Lévêque; **82** above Hugh Palmer; **82** below left Ron Sutherland/Garden Picture Library (designer Murray Collins); **82** below right Lamontange; **83** above Brigitte Thomas; **83** below left Eric Crichton; **83** below right Lamontagne; **94** Lamontagne; **96** left Joanne Pavia/Garden Picture Library; **96** centre Brigitte Thomas; **96** right Brigitte Thomas; **97** Hugh Palmer; **98** above Brigitte Thomas; **98** centre Lamontagne; **98** below Georges Lévêque; **99** Hugh Palmer; **100** above left Georges Lévêque; **100** above right Philippa Lewis/Ediface; **100** centre left Lamontagne; **100** centre right Marijke Heuff; **100** below left Lamontagne; **100** below right Houses & Interiors; **101** above left Brigitte Thomas; **101** above right Philippa Lewis/Ediface; **101** centre left Philippa Lewis/Ediface; **101** centre right Gary Chowanetz/Elizabeth Whiting & Associates; **101** below left Ron Sutherland/Garden Picture Library; **101** below right Gary Chowanetz/ Elizabeth Whiting & Associates; **102** left Hugh Palmer; **102** right Georges Lévêque; **103** above Brigitte Thomas; **103** below Gilles de Chabaneix for Terence Conran; **124** left Lamontagne; **124** centre Georges Lévêque; **124** right Lamontagne; **125** Georges Lévêque; **126** left Jerry Harpur/Elizabeth Whiting & Associates; **126** right Gary Rogers/Garden Picture Library; **127** Brigitte Thomas; **128** Jerry Harpur/ Elizabeth Whiting & Associates (designed by Clifton Nurseries); **129** above Eric Crichton; **129** below left S & O Mathews; **129** below right Georges Lévêque.

The following photographs were specially taken for Conran Octopus by **Nadia Mackenzie**:
1–7, 23–39, 53–69, 85–92, 105–121, 131–139.